Wayward Kids

❖　❖　❖　❖

Wayward
Kids

UNDERSTANDING AND TREATING

ANTISOCIAL YOUTH

❖ ❖ ❖ ❖

Delton W. Young, Ph.D.

JASON ARONSON INC.
Northvale, New Jersey
London

Production Editor: Elaine Lindenblatt

This book was set in 11 pt. Berling Roman by Alpha Graphics of Pittsfield, New Hampshire and printed and bound by Book-mart Press, Inc. of North Bergen, New Jersey.

Library of Congress Cataloging-in-Publication Data

Young, Delton W.
    Wayward kids : understanding and treating antisocial youth /
Delton W. Young.
        p.   cm.
    ISBN 0-7657-0191-X
    1. Juvenile delinquents—United States.   2. Juvenile delinquency—
United States—Prevention.   3. Problem youth—United States—
Psychology.
    HV9104.Y67 1999
    364.36'0973—dc21   99-18108

Printed in the United States of America on acid-free paper. Jason Aronson Inc. offers books and cassettes. For information and catalog write to Jason Aronson Inc., 230 Livingston Street, Northvale, New Jersey 07647-1726. Or visit our website: www.aronson.com

❖ CONTENTS ❖

❖ PREFACE ❖

There has been a sense of urgency in recent years about the prevalence of juvenile crime throughout American society and the toll it is taking on our nation's youth. The incursion of violent crime into middle-class neighborhoods, the ubiquity of gang-related graffiti in most cities, and the specter of school-yard shootings have precipitated a flurry of legislative and institutional reactions—longer prison sentences, mandatory waiver to adult court, even the death penalty for juveniles.

The study of antisocial behavior never has been the exclusive province of the behavioral sciences. Unlike clinical syndromes such as depression or attention deficit, authority to define the problem of antisocial behavior and to order interventions is not vested solely in the clinical disciplines. Psychology and psychiatry will always share the stage with the juvenile justice system. However, during these years when juvenile crime has become a national preoccupation, investigations in the behavioral sciences have quietly accomplished major advances in the capacity to understand, diagnose, and treat antisocial youth.

An adequate understanding of the development of antisocial behavior entails an especially broad range of factors involved in the pathological outcome. The social sciences have been compelled by scientific data to take account of biological factors, in particular, by making room for behavioral genetics and temperament in explaining some forms of antisocial character.[1] At the same time,

---

1. I use the term *antisocial character* in the informal sense, to indicate the presence of antisocial attitudes and behavioral habits, and not in the narrower sense of meeting diagnostic criteria for antisocial personality disorder or conduct disorder. Chapter 2 addresses diagnostic and labeling issues.

understanding the developmental insults often implicated in anti-social behavior, along with the normal interpersonal processes that build resiliency, demands examination of a wide array of social conditions. Nature and nurture can no longer be seen as separate, competing developmental forces. Contrary to the older thinking, new insights about biological factors cast in bold relief the role of psychosocial conditions, and vice versa. The most fruitful research in the years ahead will explore the crucial interactions between biological and social factors. For example, children who present an aggressive and impulsive temperament will require the most vigorous psychosocial efforts involving family, community, and school.

For years, even decades, the occurrence of antisocial behavior patterns triggered a pessimistic response from clinicians and re-searchers alike. The common wisdom was that antisocial youths could not be understood and, more important, they could not be successfully treated. Therapeutic interventions with traditional methods had generally yielded discouraging results.

All of that has changed in recent years. Our ability to discrimi-nate the different personalities of youths who commit antisocial acts is now quite sophisticated. We can chart the developmental trajectories of several subtypes of antisocial children and adoles-cents, and our methods for predicting which individuals will be-have violently are improved. Most importantly, there now are well-researched treatment strategies that are effective for the majority of antisocial youth. Success rates for comprehensive, com-munity-based treatment programs rival those for the treatment of many other behavioral and psychiatric disturbances. Hence, in most cases there are better things to do with antisocial youths than just to lock them away, and the newer methods are less costly.

This book presents the current state of our understanding and methods—our diagnostic and classification schemes, the pathways to normal and pathological development, the trajectories typically followed by the various kinds of antisocial youths, the role of psy-chiatric disorders in antisocial development and behavior, and our methods for evaluation and for treatment. Also, our understanding of antisocial development, along with an awareness of the surge in antisocial character over the past generation, compels reflection upon the social and economic conditions that are implicated in such a large-scale historical trend.

This book is intended for the broad range of professionals who come into contact with youths who behave in antisocial ways. I have made every effort to keep the material well grounded in the scientific and clinical literatures, but I avoid lengthy, technical discussions that would detract from the principal thrust of the investigations. Hence, I have strived to make these important insights about antisocial youths accessible to readers without extensive training or interest in research methodology.

❖ ACKNOWLEDGMENTS ❖

For all the sophistication of our research methods, much of our understanding of child development and psychopathology turns upon stories—the familiar stories that define what we take as typical, the stories that challenge our assumptions and make us rethink our theories, the stories that provide hope and guidance for others. I want to express my gratitude to the many individuals who have shared their stories with me—the children and adolescents seen in hospitals, detention centers, and consultation rooms, and the parents and grandparents who have responded to the troubling course their children seemed to be following. Of course, no child or parent in this book is identifiable (with the exception of cases well known through the media). Names and other identifiers have been altered; but I have preserved their stories as faithfully as possible.

I also want to thank my wife, Barbara, for her steadfast confidence in this project and the intellectual connections she facilitated. Her numerous thoughtful discussions helped to clarify my reasoning, and her critical eye corrected many lapses in expression. Thanks, as well, to my editors at Jason Aronson—to Cindy Hyden for her early support and confidence, and to Elaine Lindenblatt for her thoughtful and astute editing of the manuscript. Also, I thank my colleagues, Michael Golden and Comer Larue, whose comments on drafts of chapters considerably improved both the psychological content and the prose.

❖ CHAPTER 1 ❖

Juvenile Crime: No Place to Hide

Criminal activity by children and adolescents has been with us for a very long time, probably since social norms were first codified into laws. The prominence of juvenile crime in the public consciousness has waxed and waned over the years according to a variety of social and economic conditions and according to location. Charles Dickens's *Oliver Twist* poignantly portrays the social backdrop and the character of numerous young thieves in nineteenth-century England. During the same period in America, juvenile crime seems to have been virtually unknown in some quarters, yet a regular part of life in many cities. Closer to home, late in the twentieth century, each of the disciplines concerned with human behavior has, at one time or another, focused its attention on those children who stray far from social norms. By now, there has been amassed a considerable scientific literature on antisocial youths, ranging from psychoanalytically oriented clinical studies of pathological child development all the way to research on behavioral genetics and the role of physiological differences in the development of severe antisocial behavior.

For most of this century and for the majority of citizens, though, criminal activity by juveniles has remained something of a background noise in the hum of everyday life. Except for the occasional high-profile incident, serious juvenile crime has remained largely a distant problem, a "big city" concern, or a "minorities" issue.

The picture has changed dramatically in recent years. Alarms have been sounding for the past fifteen years about the escalating rates of serious crime by children and adolescents. Youth violence is no longer confined to inner cities or to minority neighborhoods; it is now commonplace in the suburbs. The safe havens of yesterday are now tagged with gang graffiti, and violence in schools has unnerved students, parents, and school administrators. The National Center for Educational Statistics (1995) concluded, "Unsafe conditions at school are a reality for most U.S. students" (p. 2). Adding to the alarm, even as violent crime rates decline, is the pattern of younger and younger children becoming involved in criminal behaviors, particularly in violent assaults.

We are faced with an urgent dilemma about how to respond to the youths who are responsible for such crimes. It is a dilemma with enormous ramifications for the millions of affected children and for the society we would hope to enjoy in the years ahead. With serious and violent crime eroding the quality of life throughout society, it is understandable to want to turn our backs on these kids, to lock them away, to toughen the sentences, and to build more prisons. This "get-tough" response makes good sense to many, but it entails essentially cutting loose those individuals who have so seriously violated our codes of civilized conduct, and it is well known than they rarely go away for good. In all but a few cases, they will be back sooner or later.

There are good reasons to believe that the get-tough approach will not work for long. Juvenile crime is now prevalent in virtually every sector of society. The financial cost of locking away young criminals is staggering, and it is growing. Perhaps most ominously, we know that the most serious and violent offenders often are not rehabilitated in correctional institutions, anyway. Juveniles who are committed to correctional institutions are usually released by age 21. Those who are sent to adult prison get little or no treatment, and the chances of actually changing their attitudes and behaviors are slim. Hence, unless we are willing to lock them away until middle age, we should expect them to return to our midst with antisocial attitudes intact or worse.

At some point, we need to ask, Who are these kids? How can we understand their personalities and habits? What can we do about their destructiveness? Moreover, what is it about modern society that engenders such prevalent criminality in our children? Is there perhaps a message in this epidemic of youth criminality that we as a society should be reading?

THE ESCALATION OF JUVENILE CRIME IS REAL

Rates of criminal activity by juveniles fluctuate a great deal over time according to historical conditions, depending on the methods used to report such information and on regional differences in definitions of certain crimes. In recent decades, however, there has been a sharp and unmistakable rise in the rate at which juveniles commit serious crimes.

Carefully collected statistics are tabulated by the Federal Bureau of Investigation (FBI), which publishes the Uniform Crime Reports annually; by the Office of Juvenile Justice and Delinquency Prevention (OJJDP); and by other agencies. These statistics are usually reported in terms of the rate or incidence of certain crimes—that is, the number of such crimes per 100,000 juveniles in the population. In this way, the crime rate is corrected for changes in the population of juveniles (age 10–17 years). For example, the population of juveniles declined during the 1970s and early 1980s, but has been increasing since 1984, and it will continue to rise well into the twenty-first century. Thus, even if the incidence of crimes remained stable or declined somewhat, the actual number of such crimes would increase because of the expanding population of juveniles in society (the current "echo boom").

If there is one set of data that neatly captures the problem of juvenile crime in an historical framework, it is the FBI statistics on violent juvenile crime over the past thirty years. They charted the rate of juvenile arrests for violent crime from 1965 to the mid-1990s (Figure 1–1).

In the span of a single generation, the incidence of violent crime by juveniles has tripled. Of special concern is the steep climb in arrest rates for violent crimes from the mid-1980s to the mid-1990s. The incidence of juvenile violent crime arrests increased by 98 percent from just 1985 to 1994. Beginning in 1994, overall rates of violent juvenile crime have declined, led by drops in murders and aggravated assaults. Violent sexual assault, on the other hand, has continued to rise (Sickmund et al. 1997). Large-scale, longitudinal epidemiological studies confirm the rise in antisocial behavior over the past half century. Lee Robins (1988) reported a sixfold increase in the proportion of adolescents diagnosable with conduct disorder over the past half century. Other researchers (e.g., Earls 1989) have noted

FIGURE 1–1. Violent crime arrest rates 1965–1995. Arrest Rate = Arrests per 100,000 youths age 10–17.

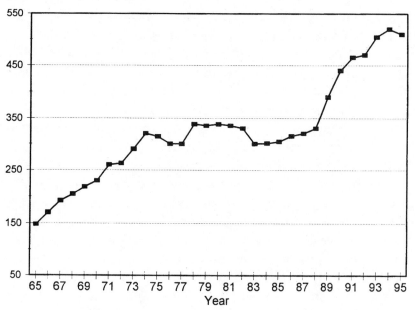

Adapted from Office of Juvenile Justice and Delinquency Prevention 1993, p. 2 and Sickmund et al. 1997.

a rise in incidence of several psychiatric conditions, including depression and bipolar disorder.

Buried within these statistics are subsets of data on specific types of crime. For example, the actual number of juvenile homicide arrests tripled between 1985 and 1994, with a 150 percent rise in incidence (accounting for population expansion). The explosion in homicide rates is closely paralleled by the expanding availability of handguns. The incidence of juvenile arrests for aggravated assault increased for the same 1985 to 1994 period by 97 percent, for weapons violations by 103 percent, and for "other assaults" by 114 percent.

The dramatic expansion in the rate of violent crime by children and adolescents is not limited just to boys. While girls account for a smaller proportion of violent crime than boys (about 1:7 in 1994 and 1995), the rate at which females (children and adults) commit violent crimes has escalated along a similar curve. From 1985 to 1994, the female arrest rate for violent crime increased by 128 percent, a higher rate of increase than for males.

The statistics presented thus far reflect crimes that are the most disturbing and worrisome, that is, violent crimes against persons. These crime numbers are especially striking when they are compared to some related trends—first, the rates of less serious crimes by juveniles, and second, the crime rates for adults.

During these same periods of time, rates of most juvenile crime climbed slowly. From 1985 to 1994, the Total Crime Index (rate of all crimes by juveniles) climbed by just 18 percent—still an unhappy trend, but not nearly so alarming. During the same period, property crimes by juveniles climbed 11 percent; and other "non-index" crimes (e.g., forgery, burglary, embezzlement, vandalism, gambling, etc.) rose by 34 percent. Some crime rates actually dropped. For example, arrest rates for burglary fell by 19 percent, for prostitution by 59 percent, and for drunkenness by 37 percent. Hence, the escalation of serious crime by juveniles over the past decade has taken place in the context of an overall crime rate that has climbed much more modestly.

While the incidence of the most violent crimes by juveniles was rising steeply, the rate of arrest of adults for the same crimes showed no such escalation. In the same 1985 to 1994 period, the murder rate for all adults rose just 11 percent (versus 150 percent for juveniles), and the murder rate by adults aged 35 to 45 fell by 25 percent!

Researchers at the U.S. Department of Justice addressed the question of future trends in juvenile crime. They took account of the fact that juveniles will make up an increasing proportion of the population in the decades ahead. For example, between 1990 and 2010, the number of children aged 10 to 14 will increase by 21 percent, and those aged 15 to 17 will increase by 31 percent. "Assuming [known] population growth and continuing increases in arrest rates, the number of juvenile violent crimes is expected to double by 2010 [from the 1995 rate]" (Snyder and Sickmund 1995, p. 111).

The picture that emerges, then, is not one of undifferentiated escalation in crime throughout society. Rather, it is serious and violent crime by children and adolescents. It is the kinds of crimes that are most frightening and anxiety-provoking to society at large—violent crime against persons, such as murder, aggravated assault, robbery, and forcible rape. Curiously, weapons violations (e.g., carrying a gun or knife to school) are not counted in the category of violent crime and they are not counted in the Violent Crime Index. But these violations have escalated parallel to those in the Violent Crime Index, and such weapons violations reflect the growth in the number and availability of deadly weapons.

The rising rates of violent crime by juveniles have sent shock waves through virtually every sector of society, but not just because of the numbers, the rates, or the statistics. Equally disturbing has been the crossing of traditional social and geographic boundaries. Frightening and violent crime is no longer confined mainly to inner cities, and it is no longer primarily a lower socioeconomic class problem. The large increases in rates of juvenile crime have occurred in urban, suburban, and rural areas, and have, to a considerable degree, invaded middle-class and even wealthier neighborhoods. Suburban areas that twenty years ago were "safe havens" today cope with youth criminality on the streets, in the schools, and even in the homes. Violent victimization of juveniles has risen sharply. For example, murders of juveniles increased 66 percent between 1985 and 1995 (Sickmund et al. 1997). Gangs have emerged in many middle-sized and smaller cities and suburbs across the country, and the gangs have become increasingly violent. A report by the National Center for Educational Statistics (NCES) concluded that the problem of gangs is not limited to either urban areas or to minority students. Sociologist Wayne Wooden (1995) chronicled an extensive and complex culture of gang-involved antisocial adolescents—many from middle-class families—throughout large suburban areas of Southern California and elsewhere.

Criminal violations in schools also have crossed the boundaries of class, race, and socioeconomic status. In a nationwide study commissioned by the NCES, it was found that, "Exposure to crime and threats at school crosses racial and ethnic boundaries. . . . Worry and victimization also did not differ by student race or racial composition" (NCES 1995, p. 4). Acts of aggression and violence were found to be commonplace even in a middle-class, predominantly white, suburban high school (Young and Larue 1998).

The Bureau of Juvenile Statistics estimated several years ago that the cost of arresting, prosecuting, and incarcerating juveniles nationwide was then about $20 billion annually. That was before the sharp rise in juvenile crime into the mid-1990s, and that number does not count the costs of resulting medical services, lost productivity, and property damage and loss. Financial loss, however, is only the narrowest measure of cost.

SOCIETY RESPONDS

The response to rising juvenile crime can be observed in two broad social arenas: first, the personal and emotional reactions of ordinary citizens, and second, institutional policies and procedures. To a large degree, the former drives the latter, via state legislatures and judicial predilections.

No one has needed charts and statistics to realize that juvenile crime was on the rise over the last decade or two. The news media routinely report (often in lurid detail) the most heinous crimes. In most cities gang graffiti is a constant reminder of the potential for harm. Lengthy, high-profile trials keep the elements of terror in the public spotlight. Frequent discussion of weapons at school engenders frantic efforts to keep children safe.

For the majority of citizens, the rising tide of serious crime is a personal concern, driven by the elemental emotions of fear and anger. The primary impulse is the most basic of all instincts—to protect one's self and loved ones from harm. The most fortunate families simply move out of neighborhoods that appear to be sliding toward social decay and crime and relocate to more distant suburbs. Personal, home, and auto security devices have proliferated. More and more citizens arm themselves against feared attack.

The increase in violent crime arrests has translated directly into many institutional changes—a rapidly rising number of juvenile court prosecutions, detentions, and commitments to correctional facilities. From 1985 through 1994, the juvenile courts disposed of 144 percent more homicides and 103 percent more aggravated assault cases (Butts et al. 1993). Also, since the mid-1980s, there has been a steady rise (by about 50 percent) in the average daily population at U.S. juvenile detention centers. By the early 1990s, nearly half of detained juveniles were being held in facilities in which the population exceeded capacity (Krisberg 1992). Needless to say, the construction and operation of detention facilities and correctional insititutions is a major growth industry nationwide. Moreover, adult prisons must be enlarged to make way for the coming cohort of criminals who now are juveniles.

The new "get-tough" attitude toward rising juvenile crime has been reflected in the matter of the juvenile court waiver. A juvenile court can, according to state statute, waive (or decline) jurisdiction in any given case, sending the case to the adult criminal court for prosecution, where procedures are less accommodating and where sentences usually are stiffer. Most states have passed laws that make waiver to adult court mandatory for certain crimes, depending on the age of the juvenile at the time of the crime. For other cases, waiver is left to the discretion of the judge.

Between 1985 and 1994 the number of cases waived to adult criminal court rose by 71 percent. As might be expected, the largest increase was in the category of crimes against persons. Increasingly, juveniles are waived by legislative action (mandated by state laws), as voters demand a more vigorous response. In many states, juveniles are protected from the death penalty even if tried in adult court. However, the matter of the death penalty for certain crimes by juveniles has been debated, and it has been imposed in certain states in over 120 cases since the mid-1980s.

ALIENS: THE CIRCLE OF DEHUMANIZATION

One of the most chilling aspects of juvenile violent crime in recent years has been the attitude that young perpetrators display toward their victims. The spectacle is now so familiar that it no longer makes the front page of the newspapers: A teen charged with murder expresses the attitude that his victim was just a thing, an incidental object to be brushed aside. Not only is there no remorse, there are no second thoughts or self-doubt. Often, a primitive sort of entitlement and self-satisfaction take the place of reflection on the deed. The attitude toward human life appears degraded to the point where a peer is viewed as merely an obstacle to immediate gratification. One can kill over a pair of sneakers if one's adversary is just a "thing." Bullets can be sprayed around a residential neighborhood if one's regard for human life is nil. Paralleling this impoverished view of human life is the disregard for one's own safety. Many antisocial adolescents express little or no expectation about having a future, and they take no precautions for their own safety. Hence, while they show no remorse or self-doubts about their crimes, they are similarly lacking in self-respect and concern for their own future. Their own life seems to hold no more value than the life of a peer who may stand in their way. The life of a peer and one's own future can be blown away in an explosive act that momentarily inflates the self-esteem.

The impoverished perspective wherein others are seen as less than human and as serving one's immediate needs (as objects of gratification or frustration) is termed dehumanization. Dehumanization is an especially pernicious defense mechanism that involves sharpening the perceived differences between "us" and "them." Such sharpening usually is accomplished by degrading the image of "them" to something less than human. Dehumanization has been employed repeatedly on a grand scale to ease the psychological strain in particularly brutal political processes. The potential pain of subjugating or destroying other human beings is eased by the convention of viewing them as if they were not fully human.

If violent youths are characterized by the habit of dehumanizing others, modern society is prepared to return the favor. Stemming from the alarm and the anger over juvenile crime, the expanding population of teens who commit serious and violent crimes tend also to be looked upon as if they were something less than human.

There are widely differing opinions in society about how best to respond to antisocial youth. There are institutions whose approach is thoroughly humanistic, whose efforts are aimed at bringing the youths back into the fold. These include psychological and medical methods as well as religious approaches. There are those who insist that such teens just need love and understanding. Others insist they need psychotherapy or the right psychotropic medication. Still others claim that what would make all the difference is a particular spiritual commitment.

These approaches try to return antisocial youths to normal society. But as fewer sectors of society seem really safe from violent crime, the predominant approach leans the other way—to sharpen the "us–them" distinctions, to look upon antisocial youths as if they were profoundly different from us, as if they were not really human, as if they were aliens. Aliens are not like us; they are not redeemable, and there's nothing we can do but to move farther away, to build higher walls, and to construct more secure prisons. This is the "aliens" approach to juvenile crime, and it entails creating various kinds of physical and psychological barriers between us and them.

It is not unreasonable to argue that antisocial youths have earned this aliens response from society. Given their attitude and behavior, perhaps they deserve to be looked upon as less than fully human. It might be argued that persons—whatever their age—who commit serious and violent crimes do not deserve the respect usually reserved for civilized human beings. After all, in a civilized society, citizens should not have to live in fear. Senior citizens should not be afraid to walk outdoors after dark, and parents should not need to worry about the safety of their children walking to and from school, or inside the school itself. It is expectable that citizens will do whatever they believe they need to do to be safe from such hazards.

NO PLACE TO HIDE

The aliens approach to antisocial youth, wherein we attempt to insulate ourselves from the dangerous ones, carries with it some ominous problems. Most obvious is the enormous financial burden. The cost of incarcerating one criminal youth ranges from about $30,000 to $50,000 per year. It is easy to compute the increasing costs of simply locking offenders away and to enumerate the many social services that need to be sacrificed in order to balance the budgets.

The more serious shortcoming of the aliens approach is that for the most part it does not really work. The effort to separate us from them has been under way for a long time across the nation. Families that fled from the city to the suburbs now find that their orderly neighborhoods are no longer safe. Youth crime has followed close behind the suburban sprawl spreading outward from most American cities. Youth crime has followed even the well-to-do behind the walls of their tightly controlled gated communities. Upscale schools are no longer free of drugs and violence. The conclusion is inescapable by now that building more walls helps only temporarily. The newest suburbs, farther out from the city, higher up into the hills, also have experienced the incursion of gangs, drugs, and violence. At some point, all these efforts to get away and to erect more walls yield diminishing returns. For the vast majority of Americans at this time, there truly is no place to hide.

Another reason why the aliens approach will not succeed with juvenile criminals is because there are two populations of antisocial kids: (1) the current population of antisocial youths—the ones we arrest, prosecute, and incarcerate today; and (2) the vast and growing population of youths who are, developmentally speaking, "in the pipeline" for becoming young offenders. These latter youths are the potential new supply of such troubled kids, and their numbers are enormous. If we apply only the aliens approach to antisocial youths, if we fail to understand the nature and sources of such antisocial patterns, and if we fail to grasp what it is about society that generates these kids in such numbers, then we can expect that the supply of antisocial youths will continue to expand.

There is yet another pitfall in the aliens approach to juvenile crime that is no less serious than the practical difficulties of creating distance and building barriers. Viewing antisocial youth as aliens and locking them away closes off reflection. But the explosion of crime by children and adolescents over the past generation demands an explanation. We want to demand that young criminals be held accountable, but as a society we too must be accountable. What does it imply about our society that so many juveniles drift into patterns of serious antisocial behavior? What does it mean that we have, by far, the highest rate of incarceration of all industrialized nations? What does it mean that we now have incarcerated such an enormous proportion of young black males?

Adolescents are a pretty good barometer of society's health because deficits in socialization and personality development can exist fairly quietly throughout much of childhood. But such deficits come out in the open during the teen years in the form of misjudgments and destructive behaviors. These data, therefore, are an invitation to examine socialization processes—to understand the early influences that make an antisocial character more likely, to understand the healthy structures that protect against untoward outcome, and to understand individual attributes that make a child more difficult to socialize.

The looming escalation of juvenile crime poses an especially complex challenge in the years ahead for citizens, social service professionals, and policymakers. First and foremost, citizens have the right to be safe in their homes, their communities, and their schools. It should be no surprise that society's principal response has been to separate us from them—to build walls, to build prisons, and to assign longer sentences. Seeing that the aliens approach is not sufficient, however, the challenge becomes more daunting than just building walls. The challenge is to respond to juvenile criminals in a way that will lead the majority of them back into civilized society. This means that we cannot just lock them away. Only building more prisons will not succeed, for dehumanizing even these most troublesome members of society will come back to haunt us. If we want juvenile criminals to become citizens who are accountable for their actions, then we must stay connected with them. We must understand who they are and what they need to advance to the level demanded by society.

The effort to stay connected with antisocial youths, to understand how they develop and what they need to become part of society—all of this falls under the rubric of a humanistic endeavor. It assumes that antisocial youths are not fundamentally different from the rest of us—in short, that they are not aliens—and that they are redeemable. The commitment to understanding and rehabilitating antisocial youths, however, is in no way soft-hearted. The principal aim is the safety of society in the long run. The goal in every case is that juveniles become responsible citizens, accountable for their actions and respectful of the rights of others. In sum, the well-being of society requires far more than the construction of prisons and the lengthening of sentences. In the long run, safety requires that juvenile criminals, whenever possible, be brought back into normal society, and that we address the root causes of such delinquency in our social fabric.

To begin to meet these challenges, we must first be conversant with the various labels and diagnoses that discriminate the different kinds of youths who commit antisocial acts, and to understand the nature and origins of those labels (Chapter 2). Chapter 3 reviews the psychosocial conditions involved in healthy versus pathological child development, as well as the biological factors that appear to be implicated in the formation of some antisocial character. Chapter 4 outlines the developmental trajectories that are typically followed by the various types of antisocial youth. Chapter 5 explicates the roles of several of the most common psychiatric disorders in antisocial behavior. The role of formal psychological evaluation of antisocial youths is reviewed in Chapter 6. The broad array of available treatments for antisocial youth is presented in Chapter 7, with an emphasis on the most effective, community-based treatment. Chapter 8 invites reflection upon the social conditions that appear to have supported the escalation of juvenile crime over the past generation in the United States.

their typical course. For example, if I state that Ms. Woods suffers from major depression, then another clinician can be reasonably confident that Ms. Woods has been enduring an extraordinarily miserable time, and that she probably is experiencing disturbed sleep and diminished appetite, energy level, and concentration. Further, the diagnosis implies that her thinking is quite negative in regard to herself and her future, and that she likely feels rather hopeless. Such a label can serve as a rough sketch of what the patient has been going through, and it can imply lines of inquiry regarding relevant background (e.g., precipitating stressors, family background/heredity) as well as the most promising treatment avenues (medications, psychotherapy).

Any tool with such professional and social potency as psychiatric diagnosis also carries some liabilities. The principal risk is that the diagnostic label can easily be taken as more real than it actually is. We like to feel, when we arrive at a diagnosis, that we know something more than we knew before, that we have identified some objective entity. It is easy to forget that the diagnosis is a socially constructed label, at best a theoretical construct. It is easy to forget that the diagnosis does not denote a discrete and natural entity, that the label is a product of human thought and wrangling. Even the sophisticated sets of diagnostic criteria in *DSM-IV* (American Psychiatric Association 1994) are voted on by committees of clinicians. When diagnosis is reified, we tend to forget the person behind the label. The worst outcome is when the rendering of a diagnosis is taken for a conclusion—whereupon inquiry ceases—instead of being the occasion for the subsequent set of questions.

Besides these concerns with diagnosis generally, there are two specific weaknesses we encounter in the diagnosis and labeling of youths who display antisocial behavior. First, there is the problem that certain diagnoses (e.g., conduct disorder) frequently include individuals whose salient behavior patterns, or "index" behaviors, are dramatically different from person to person. This problem arises because the criteria required to earn a given diagnosis range all the way from serious criminal actions (e.g., assault with a deadly weapon) to what are merely "status offenses" such as school truancy and running away from home—all of which are given equal diagnostic weight. Second, two individuals whose index behaviors are essentially the same may, in fact, be psychologically very different, with radically different family backgrounds and treatment needs, and with divergent prognoses.

The social and technical complexities of diagnosis are nowhere more in evidence than in the realm of behaviors termed "antisocial" because antisocial behavior exists at the intersection of the behavioral sciences and criminal law. It is well, therefore, to reflect on the meaning of *antisocial* and its place in our society if we are to gain a balanced understanding of youths who are so labeled.

At first glance it is perfectly obvious what is meant by the term *antisocial*. Antisocial behavior is the reason why we double check that our doors are locked at night, why we avoid walking alone at night in our cities, and why we may pass up a parking spot on a poorly lighted street. Antisocial behavior is why we have police, criminal courts, and correctional institutions. Yet a little reflection shows that these familiar instances of worry and caution capture only part of the problem. The crimes we think most about avoiding are overt, usually aggressive crimes, such as assault, robbery, and car-jacking. But there is much antisocial behavior that does not generate such anxiety and caution. A great deal of antisocial behavior is not even criminal and therefore is never prosecuted or punished.

The term *antisocial*, as it is used in psychiatry and psychology, means behaviors that violate social norms and are harmful to other persons or to society. Antisocial behaviors fall roughly into two broad categories: (1) behaviors that are overtly harmful to others (e.g., violence, theft), and (2) behaviors that are harmful to others or to society through neglect or irresponsibility. It is behaviors in category 1, the overt crimes, that are most alarming to citizens and most likely to elicit media attention. Yet the harm to society resulting from irresponsible actions should not be underestimated. Individuals or institutions that shirk responsibility for their actions wreak havoc upon society in two ways. First, there is the direct damage to individuals and families. For example, men who father children for whom they assume no responsibility leave behind a legacy of deprivation and emotional pain, which often generates long-term pathology in the affected individuals and their communities. Second, such irresponsibility serves as a model for attitudes and behavior. Children learn from their elders and from society at large, and selfishness and cynicism often are the long-lasting by-products of exposure to such influences.

There is a strong tendency to think of destructive, antisocial behaviors as the product of an identifiable class of criminal individuals. But this is only part of the truth, and it obscures the substantial damage that is wrought by a variety of institutions. The most popular institutional villain in recent years has been the tobacco industry, which has come under fire for deliberately hooking youths on its products while knowing full well that thousands of these individuals will develop serious and even fatal illnesses as a result. This is, by any definition, a pattern of antisocial behavior, as it knowingly inflicts physical harm on countless individuals, neglects to take steps to eliminate such harm, and apparently conceals what was known about the damage the tobacco industry was doing. Attorneys will debate culpability issues in litigation for years, but it is clear that the industry's endeavors were almost entirely legal. Such noncriminal antisocial pursuits often are defended by arguments that pit economic variables (jobs, profit margins) against the health and welfare of individuals and their communities—as if our society could not afford to have economic and biological health at the same time!

The tobacco industry is only the most prominent example of institutionalized irresponsibility that leads to grievous outcomes. In many instances of institutional behavior, the actions taken run through gray areas of criminal versus noncriminal, irresponsible versus responsible, and antisocial versus acceptable. In Louisiana, yet another petrochemical plant is proposed in an area where the poorest citizens already suffer high rates of serious health problems from the chemical plants located there. As always, economic arguments are pitted against the well-being of local citizens. Such projects usually are carried out in ways that are legal, so no crime is being committed. Yet it is plain that these plants inflict serious harm, usually on the citizens least able to protect themselves. Is this antisocial behavior? The irresponsibility of knowingly inflicting harm on others is antisocial to the same degree as the father who fails to pay child support or who covertly encourages substance abuse in his children.

Governmental agencies also are capable of substantial irresponsibility. During the Vietnam War, was it not antisocial behavior to knowingly mislead the American public about casualty statistics and the chances of success? At the state and local levels, government at times is complicit with actions that are directly harmful to citizens. In may instances, government agencies have needed to be sued by citizen groups to perform regulatory functions to protect the health and welfare of citizens. Such lapses of duty surely are irresponsible, but is this not also antisocial behavior? When a man fails to make child support payments, we know whom to hold accountable. But whom do we hold accountable for corporate misadventure or for the failure of government to protect? In institutional antisocial behavior, responsibility is diffused. But the difficulty in assigning responsibility does not make such irresponsibility any less harmful.

It is well to remember, then, when examining the crimes and irresponsibilities of antisocial youths, that such failure of social conscience is not limited just to that class of labeled individuals. It is well to remember that youths and their families have been exposed in many cases to professional and even institutional demonstrations of evasion of responsibility and outright dishonesty.

THE FOCUS ON OBJECTIVE BEHAVIORS

With anything so complex as human behavior, there are bound to be very different ways of labeling and categorizing the phenomena of interest. For most of this century, psychiatric diagnosis was more of an art than a science. Diagnosis was based on the clinician's impressions about the patient's personality structure or unconscious conflicts, and it depended on the training and background of the particular doctor. As a result, diagnosis was unreliable, with different clinicians frequently arriving at different labels for the same individual. Over the past three decades, however, psychiatry and psychology have moved toward a more behavioral basis for diagnosis. Psychiatric diagnosis (using *DSM-IV*, described below) is based more on observable behaviors than on inferred (i.e., unobservable) psychological processes. Patients are diagnosed less according to personality type or neurotic style than according to specific behavioral criteria and the patients' direct report of mood or thought content. The focus on objective behaviors brings psychiatric diagnosis more in line with legal definitions and criteria where fairness demands criteria based on actual behavior and self-report instead of inferred internal processes or qualities.

What is not so obvious in the lists of behavioral diagnostic criteria is that, as David Lykken (1995) puts it in regard to antisocial personality disorder, "There is no theoretical or empirical basis for supposing that this scheme carves nature at her joints" (p. 4). Because individuals may develop similar patterns of behavior through very different experiences and personalities, classifying persons just according to their behaviors is of limited clinical and scientific usefulness.

Alex, a 15-year-old tenth grader, lived with his mother and his 12-year-old sister, Lisa, in a middle-class suburb. Alex was an attractive boy with an oval face, sandy brown hair, and freckles. Up to the age of 14, Alex had appeared to be progressing about as well as most of his peers. His parents had divorced when he was 10, but he appeared to adapt well even to their unremitting tension and recrimination. Alex's grades were good, mostly B's and some C's, and he had shown no real learning difficulties. He was liked by his teachers and friends and he had a girlfriend. He participated in sports like most of his friends, including skiing and mountain biking.

During the ninth grade, however, his mother noticed a more surly and defiant attitude, and his attire more often included the familiar "gang wannabe" baggy pants and a chain. He argued more intensely over rules like curfews and homework. He was disrespectful to his mother and sister, and the time he devoted to schoolwork dropped off to nearly nothing. Alex's father, who had remarried about two years earlier, saw little of the belligerent attitude, and he suggested to Alex's mother that such behavior was probably just normal adolescent rebellion. He also implied that Alex's disrespect might stem from his mother's flawed parenting style. Father's bland attitude held up even after Alex, along with two friends, was charged by local police with possession of marijuana. His father helped to pay for a private lawyer, and he again tried to believe that Alex's behavior would just turn around. By then, Alex had a probation officer he needed to check in with regularly. Alex then was reported by the school to have been truant for sixteen days in the fall semester, and his mother and father engaged in a protracted verbal battle over why they hadn't known about the missed days, which parent should have been notified, and so on.

Alex ended the fall term with two F's and the rest C's and D's. It was much the same during the spring term, and Alex had no good explanation for the frequent absences except to say that he needed to hang out with his friends. Two brief school suspensions followed, along with several unproductive meetings at school. Alex, for his part, seemed unconcerned. He was mostly just frustrated that others kept bothering him about school and his attitude. He was reported to have been involved in two fights at school during the year, and he was suspended. On two occasions he was detained at local department stores for shoplifting. He was charged in the second case, and that case was awaiting a hearing in juvenile court when Alex was arrested for car theft. It seems that he and a new friend his parents had never met, Mike, were stopped about midnight driving about town in a car they had stolen from a nearby apartment complex.

Alex spent several days in juvenile detention, and a hearing was scheduled in court. By this time, Alex's probation officer was no longer in a mood to be lenient, and he recommended that the judge order substantial time in detention along with further evaluation by a psychiatrist or psychologist. What was puzzling to the probation

officer was the same thing that puzzled his family—how to understand this downhill pattern of behaviors over the past year in a boy
with no previous history of serious trouble. After all, this was not a
boy from a violent or deprived background. His role models were
good by every normal standard: his father was a successful attorney,
his mother was a real estate agent, and no one in Alex's family had
ever been in any real trouble.

The remainder of tenth grade and the beginning of eleventh was
an arduous and trying time for Alex's parents, for his sister, and for
Alex himself. The court was strict and made it clear that further
transgressions would be punished even more harshly. His attorney
and probation officer warned that more serious charges could lead
to substantial time in a juvenile corrections facility. Alex was sent
for individual counseling, but for several months this went nowhere,
mainly because Alex did not want to be there. Weekly family therapy
sessions helped Alex's father to give up the angry denunciations of
Alex and the blaming of his mother, and Alex's stepmother began to
have a voice in the process. Family therapies, court hearings, meetings with the probation officer, community service hours—and all
the while it was uncertain what, if anything, was going to make a
difference. But finally, after many months of such demanding work,
everyone involved began to realize that Alex's behavior and attitude
seemed to be improving. He was respecting curfews (with the court's
help), attending school (with better grades), and he surrendered some
of the defiance toward his mother. He seemed genuinely frightened
by the prospect of deeper trouble with police and courts. By the
middle of eleventh grade, Alex clearly was leaving behind the behaviors that set off the alarms the previous year. He again seemed to
focus on his future, his education, and his long-term goals.

The same basic pattern of antisocial behaviors can occur in very
different personalities, with different developmental histories, different sets of strengths and vulnerabilities, and different treatment
needs. Alex, it turned out, was responsive to clinical treatment and
ceased his untoward behaviors after extensive intervention by the

court and individual and family therapies. Relationships with his family began the long process of repair. His associate in the car theft, Mike, however, did not respond to intervention. Over subsequent months, he went on to an equally serious theft, more arrests and finally commitment in a juvenile correctional institution (i.e., prison of juveniles). The same diagnosis, conduct disorder, was applied to both boys. But the obvious question is, What was the difference between the boys that led to such divergent outcomes? This is a case where we see essentially the same pattern of index behaviors in very different boys.

In Figure 2–1 is displayed the concept of developmental trajectories. On the vertical axis is the individual's level of socialization, that is, the level of respect for and adherence to social norms and expectations; the horizontal axis is age. The area within the ellipse represents the zone of antisocial behaviors. The majority of children develop social and interpersonal capabilities without signifi-

FIGURE 2–1. Developmental trajectories

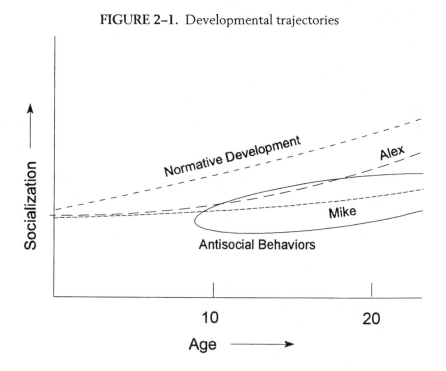

cant antisocial behaviors—normative development. It is presumed that for most purposes the behavior of young children (below about age 8) cannot meaningfully be designated as antisocial. The zone of antisocial behaviors tapers gradually after about the age of 18 to represent the fact that the incidence of criminal behavior gradually diminishes after 18. Alex's developmental trajectory is within normal limits until about the age of 13 to 14. He then shows a dip into antisocial behaviors, but he pulls out of it by the age of 16. Mike, on the other hand, traveled through essentially the same antisocial territory as Alex from about 13 to 16, but the overall trajectory is very different. Mike does not pull out of it, but instead continues within this antisocial zone into his 20s.

In retrospect, it is easy to see some key differences between Alex and Mike. Alex's attachments to his parents, while strained, were strong. After the initial phase of defiance and hostility, he was deeply pained to see their anguish, and he was tormented by the prospect of being separated from his parents and his sister. He felt loved and felt that he needed their love. He also was able, with the help of his therapist, to step back from himself, from his resentments and anger, and take stock of himself realistically. He was able to learn to think more clearly about guiding himself and making choices he could live with.

In contrast, Mike did not have strong family attachments. In addition, Mike had always had more difficulty learning; he was more impulsive and was more prone to aggressive reactions to conditions of frustration. Earlier on, he had associated with the tough crowd of boys at school. His expectations for himself were not so positive as Alex's, and he was not particularly horrified to spend several weeks in detention.

DIAGNOSES AND OTHER LABELS

The *Diagnostic and Statistical Manual of Mental Disorders,* fourth edition (*DSM-IV;* American Psychiatric Association 1994) is the official classification scheme for psychiatric diagnosis in use today.

The principal purpose of the *DSM-IV* is to facilitate reliable and agreed-upon diagnostic decisions, so that two different clinicians will have a good chance of arriving at the same diagnosis for the same patient. The *DSM*, however, has become far more than just a guide for clinical decision making. This compilation of diagnostic labels and diagnostic criteria also has become indispensable in the workings of the health insurance industry. Reimbursement of doctors and hospitals is keyed to diagnostic labels and their code numbers. Certain codes are covered by insurance plans, while others are excluded. In this age of managed care, the overseers go to great lengths to ensure that certain procedures are paid only for certain diagnostic codes, while other procedures are barred. In this way, the *DSM* has become a management tool used by the insurance industry to exert control over the decisions and practices of doctors, clinics and hospitals. In addition to the obvious role in the economics of mental health, numerous research projects in psychiatry and psychology are oriented to the diagnostic categories and their criteria that are provided by the *DSM*.

The *DSM-IV* achieves its aims by being purely descriptive and atheoretical. That is, for each disorder there are listed specific sets of diagnostic criteria that must be met in order for the diagnosis to be assigned. These criteria are purely descriptive; that is, the criteria focus on specific, observable behaviors or on the patient's report of direct experience (e.g., mood). The criteria intentionally avoid any theoretical bias or any implication about the etiology of the disorder. By basing diagnostic decisions on observable behaviors or direct reports of experience, the level of agreement among diagnosticians is strengthened.

The *DSM* has undergone considerable evolution since its inception. The first *DSM*, published by the American Psychiatric Association in 1952, reflected a very different conception of psychiatric disorder. Psychiatry at the time was strongly influenced by the psychodynamic theories of Freud and his followers. In America the most influential psychiatrists were Adolf Meyer and Karl Menninger. Meyer's psychobiological approach involved the conception of psychiatric illness as involving maladaptive reactions to life's stresses. Accordingly, he posited the view that mental illness could be understood in the terms of the individual's unique life history and his or her personal strengths and weaknesses. Similarly, Menninger (1963) taught clinicians to understand the meaning of the patient's symptoms within the context of the individual's life history and characteristic ways of coping.

The first *DSM*, then, involved the psychodynamic terms and ideas that were current in the psychiatry of the day, wherein the meaning of symptoms needed to be understood within the context of the patient's life and personal history. But by the time *DSM-II* was published in 1968, psychiatry had moved away from its emphasis on adaptation to life's stresses or on the personal meaning of symptoms. Moreover, unconscious processes had begun to fall out of favor as explanations for behavior. *DSM-II* explicitly removed reference to Meyer's term *reaction*, and other psychodynamic terms began to disappear as well. *DSM-II* moved psychiatry toward the more traditional medical conception of psychiatric illness as involving *discrete disease entities*.

The publication of *DSM-III* in 1980 marked the full remedicalization of American psychiatry. That is, with the third edition of the *DSM* there is no longer any reference to psychodynamic terms or meanings, and there is no longer any implication of continuity between illness and health. With modern psychiatry returning to its medical roots, discrete disease entities are defined purely according to descriptive signs and clusters of symptoms. This descriptive approach is most associated with Emil Kraepelin (1856–1926), the German psychiatrist who has become the spiritual father of the current classification scheme (LaBruzza and Mendez-Villarrubia 1994).

A major innovation of *DSM-III* and *DSM-IV* involves the use of five axes for diagnostic coding. On axis I are coded clinical disorders, for example, various kinds of mood disorders such as depression. On axis II are coded personality disorders—long-lasting traits of personality and behavior that are sufficiently maladaptive as to cause significant distress to the patient or others. Axis III is reserved for medical conditions. Axis IV lists psychosocial stressors (e.g., death of a loved one) that may play a role in the current clinical condition. Axis V is used to code the patient's global level of functioning—currently and in the past year (on a scale from 0 to 100).

Considering children and adolescents with antisocial behavior, there are three primary diagnostic groups of interest—oppositional defiant disorder, conduct disorder and, after the age of 17, antisocial personality disorder. The two former groups fall within the broad category of disorders usually first diagnosed in infancy, childhood, or adolescence.

The diagnosis most often assigned to juveniles who engage in substantial antisocial activity is conduct disorder. Because this is such a prevalent diagnosis, the diagnostic criteria from *DSM-IV* are presented in full in Table 2–1. Each of categories A, B, and C must be met for the diagnosis to be assigned.

The clinician is instructed by the *DSM-IV* to specify a subtype based on age of onset: childhood-onset type (at least one criterion present prior to age 10) or adolescent-onset type (absence of any criteria prior to age 10). Also, full diagnosis is to include a designation of severity: mild, moderate, or severe. The severity designation follows from the clinician's judgment about how serious are the effects of the individual's behavior on others.

The less serious, oppositional defiant disorder (ODD) involves oppositional and defiant behaviors that are sufficiently severe to be brought to the attention of a doctor or some other clinician (a not altogether reliable threshold). The diagnostic criteria for ODD are listed in Table 2–2, and each of parts A, B, C, and D must be met for the diagnosis to be assigned.

Looking into the histories of adolescents with conduct disorder, one often finds that as children they would have met the criteria of ODD before they met the criteria of conduct disorder. Similarly, in the early histories of adults with serious antisocial patterns of behavior, one typically finds disturbances of behavior, oppositionality, and aggressiveness. Such defiance and hostility can be precursors to more seriously disrupted social and interpersonal relations and even to chronic antisocial behavior patterns.

However, many children diagnosed with ODD do not go on to develop patterns of behavior that violate the rights of others, and

TABLE 2–1. *DSM-IV* Diagnostic Criteria for Conduct Disorder*

A. A repetitive and persistent pattern of behavior in which the basic rights of others or other major age-appropriate societal norms or rules are violated, as manifested by the presence of three (or more) of the following criteria in the past 12 months, with at least one criterion present in the past 6 months:

Aggression to people or animals
1. often bullies, threatens, or intimidates others
2. often initiates physical fights
3. has used a weapon that can cause serious physical harm to others (e.g., bat, brick, broken bottle, knife, gun)
4. has been physically cruel to people
5. has been physically cruel to animals
6. has stolen while confronting a victim (e.g., mugging, purse snatching, extortion, armed robbery)
7. has forced someone into sexual activity

Destruction of property
8. has deliberately engaged in fire-setting with the intention of causing serious damage
9. has deliberately destroyed others' property (other than by fire setting)

Deceitfulness or theft
10. has broken into someone else's house, building, or car
11. often lies to obtain goods or favors or to avoid obligation (i.e., "cons" others)
12. has stolen items of non-trivial value without confronting the victim (e.g., shoplifting, but without breaking and entering; forgery)

Serious violations of rules
13. often stays out at night despite parental prohibitions, beginning before the age of 13
14. has run away from home at least twice while living in parental or parental surrogate home (or once without returning for a lengthy period)
15. is often truant from school, beginning before the age of 13

B. The disturbance in behavior causes clinically significant impairment in social, academic, or occupational functioning

C. If the individual is age 18 years or older, criteria are not met for antisocial personality disorder

*Tables 2–1, 2–2, and 2–3 contain criteria reprinted with permission from the *Diagnostic and Statistical Manual of Mental Disorders, Fourth Edition.* Copyright © 1994 by the American Psychiatric Association.

TABLE 2–2. *DSM-IV* Diagnostic Criteria for Oppositional Defiant Disorder

A. A pattern of negativistic, hostile, and defiant behavior lasting at least 6 months, during which four (or more) of the following are present:
    1. often loses temper
    2. often argues with adults
    3. often actively defies or refuses to comply with adults' requests or rules
    4. often deliberately annoys people
    5. often blames others for his or her mistakes of misbehavior
    6. is often touchy and easily annoyed by others
    7. is often angry and resentful
    8. is often spiteful and vindictive

B. The disturbance in behavior causes clinically significant impairment in social, academic, or occupational functioning

C. The behaviors do not occur exclusively during the course of a psychotic or mood disorder

D. Criteria are not met for conduct disorder, and, if the individual is age 18 years or older, criteria are not met for antisocial personality disorder

these children would not earn the diagnosis of conduct disorder. Some children are simply hard to live with because of a difficult temperament (Turecki 1985), emotional stresses, or a combination of the two. Oppositional and defiant behavior can also stem from inept and coercive parenting practices (see Chapter 3).

The criteria for antisocial personality disorder (ASPD) specify that individuals under the age of 18 are ineligible for this diagnosis. Nonetheless, this is the diagnostic label most often applied to young adults who persist in behaviors that violate the rights of others, and many adolescents who have carried the conduct disorder diagnosis are diagnosed with ASPD when they turn 18. Indeed, as noted below, some degree of developmental continuity between conduct disorder and ASPD is built into the definition of the latter: the individual must have had some of the symptoms of conduct disorder before the age of 15 to be diagnosed with ASPD.

DSM-IV recognizes eleven different personality disorders. Personality disorder is defined as, "an enduring pattern of inner experience and behavior that deviates markedly from the expectations of the individual's culture, is pervasive and inflexible, has an onset in adolescence or early adulthood, is stable over time, and leads to distress or impairment" (p. 629). The premise, then, is that a personality disorder involves patterns of experience and behavior that are, to some degree, *built into* the individual's personality. Hence, personality disorders tend to be relatively stable and chronic. To diagnose an individual with ASPD, then, is to affix a label with large implications—that not only does this person engage in substantial antisocial behavior, but that he or she probably will continue to do so.

The *DSM-IV* diagnostic criteria for ASPD are listed in Table 2–3, and they are similar to those for conduct disorder. In both conduct disorder and ASPD there is listed an exclusionary criterion at the end; it is item D in ASPD. This exclusion is to ensure that clinicians do not diagnose as antisocial an individual whose aversive behavior is due to a psychotic illness. In those cases, when the psychotic illness is adequately treated, the intolerable behaviors usually abate.

Nowhere in *DSM-III*, *DSM-III-R* (revised), or *DSM-IV* are the weaknesses of the behavioral-descriptive approach to classification more apparent than in these disorders' criteria of irresponsibility and violation of others' rights. Notice in criterion A for conduct disorder that the individual must show a pattern of behavior in which *either* the basic rights of others are violated (e.g., assault with weapons, forced sex), *or* "major age appropriate societal norms or rules are violated" (p. 90) (e.g., truancy). In many cases, such violation of societal norms accompanies more overt violations of others' rights. That is, on a statistical basis, these kinds of violations tend to go together. However, given these criteria, it is possible to assign the same diagnosis to two radically different individuals—one whose problematic behaviors involve truancy, staying out at night without permission, and running away overnight; another whose behaviors involve assault with a deadly

TABLE 2–3. Diagnostic Criteria for Antisocial Personality Disorder

A. There is a pervasive pattern of disregard for and violation of the rights of others occurring since age 15 years, as indicated by three (or more) of the following:
   1. failure to conform to social norms with respect to lawful behaviors as indicated by repeatedly performing acts that are grounds for arrest
   2. deceitfulness, as indicated by repeated lying, use of aliases, or conning others for personal profit or pleasure
   3. impulsivity or failure to plan ahead
   4. irritability or aggressiveness, as indicated by repeated physical fights or assaults
   5. reckless disregard for the safety of self or others
   6. consistent irresponsibility, as indicated by repeated failure to sustain consistent work behavior or honor financial obligations
   7. lack of remorse, as indicated by being indifferent or rationalizing having hurt, mistreated, or stolen from another

B. The individual is at least age 18 years

C. There is evidence of Conduct Disorder with onset before age 15

D. The occurrence of antisocial behavior is not exclusively during the course of schizophrenia or a manic episode

---

weapon (or murder), rape, and arson. Put differently, it is possible to assign the same diagnosis to a young man who has committed the most heinous crimes several times over and to another young man whose worst "crime" was staying away from home overnight or vandalism.

The same problem appears in the ASPD diagnosis. This label can rightly be assigned to the most intractable and violent felon, but also to an individual who demonstrates dishonesty (criterion A2), impulsivity or failure to plan ahead (A3), and irresponsibility, such as failure to pay debts (A6)—in other words, as Lykken (1995) puts it, "not criminals but, rather, drifters or addicts or drunks" (p. 5).

It is no surprise, then, that such heterogeneous groups of individuals are captured by these diagnostic categories. By turning away from the individual's internal psychological structure and personality, by restricting the diagnostic gaze just to statistical clusters of observable behaviors, the person behind the behaviors is obscured. While these diagnostic labels are useful for rough groupings and for reimbursement purposes, they do not tell us much about the youths we may be working with or whose families we may need to advise. Next, we set aside the scatter-shot approach of official psychiatric diagnosis and consider some more informative terms and classifications and their histories.

PSYCHOPATHY AND SOCIOPATHY

While antisocial behavior surely has been part of the social landscape since earliest history, involvement by the medical profession and the social sciences is relatively new. During the nineteenth century, individuals who regularly violated the norms of civilized society were considered by the first American psychiatrist, Benjamin Rush (1745–1813), to suffer from "innate preternatural moral depravity" (Lykken 1995, p. 113). J. C. Pritchard (1786–1848) described these persons with the term *moral insanity*.

The term *psychopathic personality* was introduced by Kraepelin and used to refer to criminal personalities that appear to be severely lacking in moral reasoning or character. The term *psychopath* was widely applied since early in the twentieth century—usually with the connotation of some inborn or constitutional defect underlying an amoral or criminal character. However, as social and experiential factors assumed a larger role in the theories of personality development, the term *sociopath* gained in usage. In sociopathy, the emphasis was placed on social norms and limits and the developmental processes of socialization and where they go wrong. August Aichhorn (1925), for example, writing from a psychoanalytic perspective, described patterns of early experience involving emotional deprivation in sociopathic children that led to a failure of the superego (that part of the personality that normally restrains one from violating moral or social rules).

Among clinicians and researchers who devote their attentions to antisocial behavior, the old term *psychopath* has once again enjoyed wide application in recent years. In 1941, Hérvey Cleckley published his now-classic *The Mask of Sanity*, in which he described individuals from his own practice who manipulated, lied, cheated, and stole their way through life, who violated any and all norms of society, and who, by all accounts, appeared not to profit even from the painful consequences of their misadventures. Perhaps most remarkable, Cleckley observed that many such individuals appeared to have come from basically normal and healthy family backgrounds. These individuals, whose deep defects in socialization appeared not to stem from deprivation, trauma, or bad parenting, Cleckley termed psychopaths, and he systematically delineated the features that distinguish these individuals. Unlike many individuals who, from time to time, violate the rules of society, the psychopath appears to lack any shred of conscience. There is no empathic feeling for one's fellow human beings, and others can be exploited, abused, or assaulted without remorse. Other persons are viewed solely as objects for the gratification of impulses or as obstacles in the way. For Cleckley, the psychopath had failed to acquire the moral and empathic feelings that are essential in all normal socialization. Hence, the psychopath is one for whom socializing fails because of a (possibly) innate defect related to emotional experiences.

Cleckley generated a list of sixteen features that distinguish the psychopath. Several items on Cleckley's list refer to qualities of interpersonal relations, for example, superficial charm, and impersonal sex life, and untruthfulness. Other items refer to internal states such as absence of nervousness and lack of remorse or shame. Like the *DSM-IV*, Cleckley also listed exclusionary criteria (e.g., freedom from delusions) to ensure that psychotic individuals are not included.

These criteria became influential in identifying what became known as the "Cleckley psychopath"—charming, intelligent, deceitful, and devoid of normal interpersonal warmth and empathy (see, for example, Blackburn and Maybury 1985). A wide range of researchers have found that Cleckley's criteria identified a fairly homogeneous set of individuals (psychopaths) who could be distinguished even on certain physiologic variables. David Lykken, in research published in 1957, hypothesized a "fear quotient"—an innate level of fearfulness that varies from person to person. He found through empirical studies that those individuals who met Cleckley's psychopathy criteria showed lower levels of physiologic anxiety (e.g., galvanic skin response). Lykken hypothesized that the innate fearlessness of the young psychopath-to-be undermined the normal processes of socialization. The psychopath failed to learn to avoid aversive situations (e.g., punishment), and hence, had no incentive to learn to think ahead, anticipate consequences, or worry about others' feelings.

The researcher who has done the most to advance our understanding of psychopathy in recent years is R. D. Hare. His recent book *Without Conscience* (1993) provides an excellent and readable account of several criminal psychopaths as well as the more typical psychopathic behavior that is shown even by noncriminal psychopathic personalities.

Hare is best known in scientific circles for developing a reliable but simple method for the diagnosis of psychopathy. Beginning with the Cleckley criteria, Hare developed the *Psychopathy Checklist* and the *Psychopathy Checklist–Revised* (Hare 1991), which now is widely used in both clinical and research settings. The PCL-R consists of twenty items that are arranged in three factors. The first set of items is similar to Checkley's criteria and includes glibness/superficial charm and lack of remorse or guilt. The second factor includes items that are more behavioral in nature, for example, need for stimulation, a parasitic lifestyle, and impulsivity. The third set of three items is used to increase the scale's reliability and includes, for example, criminal versatility. The scale is used by rating each item: No (0), Maybe (1), or Yes (2). Item scores are summed over the entire scale to yield a full-scale score, and scores above a cut-off level are considered "psychopathic." Factors 1 and 2 correlate with one another at about $r = .50$, meaning that most cases that earn a high score on one factor will tend also to have a high score on the other factor. However, it also is possible to earn a high score on the Cleckley-like factor 1 but *not* to earn a high score on criminal-like factor 2. This fits well with the observation that not all Cleckley psychopaths lead criminal lifestyles, and with the frequent observation of "successful psychopaths"—individuals with psychopathic personalities who manage to stay just inside the law or, when they do violate the law, to avoid prosecution. We are all familiar with the white-collar criminal who straddles the world of politics and business and who, for the most part, eludes the gaze of the law; when targeted, he often manages to charm or to deceive his way out of trouble.

All the hazards of affixing labels to individuals are especially salient in the case of children and adolescents. Because they are still developing, and because their personalities are still in flux, diagnostic labels can be a considerable disservice to the child and his family. This is why the diagnosis antisocial personality disorder is reserved for individuals 18 years and over. We should avoid placing such a pejorative label on a young person who may yet develop beyond such disturbing behavior patterns. These reservations notwithstanding, there are some adolescents whose personality and behavioral history are so distinct as to warrant at least the provisional diagnosis of psychopathy. Morton, a psychopathic adolescent clearly earned that diagnosis, and his prognosis is correspondingly bleak.

I was introduced to Morton by a female staff member of the county juvenile detention facility as we started down a long, narrow hallway bordered by jail cells on either side. Some of the inmates were at the facility's school, but a few remained in their cells with the stainless steel toilets and sinks. This is the jail where children are held awaiting trial or commitment to corrections, or while they are serving brief sentences. It was apparent by the time we were seated in a tiny meeting room that Morton was alert and engaging, and that he would not be difficult to talk with. He was a few months shy of 17 years of age, but his husky build and broad face gave the appearance of being several years older. He looked me in the eye as we spoke, and he gave the impression of being totally focused on the task at hand, completely free of anxiety or distraction. His responses to my questions were direct, factual, and frank, even when describing actions that had led to painful injuries for others and probable long incarceration for himself. He was not at all egocentric, readily taking into account the point of view of the examiner, and he gave the impression of being quite intelligent.

I had been asked by Morton's probation counselor to evaluate him to assist the court in determining whether he should be tried in juvenile court or waived to adult court for trial. The key questions for a clinician in evaluations related to the waiver issue involve the sophistication and maturity of the individual, his level of dangerousness to the community, and his amenability to treatment.

Morton described with unusual clarity the events immediately before and during the armed robbery he had committed with a friend: how he had held the middle-aged woman at gunpoint in a mall parking lot while Billy (also age 17) rifled through her purse and then through her car; how he had smashed the handgun against her head as he was leaving; how he and Billy had counted the money at the far end of the parking lot; how they "hightailed it" when they heard police sirens; and how he had known he was caught only an hour later when several carloads of police showed up at his apartment.

The remarkable thing about Morton's account was the manner in which he related it. There was not a hint of the usual minimizing or rationalizing, not a moment of placing blame on someone else, and not a flicker of sentiment that he was being treated unfairly. But equally noteworthy was Morton's absence of any self-doubts, second thoughts, or anxiety. This intelligent young man knew full well the likely consequences of his actions, but he was not afraid or worried. It was as if he were incapable of regret or even reflection about his behavior. Remorse for the victim, who suffered a concussion as well as the dread she will live with for a long time? Again, it was as if Morton were incapable of such emotion. All in all, it seemed that

Morton's emotions about the crime and all that it entailed were so attenuated as to appear absent.

Reinforcing the impression of freedom from anxiety were certain scores on the Wechsler Intelligence Scale for Children (WISC-III) intelligence test. On the one subtest that is especially sensitive to the effects of anxiety (Digit Span; see Chapter 6), Morton earned an extremely high score, meaning that his was able to focus his attention in an uncommonly keen manner.

Morton went on to describe himself and his characteristic reactions. He stated that he always had difficulty in school because he was action-oriented and impulsive, and he frequently was in trouble with the teacher or the school principal. However, he learned well enough and he did not fall behind in school. He reported that he usually got into one or two fights per month, that he *liked* to fight, and that at times he actually went out looking for a fight. He stated that he never was afraid of anything, even when he was a young child, and even many instances of getting hurt or injured (e.g., a broken arm) had never slowed him down.

Among antisocial types, it is psychopaths who compose the most visible and sensational subgroup. It is psychopathic killers who murder serially, plunging whole cities into terror, as with the so-called Hillside Strangler in California, or Ted Bundy near Seattle. It is psychopathic personalities who seem so different even on physiologic variables and who, contrary to traditional conceptions, often seem not to be the products of seriously troubled childhoods. Yet for all their visibility and sensation, psychopathic criminals make up only a fraction of the antisocial individuals who wreak havoc upon society. The much larger and more diverse group of antisocial characters are termed *sociopaths*. These are the individuals who make up the largest part of the population of our jails, juvenile detentions, correctional institutions, and adult prisons. These are the common criminals who are responsible for the majority of assaults, murders, burglaries, thefts, and forgeries. It is sociopaths who are responsible for the largest proportion of common misery among victims of all sorts of crime throughout much of society.

The difference between psychopathy and sociopathy is defined most usefully in Lykken's (1995) view. He delineates the difference thus: "I am using *sociopath* to refer to persons whose lack of socialization is primarily attributable to neglectful or incompetent parenting, reserving *psychopath* for those whose antisocial behavior is due primarily to innate characteristics that either overmaster the socialization from time to time or which make them difficult to socialize even within a traditional two-parent family structure" (p. 31). Thus, according to Lykken and many other current researchers, a large part of the difference relates to the origins of these disorders. In addition, psychopaths can be distinguished by a combination of history, physiologic factors, and even psychological test variables (see, for example, Gacono and Meloy 1994 and Eysenck and Eysenck 1978).

Social science researchers being what they are, numerous subcategories have been posited, many of which make good sense. Within the large genus *sociopath*, for example, Lykken (1995) describes the common sociopath (little or no conscience, highly impulsive, never plans ahead, generally irresponsible); the alienated sociopath (unable to love or affiliate with others); the aggressive sociopath (enjoys inflicting pain and terror on others, delights in the feeling of power over the victim); and the dyssocial sociopath (normal temperament, but allegiance is to antisocial norms, e.g., Fagin's children in *Oliver Twist*). Similarly, Lykken describes subtypes of psychopaths: the distempered psychopath (may have an organic brain disorder that leads to episodic outbursts); the primary psychopath (resistant to socialization, aggressive, impulsive, does not learn from experience; derives from the middle class about as often as from the lower class); and the secondary psychopath (not only aggressive and impulsive but also introverted, shy, and guilt-prone).

The classification schemes reviewed here—both the psychiatric diagnostic groupings and the more differentiated schemes of Hare, Lykken, and others—are useful to those who work with troubled youths and their families. They provide a shorthand expression for meaningful clusters of symptoms and behaviors, and communication is thereby enhanced. However, they should not be used simply to affix a label or a diagnostic conclusion. Indeed, there is a danger in affixing such labels—the illusion that finding the right label somehow deepens our understanding of the individual. Affixing even the right diagnostic label never tells us anything more than we knew before, and we must ensure that rendering the diagnosis does not bring our questioning to a close.

❖ C H A P T E R   3 ❖

Pathways to Antisocial Behavior

PSYCHOSOCIAL DEVELOPMENT

It is nine o'clock in the morning, and the pace is heating up fast in the juvenile court building. Probation counselors and attorneys scramble from offices to courtrooms and back, papers are shuffled and exchanged, and impromptu conferences occur along the congested hallways—all in preparation for the day of hearings and trials and continuances. Fifteen-year-old Lonnie and his parents are late for a meeting with his probation counselor, Mike. When they finally arrive, Mike is already tense and he needs to hurry things along. Lonnie's mother, as she takes her seat in the cramped office, mutters something about why they were late and why her husband, Lonnie's stepfather, could not attend.

Today there will be a hearing on charges of residential burglary stemming from a recent break-in by Lonnie and one of his new friends at the apartment of a neighbor. But Mike is already familiar with Lonnie and his family. The boy had served eight months' probation for assaulting another student the previous year. Also, on Mike's desk sits an inch-thick file that contains all the usual police reports and court documents on prior and current charges. Also included in that stack of paperwork are three reports, spanning seven years, of abuse or neglect that were investigated by the state child protective service, and a lengthy case report by a state social worker documenting the history of parental violence and substance abuse, the biological father's criminal history, and learning difficulties beginning in Lonnie's early grades. An educational evaluation is included, showing average intellectual abilities but poor attention as well as impulsivity. During the previous prosecution, his mother had explained to the probation counselor how Lonnie's father was repeatedly arrested for dealing drugs, how he had physically attacked her several times, and how, after she hid herself and the children, Lonnie's father disappeared to another state. She has not received a penny of child support over these nine years, and money has always been tight. She also explained that Lonnie was "always a tough one, right from the get-go." He was difficult to calm at night, he always was more active and aggressive than other kids, and he engaged in tantrums so intense that adults often just backed off and let him have his way. Also corroborated in school reports were early difficulties with learning. He seemed to have difficulty paying attention for any sustained period of time. He had been treated on and off for attention deficit disorder (ADD), but the Ritalin (stimulant medication) seemed to help sometimes and not others, and the doctors were not sure that ADD was really the problem. Counseling had been tried on two occasions, but Lonnie was not interested, and his mother and stepfather often failed to turn up for appointments.

For Mike, there was nothing unusual about Lonnie and the picture he presented. Here was another adolescent boy from an unstable and probably violent family background, a history of school problems, association with a marginal peer group, and, finally, a pattern of crimes leading to juvenile detention, court, and trial. The potential for commitment to a long-term corrections facility (prison) loomed.

Looking more closely, however, Lonnie's history and presentation demonstrate the challenges in grasping the origins of antisocial behavior patterns. Lonnie's personal and family history are fairly typical from the perspective of the juvenile court, in that the case contains several factors that have been found to be associated with the development of antisocial behavior. These antecedent factors include having one or more antisocial parents (impact via learning and via heredity), parental incompetence or disrupted parent–child relationships, a difficult temperament, the experience of neglect and/or abuse, early difficulties in attention and learning, and association with a deviant peer group.

Our understanding falters, however, at two crucial junctures. First, despite the commonplace appearance of these factors in actual cases, and despite their frequent association with antisocial behavior, it is exceedingly difficult to specify causal connections between predisposing factors and actual antisocial behaviors. For every predisposing factor, such as having an antisocial parent or suffering learning and attention deficits, one can find individuals with those attributes who nonetheless have developed into responsible and productive citizens. For that matter, one can find individuals with several of these risk factors who have grown up well socialized.

The converse problem also weakens our ability to draw direct causal connections between antecedent conditions and antisocial behaviors: some decidedly antisocial adults have a history that reveals none of these heavily researched risk factors. Indeed, it was the appearance of deeply antisocial individuals whose histories revealed no evidence of antisocial or incompetent parents, major losses or disruptions, trauma, or learning problems that led to research on the physiological and psychological qualities of persons we now designate by the term *psychopath*. One of the features that distinguished the psychopath for Cleckley (1982) was the absence of obvious developmental insults. He found that psychopaths often were raised in what he judged to be normal and healthy families.

The second major point at which our understanding falters is this: Although we can be sure that several factors in children's histories are linked in some way to the subsequent development of antisocial behavior, it is discouragingly unclear just how these conditions and experiences lead to actual antisocial behaviors. For example, we know on a statistical basis that having an antisocial parent considerably raises the odds that a given child will develop antisocial behaviors. But the mechanism by which an antisocial parent elevates the risk of a child's becoming antisocial is not at all obvious. Several possibilities are apparent. One, it could be that the parent and the child carry a genetic loading of some kind for antisocial tendency. Two, it could be that the child was mistreated, abused, or neglected, stemming from the parent's antisocial personality, and that this led to deficits in personality development. Three, it could be that the parent modeled antisocial behavior and attitudes for the child; in other words, the child may have learned to emulate his parents. Four, the mechanism involved might be more subtle; perhaps antisocial fathers tend to father children with women whose maternal instincts are weak, and the child suffers from unstable bonding with the mother. In the complexities of the real world, the actual mechanism may involve several of these factors working in combination.

Human development, whether leading to antisocial personality or to a well-socialized citizen, is a dauntingly complex process. In all except the most contrived circumstances, we cannot specify the causes of particular behaviors. When a child exposed to a whole host of antisocial risk factors early in life develops later into a well adjusted and productive citizen, how can we account for such resiliency? And how can we explain that another child, exposed to a similar set of conditions, is deeply entrenched in a life of crime by mid-adolescence?

Because of the enormous complexity among factors implicated in antisocial behavior, along with the infinite variety of routes to successful socialization, rather than speak of the *causes* of antisocial behavior it is more useful to address the failures of socialization. In other words, since we cannot draw causal connections between salient factors and actual antisocial behaviors, it is more fruitful to ask where the normal processes of socialization go awry, and why. No matter which risk factors we consider, no matter how strongly they predispose to antisocial adjustment, they must at some level make their effects felt through the broad nexus of socialization. Thus, if we are to understand anything useful about antisocial development, we must first have a good grasp of normal, healthy development.

In framing the question of the origins of antisocial behavior and the failures of socialization, it is important to bear in mind the fact that the vast majority of children grow up to be tolerably well-socialized adults. All but a small percentage of individuals, by the time they are well into their adult years, demonstrate the principal features of a socialized personality: (1) a reasonably reliable respect for the norms and rules of society, including its laws; (2) a basic attitude of responsibility for one's actions and commitments; and (3) some capacity to care about the well-being and safety of one's fellow human beings, that is, a capacity for "prosocial" behavior and empathic attunement to the feelings of others.

The development of the human child is surely the most complex and wondrous event in nature. Even under conditions that are far less than optimal, the vast majority of children manage to adapt successfully, to grow physically, to mature emotionally and cognitively, and to take their place as competent and responsible citizens. And yet, for all the resilience and flexibility that is built into the human developmental apparatus, we also know of many events and conditions by which socialization can be blocked or undermined. Some of these are obvious hazards, catastrophic events such as severe abuse or chronic neglect, that would derail almost any child's development. Others are more subtle, such as having a depressed mother or an alcoholic father.

This chapter reviews several of the risk factors associated with antisocial development. However, to understand just how such factors exert their negative influences on the child's development, it is necessary to review some of the insights about normal child development that have been garnered over the past half century. In the study of antisocial behavior, the most relevant aspect of child development is socialization. One of the better definitions of socialization was provided by Kochanska (1993): "The gradual developmental shift from external to internal regulation that results in a child's ability to conform to societal standards of conduct and to restrain antisocial or destructive impulses, even in the absence of surveillance, is the essence and hallmark of successful socialization" (p. 325).

Successful socialization entails becoming a citizen. The concept of *citizen*, as the aim of socialization, is distinguished from other desirable aims of development, such as intellectual strength, occupational success, or having many friends. One can attain these other goals and yet behave in antisocial ways (e.g., the white-collar criminal). Also, one can be rather poorly accomplished in intellectual, social, and occupational arenas and still be a model citizen. Surely, when considering antisocial youth and adults, what we would wish for most fervently is more successful performance of the duties and responsibilities that fall under the rubric of citizenship, or, as Kochanska put it, "conforming to societal standards of conduct."

Socialization: Becoming a Citizen

Scientific exploration of child and adolescent development has expanded exponentially over the past three decades, with major contributions from psychiatric and psychological investigators. The conceptual backdrop and terminology for much research, however, derives in one way or another from the psychological theories that were dominant decades ago, that is, from psychoanalysis. Many of the most useful constructs for understanding child development and socialization (and where it can go wrong) derive from the newer forms of psychoanalytic theory that have examined the reality-oriented, adaptive ego functions and the central role of interpersonal relations in personality development. These are reviewed briefly with special attention to the constructs that are most relevant for antisocial development.

Classical psychoanalysis, as developed and taught by Freud, took as its principal focus the intrapsychic processes and conflicts within the individual. Freud's early emphasis on the drive energies of libido and aggression gave way in his later work to the tripartite structure of id, ego, and superego. The id was held to be the biological seat of instinctual drive energies—the "seething cauldron" of libido and aggression. The superego—the locus of self-restraint and respect for rules and limits—forms from resolution of the oedipal phase, and involves identification with social norms, ideals, and morality. It is the superego that so often is strikingly deficient in antisocial individuals. The ego was posited as the reality-oriented, organizing seat of personality, the executive component responsible for balancing the demands of id, superego, and reason. Even with the tripartite personality structure, however, the focus still was on individual processes, on repressed and unconscious impulses and wishes, and on the recovery of unconscious material and conflicts—all of which were difficult or impossible to explore scientifically.

Freud was well aware of the importance of interpersonal relations and the reality-based ego functions in the development of the child. However, it fell to his followers, the so-called neopsychoanalytic thinkers, to expand the scope of psychological theory so as to facilitate systematic exploration of child development. The two interconnected strands of psychological theory and research that are especially relevant for the study of normal socialization and its pitfalls are ego psychology and object relations theory. Each of these branches of theory has contributed key concepts in the ongoing effort to understand both normal development and its failure leading to antisocial character.

Ego Strengths and Defense Mechanisms

The evolution of psychoanalytic theory involved a gradual shift of focus from intrapsychic processes and unconscious conflicts to the more reality-oriented processes by which individuals adapt to the conditions and the conflicting demands of life. These involve cognitive skills such as sustaining attention, planning ahead, logical reasoning, as well as emotional regulation and the capacity to develop and sustain meaningful interpersonal relationships. For psychoanalytic theorists, the aggregate of these organizing and adaptive functions is the ego (Blanck and Blanck 1979). Psychologist Jane Loevinger (Loevinger and Wessler 1970, Loevinger et al. 1970), whose research led to the development of a sophisticated instrument for the assessment of ego development level, the Sentence Completion Test, defines the ego more specifically as *the* central organizing function: "The striving to master, to integrate, to make sense of experience is not one ego function among others but the essence of the ego" (Loevinger 1969, p. 85).

One of the earliest major steps in the study of adaptive functions was taken by Freud's daughter, Anna Freud, in her classic study, *The Ego and the Mechanisms of Defense* (1936). Here, she outlined a general theory for the understanding psychological compromises—defense mechanisms—that enable the individual to cope with the conflicting demands of external reality, internal affects, and personal wishes. Anna Freud's contribution, while clarifying the nature and functioning of defense mechanisms, still was based primarily on a model of psychic conflict.

In his landmark text, *Ego Psychology and the Problem of Adaptation* (1958), Heinz Hartmann advanced theory a step beyond where Anna Freud had taken it. He adopted an explicit focus on what he termed the "conflict-free sphere" of ego functioning. He stated, "Not every adaptation to the environment, or every learning and maturation process, is a conflict. . . . I refer to the development *outside of conflict*, of perception, language, recall-phenomena" (p. 8). Study of these reality-oriented functions has led to a broader appreciation of a range of adaptive strengths, such as the ability to perceive things accurately (reality testing), the ability to reason logically, the capacity to plan a sequence of actions toward a goal, and the ability to anticipate the consequences of one's actions— all attributes that are commonly deficient in antisocial youths. The concept of adaptation was given theoretical and empirical support through the study of resiliency (Dugan and Coles 1989). Block and Block (1980) describe a continuum in ego adaptability, ranging from "ego resiliency" to "ego brittle."

In addition to these capabilities, several nonspecific ego strengths were identified by Kernberg (1975) as especially relevant in severe personality disorders. These include the capacity to tolerate anxiety without resorting to acting out or regression (anxiety tolerance), the ability to constrain impulses (impulse control), and the development of "sublimatory channels"—some regions of special competence or creativity (e.g., skills in woodworking, art, or writing). Deficits in these ego strengths are so typical in antisocial youths that it is well to recall that the majority of adolescents *can* bear some anxiety without untoward effects; they *can* constrain most impulses most of the time, and they *do* show "islands of competence" (Brooks 1991) and creativity. Examining the psychological structure of antisocial youths, one often finds poorly developed ego strengths. It is remarkable just how frequently antisocial youth cannot point to a single area of competence they have developed, whether this be skills learned in a job, at school, or at home. Too often in interviews one hears only about "hanging out," watching TV, and playing video games—all passive and unproductive endeavors. And most antisocial youths are impulsive. Even in the absence of a psychiatric disorder, such as attention deficit, and even for children with normal intellectual functioning, the capacity to think ahead, to anticipate consequences, and to restrain emotional impulses often is impoverished in adolescents with antisocial habits.

The ego strengths that are most strikingly deficient in antisocial youths—those right at the heart of their antisocial functioning—are those whose development depends heavily on healthy and nurturing interpersonal relationships during the childhood years. Some antisocial adolescents are strong intellectually, capable of learning in school, and able to plan ahead and to efficiently learn the skills they are interested in. They possess solid strengths in some cognitive-intellectual realms. And yet, they are unable to take the point of view of another person; that is, they are *egocentric*. Egocentrism is evidenced by a young child relating an experience from his day, all the while referring casually to persons and events the listener could not possibly have known about. Typically, during the years prior to adolescence, the child comes to understand that what he knows or witnessed may not be known or witnessed by another person. The child learns to take into account the fact that the listener does not *know* Freddie from the third-grade class next door at school. In other words, the child learns to appreciate that the point of view of the other person is different from his own. In antisocial development the capacity to appreciate the point of view of other persons—and their feelings—often is impoverished.

Egocentrism can be observed in other conditions, for example, in persons suffering from psychotic disorders, where there has been a collapse of logical cognitive processing. It is most striking in anti-social youths, however, because it occurs in individuals who usu-ally are intellectually intact, and because it goes hand in hand with another ego weakness at the heart of antisocial development—*lack of empathy*. In their accounts of interactions with others, even with important persons in their lives, antisocial youths typically relate nothing about the experience or the emotions of the other person. When pressed to consider the pain or the terror they may have inflicted on a victim, their response often involves a change of subject or some bland rationalization. Examination usually reveals that this void runs throughout the individual's functioning, that there is an inability to consider and to care about the experience of another person. The other person's feelings are of no interest, and indeed the other person might just as well be an inanimate object.

Another ego strength that typically is impoverished in antiso-cial individuals is the capacity to realistically observe the actions and attributes of the self. The *observing ego* refers to that part of the mental apparatus that keeps track of one's self and one's ac-tions in the appropriate context. The normal capacity to observe oneself ensures not "losing the forest for the trees," enables one to keep track of what kinds of behaviors are appropriate in a particu-lar setting, and enables one to discern the sensible next steps. Keep-ing track of one's behaviors-in-context also helps to ensure that the needs and wishes of others are not entirely disregarded.

The principal developmental task during the adolescent years is the formation of a stable and coherent identity, a self-image and sense of self that affords the individual needed continuity through different times and settings (Young 1994). As cognitive complexity expands through these years, there is increased emphasis on internal qualities such as emotions and aspirations (Harter 1990). And, as adolescents experiment with different self-concepts or personas, there is a need to integrate these different self-concepts into an internally consistent self-image. Children who, because of high levels of stress or other impediments, fail to adequately integrate different self-concepts and attributes into a coherent identity are at risk of what Erik Erikson (1968) termed *identity diffusion*. This is an anxiety-provoking condition in which the individual feels unsure of who he is or where he belongs, and it severely undermines personality development.

To successfully negotiate the psychological tasks and demands of adolescence, to traverse the often tumultuous waters of identity formation, requires some mental anchor points. The most reliable, universal anchor is the set of ideals and values the adolescent identifies within his family and culture. The *ego ideal* is that part of the personality that identifies with and orients to such values and ideals, and this set of ideals serves as a crucial identification with the broader society. The aspiration to do good—whether in work, education, religion, or social justice—is perhaps a better guide to behavior and formation of the self than are prohibitions and threats of punishment.

Another key anchor point for development in children and adolescents, and one that is particularly important in building normal self-esteem, is what has been termed "islands of competence." This was explained most eloquently by Mary Catherine Bateson (1994):

> The safest and richest journeys through adolescence are those of children who discover some area of skill that becomes their very own, focusing energies and demanding for at least part of the day a honed and delicious alertness. Building model planes, ballet dancing, riding, computer hacking . . . any of these, whether or not it promises a way to make a living later in life, can become a standard for feeling fully alive. [p. 202]

Adolescents who readily identify with the ideals and aspirations of society and who seem naturally to develop some special areas of competence make it look easy. It is remarkable, then, to see how regularly adolescents labeled antisocial are altogether lacking in such ideals and competencies. For so many antisocial youths, there are no reliable beacons out there to help guide them, no reliable ideals and values, no special skills or pursuits. What ideals do appear often are with sports superstars—images that function more like fantasy figures than real people one might learn from.

Whatever strengths and resources the individual can call upon enable her to adapt to her life in the most satisfying manner possible. But adaptation is seldom smooth and it is never fully harmonious. For all of us, but especially for persons whose life circumstances are difficult or painful, there is a need for psychological compromises—defense mechanisms. In his masterful exposition of the psychology of defense mechanisms, psychiatrist George Vaillant (1993) states, "Our minds distort inner and outer reality so that an observer might accuse us of denial, self-deception, even dishonesty. But such mental defenses creatively rearrange the sources of our conflict so that they become manageable and we may survive. The mind's defenses—like the body's immune mechanisms—protect us by providing a variety of illusions to filter pain and to allow self-soothing" (p. 1).

The mention of defense mechanisms often carries a pejorative tone. We think of the denial of the alcoholic, the projection of the paranoid, or the acting out of the character disordered patient. However, as Vaillant makes clear, defenses also serve an adaptive and stabilizing function, rendering bearable aspects of our experience that might otherwise be too painful and anxiety provoking. Nowhere are the psychic benefits of defenses more clear than in normal child development. An illustration of the stabilizing function of normal defenses was provided by a colleague, about his 8-year-old son, Jeffrey.

There was a buzz of excitement around the house the day that Jeffrey's sister came home with her 14-inch baby corn snake. Jeffrey was curious, and he learned, among other things, that corn snakes do not eat the crickets that make up the daily fare for his lizard. Corn snakes eat mice, and almost nothing else. All was well for awhile, for the snake had eaten the day before purchase, and would not need to feed again for several days. Then, the day came for the first feeding at home. A short stop at the pet shop produced a "pinky"—a small and helpless baby mouse. Jeffrey watched with awe, then with a darkening expression, as the small snake circled then constricted the immobile little mouse. At the sight of that helpless mouse being held, then swallowed by the snake, Jeffrey's expression changed to horror. He ran from the room in tears, and needed some consoling. His mother offered him various explanations—like how the baby mouse doesn't even know what's happening, and "that's nature's way."

Jeffrey was present for the next feeding a few days later. Right after the pinky disappeared into the snake, Jeffrey was heard, on his way through the kitchen with his neighbor friend, explaining in the most casual tone, "Oh, the baby mouse doesn't even know what's happening. It doesn't even hurt him."

Freud saw defense mechanisms as largely pathological, and the aim of psychoanalysis was to enable the patient to overcome the reliance on such defenses. Vaillant, however, in the tradition of modern ego psychology, is more interested in the adaptive and creative aspects of psychological defenses. Modern research has demonstrated that there is a continuum between defense mechanisms that are maladaptive and defenses that are more adaptive and healthy. Indeed, this continuum is included as a provisional diagnostic dimension in the *DSM-IV* (American Psychiatric Association 1994).

In the concluding chapter of Charles Frazier's (1997) novel, *Cold Mountain*, the protagonist reflects upon the horrific losses and pain of the Civil War. His narrative provides a good description of the pragmatics of coping and the need for defenses:

You could grieve endlessly for the loss of time and for the damage done therein. For the dead and for your own lost self. But what the wisdom of the ages says is that we do well not to grieve on and on. And those old ones knew a thing or two . . . for you can grieve your heart out and in the end you are still where you were. All your grief hasn't changed a thing. What you have lost will not be returned to you. It will always be lost. You're left with only your scars to mark the void. All you can choose is to go on or not. [p. 334]

In the following chapters there are references to psychological attributes of antisocial youths, including personal styles of psychological compromises—the defense mechanisms and coping strategies. Hence, it will be worthwhile reviewing Vaillant's (1993) scheme for understanding some of the more commonly observed defenses.

Vaillant arranged defense mechanisms on a rough continuum, ranging from the immature defenses that distort one's reality testing and lead to conflicts, to the mature defenses that are employed by healthy and well-adapted individuals. He presents as an example a young man's conflictual, painful awareness that he hates his father. The young man might employ the immature defense of projection. In projection, the individual attributes to another person some emotionally charged quality that he himself experiences. In other words, he unconsciously distorts the reality of the situation. In that case, he might feel "My father hates me." Another immature defense is acting out. Acting out involves, just like it sounds, putting into action the conflicted emotion. The young man might attack his father in some fashion.

At a higher level of functioning, the young man might employ one of several intermediate-level defenses such as displacement. He might kick the father's dog. He might use the more common defense of repression, whereby he would no longer recognize his hatred for his father. Instead, he would feel uncomfortable or nervous but not know why. Or, he might rely upon dissociation—the disconnection of the conscious self from some experience or emotion. Dissociation is particularly prominent among incarcerated youths because of the role of this defense in coping with trauma and abuse. At the highest level of functioning, the young man might employ the mature defenses of sublimation, altruism, or humor.

The primitive defense of denial is evidenced, for example, by the alcoholic who, despite incontrovertible evidence of alcohol addiction, insists with a straight face that he has no real problem with alcohol. Denial frequently is a feature of youthful offenders; they seem often to believe their own highly distorted accounts. Because denial involves such a break with plain reality, Vaillant classifies it with the psychotic defenses. However, in the vast majority of cases of denial among antisocial youths, there is no psychotic disorder. Denial is a defense that can be employed by almost anyone under the right circumstances of stress.

A central feature of many defense mechanisms is that they alter or distort the way others are perceived and understood. The paranoid's use of projection, for example, leads him to misread social cues and to perceive malicious intentions that may not be present. In many antisocial youths, this brings about an "attributional bias"—habitual hypervigilance toward hostile interpersonal cues and a tendency to perceive hostile intentions where none exist. Moreover, it is not just individuals who distort reality in these ways. In his book, *The Family's Construction of Reality* (1981), psychiatrist David Reiss describes how families and other social groupings can collectively distort the image and intentions of outsiders. Such group defenses also apply in the everyday life of youth gangs, peer groups, and even many political factions. While such distorting defenses can be a normal part of group life, they also can lead to enormously destructive processes, including persecution of other groups and even to wars.

Object Relations

Of all the strengths that lead in the direction of successful socialization, the one that forms a developmental bedrock upon which all the others are built is the capacity for healthy interpersonal relations. The capacity to develop and sustain meaningful relationships is a strength whose earliest origins are in infancy, in the relationship to the mother and/or other parental figures. The personality defects we find in antisocial individuals almost invariably involve deficits in this crucial matrix of personality strengths referred to as object relations. The awkward term *object* derives from the translation of Freud's text from the German. It refers, in his writings, to the target at which the instinctual drives aim for gratification. The central role ascribed to early interpersonal relations was described by British child psychiatrist John Bowlby (1958): "The child's first object relations [forms] the foundation stone of his personality" (p. 350).

Freud expressed the idea that the ego and the superego derive from the child's internalization of the relationship with the mother (Slipp 1988). Here was an early indication of the central role of interpersonal relations in psychological development. Once again, however, it fell to Freud's followers to develop these ideas outside the realm of instinctual drives and unconscious conflict. Melanie Klein (1934) postulated that the motivating force behind personality development was not conflict over instinctual drives, but an innate need to relate to the mother. Similarly, the British psychiatrist Ronald Fairbairn (1952) set aside the whole idea of libidinal drives and their associated conflicts. He too insisted that the ego developed primarily out of the infant's need for a relationship with the mother. Psychiatrist D. W. Winnicott (1958) also focused upon the rich dynamics of the mother–infant bond, and he developed the concept of the "holding environment"—that arena of security and limits that is configured by the parent within which the infant/child can begin to explore the world and build an early sense of self.

Freud's method of studying the mother–infant relationship was through the imperfect lens of psychoanalysis—meaning through the memories, dreams, and fantasies of the (usually) adult patient. It seems not to have occurred to early analysts that studying the mother–infant relationship directly, that is, empirically, could yield enormous rewards of understanding personality development. This was the contribution of the early object relations school of psychoanalysis. While not rejecting all of Freud's tenets, the emphasis shifted to the infant's earliest interpersonal relations and, most importantly, to the direct study of the real relationship (as opposed to the relationship of memory or fantasy) of mother and child. This novel approach involved for the first time the direct and systematic observation of infants and their mothers in interaction. This line of empirical research has strengthened in recent decades; and there is now a considerable and growing volume of data available on parent–child processes in both normal and pathological development.

During the same period that object relations theorists were arguing for the primacy of the interpersonal relations in child development, systematic observations of real infants and children were getting under way. Not surprisingly, clinical investigations during that era focused on some of the most severe developmental insults with the most obvious consequences. Psychiatrist Rene Spitz (1945) seized the opportunity imposed on England by the Second World War to study the effects on infants of prolonged separation from their mothers. He studied in detail the "emotional deficiency diseases" in infants who were separated from their mothers in the second half of the first year. He described a syndrome of "anaclitic depression" consisting of motor retardation, passivity, vacuous facial expression, defective eye coordination, and bizarre finger movements. He concluded, "Absence of mothering equals emotional starvation. . . . This leads to progressive deterioration engulfing the child's whole person" (1965, p. 281). Children who lost a mother after having established a person-specific relationship (usually after about 8 months of age) were seen by Spitz to suffer early and possibly irreversible damage to that "foundation stone" of personality. Such early damage led to two possible outcomes—progressive withdrawal, apathy, and depression; or aggressiveness, sensation-seeking, and antisocial character (Spitz 1945, 1949). A range of empirical studies seemed to bear this out.

John Bowlby (1940) wrote, "For a long time broken homes have been suspected of increasing a child's conflicts and making in particular for delinquency. An investigation of this problem [shows] that it is not so much the child's home being broken . . . but the separation of the child from his mother" (p. 158). Bowlby went on to describe the psychological characteristics of such deprived children, noting that they often fail to make emotional ties with others, they are sometimes sociable but without emotional ties, they are "hard-boiled," and "nothing you say or do has any effect." Bowlby was describing what we would today describe as a sociopathic personality. Similarly, in his classic study, "Forty-four Juvenile Thieves: Their Character and Home Life" (1944), Bowlby found the most severe cases of delinquency—what Spitz (1950) termed "affectionless thieves"—in children who had been subjected to prolonged separation from their mothers early in life. Other investigators reported similar findings. Psychiatrist Ralph Rabinivitch (1950), for example, reported, "In cases with the longest and most complete isolation and neglect we find the most severe distortion with gross asocial psychopathic personality development. . . . there is a total absence of anxiety and capacity to feel guilt" (p. 233). These descriptions are remarkably close to the accounts of sociopathic and psychopathic personality from present-day researchers.

These early investigations were crude by the standards of today's scientific methods. For the most part there were no experimental controls, and statistical analysis was scant. Their conclusions would need amending today to take account of newer findings, for example, on the effects of innate temperament and the influence of the modern media. Such reservations notwithstanding, however, the fundamental insights posited by this early group of researchers hold up well—that the early bond with mother and/or father is critical in laying the groundwork for subsequent socialization, and that serious disruption of that bond can result in marked deficits in those aspects of personality development directly implicated in the development of antisocial character.

Modern research has examined empirically the damaging effects of disrupted early attachments. Kobak and Sceery (1988), for example, reported that children with more secure early attachments showed greater resiliency later in life, and that those with insecure attachments more often displayed anxiety and personality disorder. Another study (Kolvin et al. 1988) reported a thirty-three-year follow-up that correlated the extent of early disruption in attachments to later antisocial behavior (i.e., convictions). The boys who suffered greater deprivation were more often convicted of crimes. Moreover, a "dose-response" effect emerged: the greater the degree of disruption in early attachments, the greater the number of convictions for crimes.

One need not look far to find present-day examples of the damage stemming from the experience of early deprivation. State social workers and juvenile probation counselors see such cases regularly. In actual practice, it usually is impossible to disentangle the developmental effects of maternal/paternal deprivation and loss, physical and/or sexual abuse, repeated displacement from one residential setting to another, and the damaging in utero effects of substance abuse by the mother. The case of an adolescent boy referred for evaluation by the state social worker illustrates a familiar configuration of (1) unreliable/disrupted maternal relations (and an absent father) ending in termination of mother's parental rights, with (2) a deepening pattern of antisocial behaviors that give every appearance of leading toward a stable antisocial character.

Several days prior to the first appointment with 13–year-old Marcus and his foster father, a heavy manila envelope arrived, bearing reports by social workers, pediatricians, school administrators, and school psychologists. The stack of documents covered almost all of the boy's life, beginning with the first investigation by the state into child neglect when Marcus was less than 2 years old. He was born to a 17-year-old girl who had a pattern of stormy and sometimes violent relationships with older men, a history of drug abuse, and no family to rely upon. Marcus's biological father remained with Marcus's mother for only a few months; then, following an assault on the mother, he disappeared and had not been heard from since.

A series of investigations by the state culminated in termination of the mother's parental rights by the court when the boy was 3. Young Marcus had twice been left with friends for several-week periods during which the mother and her boyfriend were in other states for reasons that were never explained. Reports indicated that at his second birthday Marcus was communicating only in grunts and gestures, and that he appeared alternately apathetic and depressed, then driven to fits of rage over the slightest frustration. He showed a disturbing pattern of excessive physical closeness, lacking boundaries or wariness of strangers, for example, hugging tightly to adults he had just met. A series of nine foster placements ensued, leading to the current residence with the Jamesons—which brings us to the reason for the evaluation.

A lineage of several social workers had struggled to arrange placements as Marcus had proven too much for one family after another. He was clingy and emotionally needy, but also volatile and explosive, and he repeatedly blew out his placements by assaulting other children. At school, attention and learning difficulties had been a constant drain on resources, and peer conflicts regularly interrupted the classroom. After nearly two years with the Jamesons, they too were near the end of their tether. Marcus had gotten the assaultiveness under control, but his searing hostility to the foster mother was rapidly burning out the placement. Most recently he had threatened her, saying at one point, "I'm gonna slit your throat while you're asleep," and he had been stealing from the family for several months. It was reported that Marcus wanted to remain with the Jamesons, and he appeared at times remorseful about the recurrent behaviors that threatened the placement. Like so many children who carry deep resentment over failure of parental bonds, Marcus took out his anger on the people closest to him. With such angry and hurt kids, it is as if the felt experience of a loving, nurturing relationship stirs up all the pain and anguish from years of heart-breaking disappointments. Even when youths like Marcus consciously want to remain attached, and even when they know there's no good reason to be hostile, the rage overcomes them. They end up destroying the thing they want the most.

From the moment of initial greetings in the waiting room, Marcus's manner and appearance betrayed the emotional weight of a childhood that never was. His greeting of the examiner—that first few seconds of contact—was weak and clouded. The normal gestures of interpersonal acknowledgment (eye contact, facial expression, handshake)—gestures that one expects even in disturbed individuals—seemed faded, not out of disrespect or resentment, but by simple depletion of the emotional resources upon which all personality develops. Marcus's posture was poor, his hands were dirty, and he was ungroomed (despite the efforts of the foster parents). And, as he took his seat, Marcus curled slightly in his chair with his head tipping to the side. For a while, he gave the appearance of a teenage-sized version of Spitz's infants suffering anaclitic depression—curled up, withdrawn, and apathetic.

Like so many children whose early attachments had altogether failed them, Marcus consistently had difficulty sustaining attention, and by age 4 he was diagnosed with attention deficit/hyperactivity disorder (ADHD). He had been treated with various stimulant medications (for example, Ritalin) with mixed results. But he had been assigned a variety of other diagnoses as well, and several other medications had also been tried. Neither the medications nor the on-and-off psychotherapy could alter the pattern of hostility and destructiveness.

The outcome for Marcus was the same as for countless other children who cannot overcome the early damage to that foundation stone of personality development. He finally was sent to live in a more structured and impersonal residential setting, a group home, where the emotional dynamics of dependent bonds are less potent. Reports issued later indicated that Marcus no longer unleashed such furious hostility on others, though his learning difficulties and peer conflicts continued. The most prominent feature later was that Marcus more often appeared depressed and lethargic.

Infant–Mother Research

Several researchers working within the object relations framework provided key insights into the phases of infant and child development. Perhaps best known is the work of Margaret Mahler, whose studies of the "separation-individuation" phase of infant–mother interaction shed light on early processes related to personality disorder development. These insights became clinically useful tools in the understanding and treatment of such conditions. However, many of these studies were not empirically rigorous, and their validation remains only partially fulfilled.

Increasingly, research on child development is no longer rooted in psychoanalytic object relations theory. By the late 1980s an imposing industry of child development research had taken its place on the social science landscape. The hallmark of this research is methodological rigor and sophisticated analytic techniques. At the same time as scientific rigor has been gained, however, some of this research is conceptually constricted and its "ecological validity" (Bronfenbrenner 1977) doubtful. There is a considerable gap at times between theoretical constructs and empirical findings, on the one hand, and the real world of developing children and families, on the other. In those instances, research findings relate best only to other such research. The issue of ecological validity occasionally gains considerable attention as, for example, when laboratory research on memory led to the conclusion that abused children could not forget their trauma and then recall it later in life. In contrast, clinical investigations of real children demonstrated that this is indeed possible, and is part of the life histories of many traumatized individuals.

One body of research that is especially important for understanding both normal and antisocial child development is that of child psychiatrist and psychoanalyst Stanley Greenspan. For over thirty years, Greenspan and his colleagues have closely investigated the parent–child interactions involved in the earliest layers of personality formation and cognitive development. Their findings have invalidated some of the most pervasive assumptions about early psychological development.

As far back as the ancient Greek philosophers, Western intellectual tradition has embraced the notion of the mind and the body as being separate, sometimes conflicting aspects of human nature. This mind–body dualism generally has involved the elevation of the rational and intellectual over the emotional. Even Freud's tripartite structure of personality involved the notion of the ego as the rational "rider" on the id with all its unruly passions and irrationalities. Some modern thinkers, such as the phenomenologist Merleau-Ponty (1962), have examined just how rooted in the body are our cognitive processes such as perception. And Piaget's (1952) theory of cognitive development describes the ways logical thinking processes grow out of the sensorimotor stages of early bodily sensations and reactions. Yet the primacy of the intellectual continues to be asserted, as implied in the so-called cognitive revolution.

In examining critical early experiences that form the basis for cognitive and personality development, Greenspan (1997) found, "Contrary to traditional notions, these experiences are not cognitive but are types of subtle emotional exchanges. In fact, emotions, not cognitive stimulation, serve as the mind's primary architect" (p. 1). He found that even intellectual development can proceed normally only on a pattern of regular and extensive emotional exchanges with the mother or other caregivers. Greenspan found the basic unit of intelligence in the early months of infant development to be the mental connection between an emotion or desire and an action or a symbol. "When a gesture or a bit of language is related in some way to the child's feelings or desires . . . she can learn to use it appropriately and effectively" (p. 16). The most fundamental organization of thinking and memory is laid down according to the emotional significance of experience. Greenspan found that many individuals with organic brain damage (from trauma, strokes, toxins, or other severe insults to neurologic functioning) lose their affective (emotional) organizing capacity. Such neurologically handicapped persons (such as those with autism) tend to operate in a concrete and rote fashion, lacking the ability to assess the significance of a situation or an object because that significance is based in emotional experience. While there surely is, in such cases, a failure of logical thinking, it is more accurate to understand this as a failure of emotional organization that enables logical thinking to proceed.

Greenspan (1997) explicates the mind's deepest "structural components" that are the foundation of all subsequent psychological development. He shows at each stage how healthy mental and emotional development stems from secure and active emotional engagement with caregivers. In the earliest stage of development, through neurologic development in conjunction with interaction with the mother, the infant learns to organize the myriad of confusing sensations and bodily movements. The child gradually is able to make patterns emerge and to make sense of sights, sounds, and rhythms. The most basic level of security is grounded in this ability to decipher sights, sounds, and patterns, that is, to begin to make sense of the immediate world through organized perception.

At the same time as the infant is learning to make sense of what William James called the "blooming, buzzing confusion," there is a growing sense of secure and continuous engagement with the mother. The mother provides not only love and excitement, but also a safe zone within which the infant can experience her bold assertions of rage and frustration—what Winnicott termed the "holding environment."

In the next of Greenspan's developmental stages, the child, having gained the capacity for calm attention and organized perception, is capable of participating in the construction of an intimate relationship. Through the normal process of "ecstatic wooing" by a loving adult, the infant comes to the magnetic pull of interpersonal relations and begins to see others as fully human beings, just as she is. Individuals who, because of a deficient nervous system or failure of caregivers, are unable to engage fully in such intense loving experiences are at risk of becoming unfeeling, self-centered, or aggressive individuals lacking any sense of shared humanity.

In the second half of the first year, the infant traverses the third of Greenspan's phases, that involving the willful and coordinated exchanges of preverbal signals and reactions—that is, early back-and-forth communication. It is in this phase that the children first come to recognize that they are part of a two-way dialogue of sorts. From these key experiences, they begin to understand that their own signals and gestures can elicit a response from another, and that the *other* is separate from themselves. Here is the earliest foundation for the subjective boundary between the self and the not-self. The incipient grasp of a reality outside the self is born. The complexity of interaction with the mother expands over the months as gesturing becomes reciprocal and the infant begins to discern meaningful patterns in the reactions of mother and others. She learns to discriminate among emotional cues in others, for example, between an approving smile and nod versus gestures and tones that suggest disapproval. And she learns what psychoanalysts term "object constancy"—the recognition that the mother she is enraged with is the same mother who loves and holds her. Until such constancy is achieved, infants behave as if these were different persons.

When emotional development goes awry in these early months, the result can be long-lasting. For example, Greenspan describes the case of a 12-month-old whose vigorous demands for closeness the mother finds too intense. Her tendency to withdraw from his advances leaves him frustrated, and he learns to seek through stimulation the satisfaction he could not gain through intimacy with his mother. The emotional and behavioral habits he learns then tend to be replicated later in life: he reacts aggressively and angrily to loss or rejection and becomes counterdependent—not needing anyone.

During the second and third year emerges the child's internal world of ideas and symbols. The ideas that a sound can stand for a thing, that one thing can stand for another, is the birth of symbolic processes. Even emotions can be given symbolic representation through words. Thus, the child who develops normally learns that he can *tell* his father that he is afraid instead of just screaming in fear, and a satisfying response makes the child's life all the more pleasant. The key to such symbolic development again is a close, emotionally rich relationship with a loving adult, one who encourages the use of such signals. Similarly, reflection on the self and one's thoughts and emotions is born out of intimate interaction with parents who encourage the child to think about his intentions and wishes. Such reflection facilitates the use of symbols, and symbolic development enables even deeper forms of self-reflection. "The child can develop a rich inner life only if she has experiences from which she can derive and refine inner images" (Greenspan 1997, p. 84).

Psychologist Gerry Patterson's research on coercive parenting practices is discussed below. Patterson's findings on how harsh and inconsistent discipline fosters aggressive habits in children are consistent with Greenspan's observations about the key role played by parents encouraging reflection and symbolic development—and the aggressive hostility that can emerge when needs for secure emotional relatedness are frustrated.

The cognitive development that links ideas and symbols with events and objects allows the child to begin to anticipate consequences. Hence, the ability to anticipate outcomes supplants simple fear and apprehension. Similarly, the ability to observe the self—the observing ego—derives from the symbolic representation of one's actions and one's emotions. "All thought and endeavor thus ultimately grow out of the ability to create symbols and to forge connections among them" (Greenspan 1997, p. 86). On the other hand, failure to take pleasure in symbolic representation and self-reflection tends to lock people into rigid and inflexible modes of conducting themselves. Rather than reflecting on themselves and their own emotions, they often tend to repeat the same patterns of unproductive behavior, and they often then habitually try to make others conform to their own wishes.

Greenspan's research is especially salient for understanding youths at risk of developing antisocial patterns of behavior. Recognizing the roots of cognitive development in the earliest patterns of emotional exchange between infant and parent helps to comprehend the source of those psychological traits that are so sorely lacking in many antisocial individuals. Empathy and regard for the feelings of others "develops from a shared sense of humanity. This capacity develops only in a baby who has the chance to interact . . . with an admiring, supportive caregiver" (p. 119). The experience of being lovingly nurtured and guided eventually becomes the foundation for true empathy.

Of course, there is a second ingredient that goes hand in hand with emotional relatedness in developing moral citizens—respect for clear limits and authority. Children from babyhood onward derive a sense of security from knowing where the limits are, what is expected of them, and what are the predictable consequences of disregarding them. Over the childhood years, growing respect for society's rules and for (legitimate) authority contributes to self-esteem as the child identifies with the need for such authority, rules, and guidance. Identification with, and respect for, social norms and limits encourages the child to appreciate the needs and the emotions of the other, that is, the development of empathy.

A friend wrote the following about his 7-year-old:

> Working in the study one evening, my attention was interrupted by the sound of Daniel crying downstairs. Instinctively, I tried to discern what *type* of cry I was hearing. Right away, I ruled out the possibility that Daniel was really hurt. It was not that kind of cry, the kind that a parent must respond to with great haste and a certain amount of ceremony. But neither was it the cry of everyday bumps and stubbed toes. It was something different, this cry. I sat back from the computer screen and listened a little longer. The wailing grew more intense. There was anguish in those wails, some kind of emotional hurt. I thought his mother was supposed to be reading to him before bedtime. What was going on? Puzzled, I popped up and descended the stairs not quite in a hurry.
>
> As I walked into his room, there was Daniel, sitting on his mother's lap and holding on to her, sobbing the most heartfelt sobs. Relieved to see that there were no serious injuries, and no sign of bad news over the telephone, I was free to just reach out. When I asked what was the matter, Daniel turned a tearful face up to his mother— who also was in tears—and said, "You tell him, Mom; it's too sad." His mom reached over and held up Daniel's paperback copy of *Charlotte's Web*. She explained, in a tone that accounted for all the tears, "We just finished the story and, you know, Charlotte dies in the end."

His mother's explanation was not quite good enough for Daniel who, by now, had something to say. In a voice that seemed to carry much of the pain and indignation for life's injustices, Daniel explained through his tears, "After all she did. She saved Wilbur, and then she *died*." Then he pronounced the final tragedy in this powerful children's book: "I understand about having to die, but why did she have to die before she even got to see her babies?"

Daniel was consoled by his parents for a while and talked more about what a fine "person" Charlotte was and how sad was the ending crafted by E. B. White. Daniel was, by any measure, a pretty regular kid for his age. Like most first-grade boys, he found it difficult to sit still for long in school, and his real passions ran as much to baseball and weaponry as to stories. But like most children, Daniel was capable of an emotional response to the loss or plight of others. The *Charlotte's Web* episode displayed the capacity for empathy that will be evident in most children in countless, less dramatic ways in everyday life. This normal capacity for experiencing strong feelings for others—nurtured over years of loving and respectful relations with parents and others—is a powerful force against antisocial development. That capacity, along with some measure of fear of punishment and retribution, becomes the bedrock of conscience.

A Note on Moral Development

Greenspan's theory describes a process whereby the nurturing and protective relationship with the parents—along with respect for limits—is internalized. The focus on the emotional relationship with the parents explains more than a purely cognitive approach to moral development. For example, Lawrence Kohlberg (1964) extensively studied the complex development of moral reasoning in children. However, children's strategies for reasoning about the perspective of others or for deploying advanced social skills misses the most essential ingredient in the character of a moral and ethical citizen. All too familiar are individuals with sophisticated cognitive and social skills who apply their talents in the exploitation of others. The irreducible ingredient in moral development is not the level of intellectual and cognitive maturity, but the quality of compassion and caring that is nurtured in positive early emotional experience. Even persons quite limited intellectually, for example, with serious learning disabilities or low IQs, can be fully capable of a morally guided lifestyle. Greenspan (1997) summarizes his concepts of moral development:

> The morally responsible person whom conservatives admire can only grow out of the affectionate and secure family that liberals demand. The two basic features of families that work—empathic, sensitive nurturing combined with clear, firm limits—can flourish in an array of social, cultural, religious, and economic settings. But no child can become a morally responsible adult without experiencing both. (p. 195)

The Cycle of Violence

In the arena of violence and antisocial development, perhaps no set of beliefs is more widely shared than the idea that violence begets violence. This is the commonsense notion of the intergenerational transmission of violence—the belief that children who experience violence early in life tend to become aggressive and violent themselves (Widom 1989b, 1990). In published reports and in clinical practice one can find numerous examples of delinquent and aggressive youths who report having been physically abused as children.

The unqualified acceptance of the cycle of violence hypothesis has eroded in recent years, however, beginning with the recognition that the relationship between child maltreatment and later aggression is more complex than just "violence leads to violence." Numerous findings have indicated that we need to look more closely at the array of factors involved in what appears to be the cycle of violence. For example, we know that the majority of physically abused children do not become violent or delinquent, and we know that many or even the majority of delinquents were not physically abused as children (Widom 1989a,b). We also know that *rejected* children have high rates of delinquency and violence, perhaps equal to the rates for physically abused children. And it is well established that the outcome for abused children varies by gender, with girls tending to develop "internalizing" problems such as depression and withdrawal, with boys more likely to develop "externalizing" problems such as aggression. In addition to these complications, there are vexing methodological problems. For example, physical abuse of children tends to occur more often in lower socioeconomic classes, in single-parent families, and in families in which there also is marital violence. Thus, when abused children become aggressive adolescents we cannot be sure whether the aggressive behaviors stem directly from the abuse itself or whether the aggression might be the by-product of low socioeconomic status (SES), family stress, or witnessing violence in the home. Also, it is important to be clear about what level of violence we are referring to, because the term *violence* is assigned to family situations spanning a wide range of types and severity of mistreatment. Would we include, for example, the kind of verbal assaults that might be termed emotional abuse? Or would we wish to restrict the term to situations of overt physical aggression?

Stemming from such concerns as these, psychiatrists Kaufman and Zigler (1987) stated that the unqualified faith in the cycle of violence hypothesis was unfounded. Subsequently, carefully designed research has led to substantial gains in our understanding of the complex relationships among negative early influences and later development of antisocial behavior. In a controlled study of the effects of abuse and neglect on later violence, psychologists Beverly Rivera and Cathy Widom (1990) identified 908 cases of abuse and neglect through systematic review of court records in a metropolitan area in the Midwest, and they assembled a control group of 667 children (matched to the index cases according to age, sex, and race) who had not suffered such abuse (at least according to official records). They then searched the official arrest records for juveniles and adults at the local, state, and federal levels to determine which children actually committed violent and delinquent acts in adolescent or young adult years.

Rivera and Widom reported, as predicted, that abused and neglected children show significantly higher arrest rates for delinquency, for adult criminal behavior, and for violent criminal behavior than do the non–abused/neglected controls. They analyzed the data in ways that statistically control for the effects of age, sex, and socioeconomic factors, ensuring that the results were not due to these confounding factors. The abused and neglected group showed (1) a larger number of offenses; (2) an earlier average age at first arrest; and (3) a higher proportion of chronic offenders, those charged with five or more offenses. They also found that although females in general have lower rates of arrest for violent offenses, those who were abused and neglected in childhood showed higher rates of violence later on. Rivera and Widom also separated the effects of physical abuse from the effects of neglect. They found that physical abuse alone led to the highest rates of arrest for violent behavior, but that the rate of violence in the abuse-only group was followed closely by the rate of violence for the neglect-only group. This supports the impressions of some researchers and clinicians that neglect, by itself, can be a powerful factor in the development of antisocial behavior.

The next logical question in understanding the pathway from early victimization to later antisocial behavior involves the mechanism by which these effects occur. In another controlled, prospective study, Kenneth Dodge and associates (1991) studied the behavior patterns and the information processing styles of abused and nonabused children. These researchers found that physical abuse, by itself, led to markedly higher levels of aggressiveness, and this effect held up even when family ecological variables (SES, marital conflict, etc.) were controlled. Also, these findings held up when the child's biological variables, such as difficult temperament and health problems, were controlled. Similarly, a study of twenty adolescent murderers found especially high incidence of family violence, violent fathers, and physical and sexual violence directed at the child (Bailey 1996). A host of other studies in recent years continue to find that the relationship between early exposure to violence and later aggression and violence is substantial (e.g., Spaccarelli et al. 1995). Hence, the cycle-of-violence hypothesis has been affirmed, but with some qualifications.

In an illuminating adjunct to the main study, Dodge and colleagues (1991) also assessed the extent to which a child's individual factors correlated with victimization. Some research has suggested that children with more difficult temperaments (more fussy, more resistant, etc.) may provoke more angry and abusive reactions from parents, thereby setting in motion a pattern of abuse and behavioral disorder. Dodge and colleagues found that the child's temperament and other individual factors did *not* predict abuse. They wrote, therefore, "There is no evidence in our data for blaming the victim of abuse" (p. 1682).

Besides the direct line from abuse to later violent behavior, the Dodge study shed some light on the mechanism by which early abuse leads to later violence. They found that abused children develop biased and deficient patterns for processing social information. In a pattern that is familiar to clinicians working with antisocial youths, the researchers found that abused youths fail to attend to the relevant interpersonal cues, and that they frequently attribute hostile intentions where none exist. As a result of such misreading of social cues and information, abused children fail to develop healthy social skills, are frequently frustrated, and more often resort to aggression to solve problems. The abused child, in short, comes to conceptualize the social world as a hostile and dangerous place, a place in which aggression would be the appropriate response. There is, then, some self-fulfilling prophecy for such individuals who, because of their habit of misattributing hostile intent, create their own hostile social nexus.

Dodge and colleagues also found that abused girls are at risk for high rates of internalizing problems such as withdrawal, isolation, and depression. Again, such psychological problems in girls appeared to result from abuse even when the effects of family ecological variables are accounted for.

For over two decades, psychologist Gerald Patterson, at the Oregon Social Learning Center, has studied the development of antisocial behavior patterns in children and adolescents. His "social-interactional" approach applies the behavioral principles of operant conditioning to the complex problems of interpersonal interaction (Reid and Patterson 1989). Operant conditioning is the behavioral principle that states that behaviors that are reinforced will tend to recur more frequently. Operant conditioning is contrasted with classical conditioning, wherein a stimulus (e.g., a bell) that regularly precedes another stimulus (e.g., food) will tend to elicit the response (e.g., salivating) appropriate to the latter stimulus. In what he terms "coercive family processes," Patterson finds that family members "train" the child to engage in antisocial behaviors by inadvertently reinforcing aversive and aggressive behaviors and by failing to consistently reinforce prosocial ones (Patterson 1982, Patterson and Capaldi 1991). He finds that some coercive behaviors are directly reinforced by family members (by attending, laughing, or approving). But the most potent learning stems from what he terms "escape conditioning" sequences (Patterson 1992, Patterson et al. 1989). In escape conditioning contingencies, the child learns to employ aversive behaviors (tantrums, aggression) to get parents to terminate their interventions (i.e., back off). In such families, aversive behaviors work effectively for children who want to punish their parents for intervening, and the parents soon learn not to intervene. "This kind of punishment by the problem child teaches many mothers to stop trying, particularly if they are pain-avoidant types" (Patterson 1992, p. 84).

As this interaction pattern progresses over the years, the child gains greater control over household processes. Parents become increasingly hesitant to enter into a struggle they feel they cannot win. "Having defeated the parents, children are free to explore the delights of a variety of avoidance arrangements (e.g., avoid boredom by skipping school, avoid work by stealing, avoid negative sanctions by lying)" (p. 85). At the same time, they are free to explore the positive reinforcement of the "rush" involved in theft or assault or drug abuse.

In countless close observations of such families, Patterson also observed a dearth of training in, and reinforcement for, prosocial behaviors. Prosocial acts in these families tend to be ignored or responded to inappropriately. The result for children in such families is a double liability: they develop antisocial habits (aversive and aggressive response patterns) and they lack social skills for the development of normal peer relations. This leads to the second stage of Patterson's four-stage process in the development of chronic antisocial behavior.

The child's conduct problems and lack of social skills leads, during the highly formative early school years, to two highly predictable outcomes—rejection by the normal peer group and the beginnings of academic failure. Several studies have documented the poor academic progress of children with incipient antisocial habits (e.g., Hawkins and Lishner 1987). Antisocial children are seen to spend less time on task than their nondeviant peers; they also are poorer at attending, remaining in their seats, and answering questions, and they more often fail to complete homework assignments (Cobb 1972, Dishion et al. 1983, Loeber and Dishion 1983, Loeber et al. 1995). At the same time that the academic deficiencies are expanding, these antisocial children are being rejected by their normal peers. Several studies have documented that the child's aggressive behavior patterns lead to rejection. Such rejected children are found to be deficient in social skills. They do not know how to enter groups, they fail to understand peer group norms for behavior, they respond inappropriately to provocation, and they consistently misread social cues (Patterson et al. 1989). It has been surmised that peer rejection and academic failure are the causes rather than the results of antisocial habits. However, it seems most often to go the other way. It has been found, for example, that improving the academic skills of antisocial children has not led to reductions in antisocial behaviors, and the same pattern has been observed in regard to social skills training (Kazdin 1987).

Academic failure and rejection by normal peers leads reliably to the third of Patterson's stages—commitment to a deviant peer group. Aided by lax parental supervision, such rejected children, by early adolescent years, begin to affiliate more and more with peers who train them in the attitudes and rationalizations that support the ongoing development of delinquency. The early anti-social child tends to select individuals and settings at school and in the neighborhood that are most likely to reward aggressive and coercive behaviors. Several studies indicate that such a delinquent peer group is the primary training mode for early delinquent acts and for substance abuse (Elliott et al. 1985). As Patterson points out, the delinquent peer group may be thought of as the "positive feedback" factor that serves to maintain the process. "The members of the deviant peer group are the proximal agents of change that directly transform childhood behaviors to delinquent acts" (Patterson 1992, p. 98). With parents paying little attention (having been "defeated" years earlier), such children are out on the streets several years earlier than normal peers. And, in that context, there is ample training for new forms of delinquency.

In Patterson's model, as with other research on antisocial development, there is always the question of whether the actual cause of the antisocial habits is the factors we are studying or if the cause is some "contextual" factors that underlie the variables we have studied. We know, for example, that the inept parenting practices leading to early antisocial behavior tend to occur in families in lower socioeconomic levels and in families with less parental education and fewer financial resources. Other family stressors such as unemployment, marital discord, and divorce also are associated with increased likelihood of antisocial development. Patterson and his colleagues (1992) conducted a series of sophisticated studies to address these questions. The result was, as they predicted, that the effects of such family contextual variables and stressors were mediated by actual parental practices. In other words, divorce, unemployment and financial stress, and poor parental education level all had their effects on the child's development by way of the parenting practices employed. Hence, it appears that it is not marital discord by itself or financial stress by itself that leads to antisocial practices, but rather that such stressors predispose the parents to be more irritable, intrusive, and coercive in their parenting practices (see also Florsheim et al. 1996 for similar investigations and results).

BIOLOGICAL FACTORS

It has been recognized since the ancient Greeks and Romans that some psychiatric disorders have a hereditary component. Hippocrates (460–377 B.C.), for example, observed that melancholia (depression) seems to run in families; and casual observation, even by an untrained eye, reveals that certain family lineages are afflicted with far more than their share of mental and emotional misfortune. Systematic research over the past three decades has confirmed genetic contributions in the etiology of several psychiatric disorders, for example, in bipolar disorder and in attention deficit/hyperactivity disorder. In one way or another, each these investigations has involved correlating the degree of known genetic similarity between individuals with the measured risk of developing the same disorder. In this way, for example, bipolar disorder is found to be more likely in closely related family members of "index" individuals who have the disorder.

Given the abundance of physical and physiological attributes and psychiatric disorders that have some genetic link, it is a reasonable question whether genetic liabilities play a role in the etiology of antisocial character and behavior. The dominant view in the nineteenth century was that antisocial individuals suffered from an innate moral deficiency, the result of an inborn defect in character. Cesare Lombroso (1836–1909) described the "criminal man"— an individual whose character was presumed to be innately criminal. But in the twentieth century, the pendulum of accepted opinion swung far in the opposite direction.

By the 1950s, the dominant psychological theories were psychoanalysis and behaviorism, each of which emphasized the experiential roots of behavior patterns and, correspondingly, paid no attention to inborn qualities that might contribute to emotional and behavioral problems. Psychiatric disorders stemmed from the internal conflicts arising from disturbed early relationships and developmental insults, or else they were the predictable consequences of stimulus-response conditioning (classical conditioning) or behavioral reinforcement contingencies (operant conditioning). In both psychodynamic theories and in behaviorism, there was assumed to be nearly limitless plasticity in human character and behavioral habits, and there was therefore no need to take account of the genetic or constitutional characteristics of the individual. This extreme environmentalist assumption was so pervasive for many years that theory and research on innate or genetic factors was unwelcome in many quarters.

Over the past two decades, there has accumulated a considerable body of respectable research data from the United States and other countries that supports some genetically inherited disposition for some kinds of antisocial development and behavior. Developmental theories and psychopathology, on the basis of such data, now are compelled to "find room for behavioral genetics" (McGue 1994, p. 105), despite a history of passive resistance to these findings.

Social scientists tend to be loyal to the theoretical framework they were trained in. The paradigm that a given investigator works within, and the language specific to that paradigm, prefigures the kinds of information she will gather and the kinds of interpretations she ultimately will offer. In other words, scientific paradigms tend to be conservative and to change only in response to considerable countervailing evidence. But there are other good reasons why much of the social science community has long eschewed genetic factors as even a partial explanation for antisocial behavior.

Antisocial character exists in that murky zone where psychiatry and medicine intersect with social problems. Antisocial behavior is defined, in large measure, by social norms and expectations, not by traditional medical or psychiatric designations; and the question of whether to assign a medical diagnosis carries weighty implications. If antisocial behavior is largely a social problem stemming from social-historical conditions, then medicalizing such behavior—framing it as an individual biological problem—might lead to neglect of the responsible social conditions while attributing the problem to "bad genes." Also, if antisocial behavior primarily involves a conscious choice to do bad things, then medicalizing it might be used as a way to absolve the perpetrators of responsibility for their behavior. Hence, it is not at all obvious that individuals who are habitually dishonest, exploitative, or violent should earn a diagnosis that implies that they are afflicted with some disease. Rather, some would say, it is society that is afflicted—by the choices these persons make about how to conduct themselves. They are not ill or crazy; they are badly behaved.

Psychiatric and psychological researchers have a long tradition of investigating the nature and course of antisocial character. According to this history, antisocial character ought to be seen within the purview of these psychological and medical sciences. On this side of the argument are researchers such as Lee Robins, whose research over three decades has contributed vastly to the epidemiology of psychiatric disorders in America (e.g., Robins 1966, Robins and Regier 1991). Robins's research leads her (and others) to conclude, "Antisocial personality seems to be a real syndrome in American males" (1978b, p. 620). She based her conclusions on findings that patterns of antisocial acting out are remarkably stable from adolescence through adulthood (Olweus 1979, Robins 1985) and that "these patterns of childhood antisocial behavior are transmitted from one generation to the next" (Robins 1978b, p. 620), all of which amounts to claiming that antisocial character is a real psychiatric disorder and therefore ought to be within the province of the social and medical sciences.

There is an understandable aversion to genetic explanations of behavioral differences in an era when the most barbaric political adventures have been justified on the basis of putative racial (genetic) inferiority. Hitler's programs of racial extermination, rationalized on the basis of such genetic claims, must have seemed compelling at the time, for they were accepted by a large proportion of his countrymen. More recently, the Western world was horrified as similar claims of racial inferiority were used to justify "ethnic cleansing" campaigns of murder and dislocation in Bosnia.

Closer to home, on the scientific front, Hernstein and Murray (1994) claimed that the lower IQ scores of African-Americans as compared with whites is due to genetic inferiority in this realm of functioning. The policy recommendations that might stem from such racial-genetic claims are disturbing. For example, if African-Americans' lower intelligence test scores are due to genetic traits, then perhaps compensatory education is unlikely to be helpful. It is not much of a stretch to imagine more overtly racist conclusions and policies stemming from such putative genetic differences between races. Critiques of the Hernstein and Murray's conclusions (Block 1995, Rutter 1997) point out two fatal fallacies in their book, *The Bell Curve*. First, estimates of heritability (the proportion of variance attributable to genetic differences) are specific to the particular time frame and the samples employed, and such differences cannot be generalized to racial differences outside the context of the culture they are embedded in. As Lykken (1995) puts it, "The heritability of a trait often tells us as much about the culture as it does about human nature" (p. 88). Second, even when a given trait does have a genetic component, this in no way implies that changes in the environment and experience cannot engender large changes. It is the geneticists, themselves, who have been most forceful on this issue. In their study of the genetics of various diseases, for example, geneticists Kathleen Merikangas and David Kupfer (1995) state, "The knowledge of the role of genetic factors may lead to prevention and amelioration of the diseases by purely environmental methods" (p. 1102). Rutter (1997) makes the same point in regard to intelligence: "Even very high heritability estimates do not imply that changes in the environment cannot bring about big effects" (p. 391). (See also Zuckerman [1990] for a critique of research on racial differences.)

To the extent that genetic differences are employed to account for social problems, society and its leaders are absolved of responsibility for creating or for ameliorating those problems. If blacks score lower on IQ tests because of inferior genes, then society need not be concerned with the effects of several generations of racial subjugation on the intellectual functioning of children. If poor people are genetically inferior, then their poverty cannot be attributed to social and economic policies. Moreover, there is no need to provide better education, nutrition, and safety for children in such neighborhoods. This kind of reasoning would be the most diabolical purpose to which social science research could be put—to blame the victims of social and political policies and to provide rationalizations to the privileged.

It is no surprise that social scientists have been slow to embrace the findings of early genetics researchers on the topic of antisocial character development. The last thing researchers would want to see is for a conclusion of genetic causality to lead to blaming the victims of social inequities, to therapeutic nihilism ("there's nothing that can be done"), or to the illusion that social and economic factors need not be addressed. As will be seen in the following sections, however, making room for genetics in the psychology of antisocial development makes more clear the kinds of environmental interventions that *are* most likely to prevent or to ameliorate these problems.

A considerable body of research data—findings to be reviewed later in this chapter—now supports the position that there is some genetic component in the development of some forms of antisocial behavior. The next question is, What is it that is genetically transmitted that predisposes some children to antisocial development? Genes cannot code for anything corresponding to laws and norms of socialized conduct, for these are socially constructed categories, not biologically determined dimensions. Genes cannot prefigure an individual's proclivity for telling the truth versus deceiving others, any more than they can determine whether one's aggressiveness occurs within the bounds of socially sanctioned violence (e.g., football or hockey), or whether it occurs on the street and brings harm to unsuspecting persons. Similarly, genes cannot predetermine whether one's complex financial transactions are honest and legal or whether they are representing a scheme of white-collar crime involving deception and theft. The line between the two can be obscure, and the psychological traits that lead to success in the realm of legal business transactions are not very different from those leading along a path of deception, fraud, and exploitation.

The inborn individual traits that make a child more prone to unacceptable forms of aggression, more prone to lack conscience, and more prone to deploy social skills in deception and exploitation—in short, those traits that make a child more difficult to socialize—this is the domain of temperament studies.

Temperament

Ask a mother who has raised several children whether her children came into the world with distinct personality styles or whether they were all the same, and you are likely to hear about what researchers term temperament—styles of reactivity and arousal that often are evident in the first or second year and that often persist well into childhood and even into the adult years. You may hear about one child being an "easy" baby while another child "always was fussy and easily upset." You may hear about a child who was adventurous and aggressive right from the beginning and "nothing ever seemed to hurt him," or about another child who always seemed to be cautious, "slow to warm up," inhibited, and shy.

During the years of dominance by psychodynamic and behavioral theories, not much attention was paid to such apparently inborn differences. Indeed, when such distinct personality styles were observed, they usually were attributed to subtle differences in parenting styles or to distorted perception or recall by the parents. However, by the 1960s a series of studies by Alexander Thomas and Stella Chess had established temperament as a legitimate arena of child research (Thomas and Chess 1989). By the 1970s they had described nine dimensions of temperamental difference that could be reliably distinguished—approach versus withdrawal from new situations (i.e., shyness), energy level, happy versus irritability, attention span, and others (Kagan 1996). To specify temperamental dimensions that were stable through most of childhood, Chess and Thomas collapsed the nine dimensions into three broad and familiar categories. Roughly 40 percent of babies/children were termed "easy," about 15 percent were termed "slow to warm up" (shy, wary, inhibited), and about 10 percent were termed "difficult" (irritable, withdrawing from novelty, poor adaptation). Chess and Thomas's categories make intuitive sense to many parents, and several books designed to assist parents with their challenging children have been very popular with parents and pediatricians (e.g., Kurcinka 1991, Turecki 1985).

Jerome Kagan (1996) has focused much of his effort on a single, overarching dimension of temperament—inhibited versus uninhibited. He and his colleagues have found that about 15 to 20 percent of healthy children can be reliably classified as inhibited, showing "a consistent tendency to withdraw and to become emotionally subdued, restrained and timid in the presence of unfamiliar situations, people or objects" (p. 271). About 30 percent of children show the opposite characteristics, being uninhibited. These children show a relatively rapid approach to novel situations as well as considerable "spontaneous emotion." He found that about 75 percent of children classified as inhibited or uninhibited in the second year of life retain those qualities in the eighth year of life. Supporting the biological basis of temperamental differences, Kagan and his colleagues have turned up reliable physiological differences between inhibited and uninhibited children, differences that appear to involve the operation of the sympathetic nervous system. For example, inhibited children show greater cardiac acceleration and pupil dilation to mild stress, and larger rises in diastolic blood pressure when changing posture from sitting to standing. Inhibited children are more likely to cool on the right side of the face to mild stress, due to constriction of the arterioles mediated by alpha-adrenergic receptors (Kagan 1996). Kagan conceives of temperamental differences as genetic in origin, and this is how he defines such individual differences. In addition to the physiologic differences in temperament, he points to twin studies at the University of Minnesota that suggest heritabilities (the proportion of total variance attributed to genetic variability) of 0.5 for inhibited behavior and 0.4 for uninhibited behavior—more evidence supporting the genetic basis of these temperament differences.

Several dimensions of temperament have been investigated for their possible role in the development of antisocial behavior—aggressiveness, lack of control, impulsivity, and fearlessness. The key question in such research is not what innate differences cause antisocial behavior, for there is no such causal connection. The proper question is: What individual attributes make a child harder to socialize and therefore more likely to display behavioral traits we would label antisocial? The various temperamental dimensions that have been investigated differ somewhat from one study to the next. For example, so-called externalizing problems are similar to but somewhat different from aggressivity and impulsivity. Such research inconsistencies make it more difficult to interpret the findings. Nonetheless, taken as a whole, the research on temperament in antisocial behavior sheds light on crucial variables that must be taken into account if we are to understand the development of such vexing and destructive behaviors.

Aggressiveness

Other things being equal, we would expect that children who are characteristically more aggressive in their dealings with others (verbally or physically) would be more likely to earn a label of antisocial during their adolescent or adult years, for two reasons. First, children who are more prone to aggressive reactions tend to be harder to socialize. The parents of aggressive children are therefore more likely to back off or to react aggressively themselves, leading to the coercive cycles described by Gerald Patterson. Second, aggressivity is one of the principal behavioral features that earns a label of antisocial. Adolescents who employ aggression—verbal threats, intimidation, or overt violence—are more likely to be diagnosed with conduct disorder and to show the habits more likely to lead to the functioning of antisocial personality. In fact, this is just what has been found, that children who are especially aggressive in childhood more often tend to become violent adolescents and adults (Farrington 1991, Reiss and Roth 1993).

A key question is the extent to which such aggressive traits in childhood are inborn temperamental features versus the extent to which they represent learned patterns of behavior. The idea of inborn aggressiveness fell out of favor during the dominance of psychodynamic and behavioral theories. Accordingly, aggression was seen solely as the result of frustration, conditioning, and learning. However, temperament and genetic studies now suggest that there is, at least in some cases, a temperamental predisposition to aggressiveness. Resistance to the idea of innate aggressiveness stems from the aversion to any suggestion that some children are "born to be bad." However, even if some aggressiveness does have an innate component, this in no way condemns the child to an antisocial lifestyle. An aggressive temperament may make the child more difficult to socialize, but there are numerous socially acceptable pursuits into which the child's energies might be channeled. So-called aggressiveness, with appropriate socializing, becomes the culturally valued attribute competitiveness, which serves well in many sports and even in professional endeavors, for example, law, politics, and business.

One body of research findings that supports the idea of an innate predisposition for aggressiveness is that individual differences in aggressiveness appear to be remarkably stable over time (Eron and Huesmann 1984, 1990, Olweus 1979, 1980). We know that there is considerable plasticity in behavioral patterns, and aggressiveness surely can be successfully modified in a variety of ways (Pepler and Rubin 1991). Nonetheless, it is consistently found that children who characteristically respond with aggression often are found to use aggression habitually in the adolescent years, and aggressive adolescents tend to be aggressive adults (Loeber 1991). Acknowledging the difficulty in separating genetic from learned patterns of behavior, Huesmann and colleagues (1984) state, "What is not arguable is that aggressive behavior, however engendered, once established, remains remarkably stable across time, situation, and even generations" (p. 1133).

Regarding heritability, findings have varied a great deal in regard to just how genetically determined is such aggressiveness (Gottesman and Goldsmith 1994). Huesmann and his colleagues (1984) report that children's rated aggressiveness correlated .65 with their *parents'* rated aggressiveness when the parents were 8 years old. In a twin study of self-reported aggressiveness, McGue and colleagues (1992) found remarkably high heritability for aggressiveness (about .80). Other twin studies and adoptions studies have also found a genetic factor in such aggressiveness, but at far more modest levels of genetic influence.

Lack of Control/Difficult Temperament

Another temperament dimension, one that overlaps with aggressiveness, but is better described as poor self-regulation, is termed "lack of control" (composed of inattention, negativity, and impulsivity; Gottesman and Goldsmith 1994). In a study of 800 New Zealand children, researchers (Caspi et al. 1995) there found that high ratings on "lack of control" at age 3 and 5 years predicted (with modest correlations) antisocial behavior ratings at age 9 and 11. In a later study (Henry et al. 1996) it was found that the "lack of control" dimension was specifically associated with conviction for violent offenses by age 18 but not with conviction for nonviolent offenses. Hence, this temperament dimension seemed to discriminate between offenders likely to act out violently and those more likely to commit nonviolent crimes—a finding that may have important implications in the effort to identify children who are especially at risk for antisocial violence.

A dimension of temperament that involves poor self-regulation of mood and impulse and also seems to relate to possible antisocial behavior is termed "difficult temperament." Researchers in Indiana used parents' reports of their children's frequent and intense displays of negative emotion (even from the age of 6 months) to determine difficult temperament. High ratings of difficult temperament in the first year or two predicted externalizing behavior problems (verbal and physical aggressiveness) at ages 3, 5, 6, 7, and 8 years of age (Bates et al. 1991). Of course, whether these children actually become antisocial adolescents and adults is unclear. In some research, children rated as showing difficult temperament were at risk for developing other conditions such as depression and anxiety.

It should be recalled, with regard to these dimensions of temperament, that it is not always clear in the research reports whether these attributes represent temperament in the proper sense of genetically determined individual differences in arousal and responsiveness. It may be, for example, that some children who score high on aggressiveness or lack of control do so because of poor early parenting practices. Nonetheless, there is good evidence to support the contention that at least some of these aggressive or poorly controlled children are so because of genetically inherited attributes.

Fearlessness

In general, fearfulness and inhibition do not go well with a criminal lifestyle. Inhibited children tend to shy away from risky situations and not to take risks, and their whole social developmental trajectory is toward avoidance of conflict and aggression (harm avoidance). At the opposite end of this dimension are children who seemed innately—as in Kagan's research—to be fearless and adventurous. Such children seem not to learn from painful consequences, and punishment typically has less effect on their patterns of behavior than parents and other adults would wish. The contribution of such fearlessness to antisocial development was shown in the Cambridge Study in Delinquent Development (Farrington 1986). It was found there that ratings of being "daring" at ages 8 and 10 strongly predicted criminal convictions at ages 14 to 16. Subsequently, the best predictor of convictions at ages 21 to 24 was criminal convictions at ages 14 to 16. As with aggressiveness, fearlessness seems also to have at least some genetic heritability, as revealed by Kagan's studies but also in a twin study reported by McGue and colleagues (1992).

In addition to the empirical research on fearlessness, there is a long tradition of clinical reports on chronically antisocial individuals who seem always to have been lacking in normal fearfulness. Clinical lore is rich in accounts of fearless children who would try anything and who seemed not to be restrained by anticipating the painful consequences of their actions. The most interesting work in this area has focused on the most antisocial persons of all, the psychopathic personality.

Temperament of the Psychopath

In his classic 1941 work on the psychopath, Cleckley listed as a discriminating feature a "general poverty of major affective reactions." He described a shallowness of emotional responsiveness, and stated, "The conviction dawns on those who observe him carefully that here we deal with a readiness of expression rather than a strength of feeling" (1983, p. 348). More specifically, though, Cleckley and others following him have pointed to a remarkable lack of anxiety, by which he meant very little "remorse, uneasy anticipation, apprehensive scrupulousness, the sense of being under stress or strain" (p. 257). Robert Hare, whose book *Without Conscience* (1993) presents rich accounts of psychopathic character, writes "Psychopaths have little aptitude for experiencing the emotional responses—fear and anxiety—that are the mainsprings of conscience" (p. 76). Here, Hare ties what seems to be a temperamental quality—lack of fear and anxiety—directly to socialization. He suggests that socialization is nearly hamstrung if the child cannot experience these uncomfortable emotions.

Recognition of the contribution of innate endowment to the most severe forms of antisocial character is not solely a modern insight. In Shakespeare's *Tempest*, Prospero unleashes his exasperation over the temperament of the "savage," Caliban:

> A devil, a born devil, on whose nature
> Nurture can never stick, on whom my pains,
> Humanely taken, all, all lost, quite lost. [Act IV]

Anxiety is the surest poison to keen attention. On psychological tests that tap concentration and immediate recall, anxiety markedly diminishes performance. Hence, if psychopaths are free of anxiety, we would expect them to show high performance on tests of attention. And this is just what clinicians have consistently found. Hare likens the psychopath's capacity for focusing attention to a "narrow-beam searchlight," and others refer to the psychopath's concentration being like that of a "predator stalking its prey."

The capacity for keen attention cannot be all bad, of course, and the ability to focus one's gaze is highly valued in sports and in academics. How else would a professional baseball player manage to hit a 96-mile-per-hour fastball? And surely such capacity for focusing attention is prerequisite for success in higher math and science. Yet there seems to be something different, something uncanny and disturbing in the psychopath's prowess in focusing his attention. This relates to the absence of emotional accompaniment that the baseball player or the physicist would feel and display. It seems that the psychopath, being unencumbered by feelings of attachment, doubt, and worry, is free to deploy his attention especially keenly, and not to be distracted by the thoughts and emotions that would affect most of us. Hare (1993) writes, "The psychopath carries out his evaluation of a situation . . . without the usual anxieties, doubts and concerns about being humiliated, causing pain, sabotaging future plans, in short, the infinite possibilities that people of conscience consider when deliberating possible actions" (p. 78).

In 1957, Lykken published a research paper that demonstrated distinct and measurable physiological differences—differences presumed to have genetic origins—shown by psychopathic offenders. Lykken's hypothesis was that psychopaths were especially difficult to socialize because of a lack of anxiety and fear—the "low-fear hypothesis." He tested three groups—(1) a group of nineteen "primary psychopaths," incarcerated offenders who met all of Cleckley's criteria; (2) twenty offenders with long criminal histories who did not meet Cleckley's criteria; and (3) fifteen normal subjects who were matched with the other groups for age and education. Lykken used electrodes to measure the electrodermal response (EDR; a physiologic measure of stress) of the subjects when presented with a conditioned stimulus associated with electric shock. He found that the primary psychopaths showed significantly less EDR reactivity to the stressful situation of anticipating electric shock. In addition, when provided the opportunity to learn to avoid the aversive stimulus by learning mazes, the primary psychopaths (despite being just as intelligent as the other groups) were far slower at this avoidance learning. It seemed that the psychopaths were less bothered (physiologically) by the painful stimulus, and that they were less motivated to learn how to avoid it (less harm-avoidance). Lykken's findings have been replicated by other investigators and there is now a general consensus that "the psychopath's anticipation of a disturbing or aversive event seems to generate less fearful apprehension than the same situation produces in non psychopaths" (Lykken 1995, p. 165). Similar findings have been reported by other researchers (e.g., Ogloff and Wong 1990, Patrick 1994). One of the more interesting findings has been Hare's discovery that psychopaths, despite showing less EDR reactivity to aversive stimuli, produce greater cardiac acceleration! Ogloff and Wong (1990) reported similar findings. Perhaps cardiac acceleration represents a physiological defense mechanism that weakens the impact of an aversive event. Lykken, following these findings, found that relatively fearless subjects show more cardiac acceleration than average subjects prior to painful shock, but then they show less response to the shock itself.

It is well established, then, that genetically influenced individual traits—temperamental qualities—can play some role in the development of antisocial behavior. Traits such as aggressiveness and lack of control contribute to antisocial development (see also Raine and Duncan 1990, Raine and Jones 1987). Even several physiological variables are shown to reflect the temperament of the most severely antisocial individuals. When researchers include both temperament and environmental variables in their investigations, however, the single most consistent conclusion is that "it is the combination of lack of social regulation and lack of self regulation that sets the stage for serious offending" (Henry et al. 1996, p. 622). While a predisposing temperament may have independent statistical effects leading to sociopathy, it is the interaction of predisposing temperament with family and social factors that is the most powerful factor in the development of antisocial character. As Dan Olweus (1980) put it, "A boy with an impetuous and active temperament may to some extent exhaust his mother, resulting in her becoming more permissive of the boy's aggression, which in turn may be conducive to a higher level of aggression in the boy" (p. 658).

Genetics Research

Several strategies are possible in assessing the genetic contribution to a given trait. In the most straightforward approach, termed family aggregation, we determine to what extent a trait tends to run in families as opposed to being randomly distributed throughout the population. This was the method used by Hippocrates when he observed that melancholia tended to cluster in certain family lineages. The weakness of the family aggregation method is that it mixes together genetic factors with environmental factors. Members of the same family share not only a good deal of the same genetic material, but they also share the same home, language, community, socioeconomic status, and, to a large extent, they share the same values, religion, and social attitudes. Such social-environmental influences are not much of a threat to the study of physical traits such as height. We assume that, given basically good nutrition and decent physical surroundings, an individual's height will not be much affected by the social and cultural values of his family. On the other hand, when the question is about psychological and behavioral traits, we are wise to assume that family and social influences can have a substantial effect. Individuals learn from their families, their communities, and their culture, and their behavioral patterns can be heavily influenced by such exposure and learning.

Two basic approaches have been employed in the effort to disentangle the effects of genetic endowment from those of shared family and social environments. In perhaps the most straight-forward strategy, the behavioral similarity of parents and their adopted-away offspring are compared. Such adoption studies re-move the effects of children being reared in the same family and social environment that is bestowed by their parents. Since the possibility of learning from the biological parents is removed, any aggregation for the psychological trait of interest (above that ex-pected by chance) presumably can—with certain limitations enu-merated below—be attributed to genetic influences on psychologi-cal development.

The second approach to separating genetic from environmental influences on development involves the study of twins. Because we know that monozygotic (identical) twins share 100 percent of the same genetic material, and dizygotic (fraternal) twins share about 50 percent, we can systematically assess the association of genetic similarity with the occurrence or strength of a given psy-chological trait. If a trait were entirely genetic in origin, then monozy-gotic (MZ) twins would show a near-perfect concordance, whereas dizygotic (DZ) twins (and other siblings) would show a substan-tially lower concordance. The difference between MZ and DZ concordance has been used in numerous investigations to estimate the heritability of various traits, including criminality and antisocial character.

Throughout the substantial body of scholarly studies on genetic influences on behavior, the aim often has been to determine the extent to which a trait is genetically determined versus the extent to which it is environmentally determined—"nature versus nur-ture." For any given trait, say criminality, the extent to which that trait varies throughout the population is the trait's variance. The total variance of that trait among people can be thought of as the sum of the variance stemming from genetic factors plus the vari-ance stemming from environmental factors. The heritability of a trait, then, is the proportion of the total variance in the trait that is due to genetic causes. The heritability of height, for example is estimated to be around .90; the heritability of IQ (as measured by standardized intelligence tests) is estimated from various studies to be about .75. When it comes to more environmentally sensitive traits, however, such as school achievement or social attitudes, heritability estimates are much weaker.

One major limitation of heritability studies, discussed cogently by Lykken (1995), involves this crucial fact: the proportion of variance attributed to genetic factors varies inversely to the degree of environmental variance of the population studied. In other words, if there is little variance in the quality of families under study, then whatever variance is discovered in the trait will necessarily be attributed to genetic causes. Conversely, when there is great variance in the quality of the family environments studied, then the proportion of variance attributed to genetic causes will be diminished (assuming that the environment has some effects on the trait), all of which means that when we see high heritability estimates for psychological traits, we must be careful to assess the population within which the study was conducted.

As an example, consider the trait sociopathy being studied by an adoption design. Suppose we follow up and systematically study the adopted-away offspring of sociopathic parents, and we include a control group of adopted-away children of parents free of sociopathy. And suppose that we find that virtually all of the children were adopted into stable, middle-class families (which often has been the case, due to selection criteria for adoption). Now suppose that we find that when there is sociopathy in the children it is associated with having a biological parent who is sociopathic. Can we now conclude that sociopathy is highly heritable? Because of the way our group of adoptive families was constituted, there is little or no variance in the qualities of the families that are most likely to contribute to sociopathy. In short, if there is no variance among adoptive families, then there is no chance of finding any environmental effects on sociopathy. On the other hand, if the adopted-away children were taken into very different kinds of homes, homes that varied a great deal in stability, mental health, socioeconomic status, and (most important) adoptive parent sociopathy, then we are likely to find a great deal more environmental effects, and our heritability estimate would be correspondingly lower.

The most powerful research design for determining the genetic contribution to a psychological trait is to study MZ twins reared apart. Since they share 100 percent of the same genetic material, any observed differences can be attributed to environmental effects. The difficulty is that the numbers of reared-apart MZ twins is small, and the number of reared-apart MZ twins with the traits we are interested in is very small.

Several twin studies, conducted over three decades, have consistently found concordance rates for criminality to be greater for MZ twins than for DZ twins, meaning that the genetic contribution to criminality in those samples was substantial. More recent studies have found MZ and DZ concordances of 51 percent and 30 percent, respectively, yielding heritability estimates of about .50 (Cloninger and Gottesman 1987) or, according to reinterpretations of the data, about .40 (Carey 1992). Notably, the MZ and DZ concordance rates are far higher for male co-twins than for female co-twins, which poses another set of questions about the interaction of genetic factors with gender in the study of criminality (Rushton 1996). In another study, this one from the Washington University Twin Study of Psychopathology (DiLalla and Gottesman 1989), MZ concordance for antisocial personality was reported to be .65, while DZ concordance was .40—yielding a heritability estimate of about .30, again a substantial but not overwhelming contribution. It should be noted that these studies often are studying somewhat different constructs. For example, we know that one can be diagnosed with antisocial personality (ASP) without ever being convicted of a crime, and one can be a convicted felon and not meet full ASP diagnostic criteria. Thus, the estimates of heritability will vary not only according to the population and sample under investigation, but also according to the definition of the trait in question.

Adoption studies also have found a substantial contribution of genetics to the development of antisocial and criminal behavior. As early as the 1970s investigators compared the criminality in adopted-away offspring with criminality in their biological parents (Cadoret et al. 1983, Crowe 1974, Hutchings and Mednick 1977).

In the latter study, having a criminal biological father doubled the risk that an adopted-away son would be convicted of criminal acts. As in other research, that hereditary connection did not hold for females. Similarly, Cadoret (1978), when he examined the histories of 246 adopted-away children from ages 10 to 37 years, found a significant correlation of antisocial diagnosis in adoptees with antisocial diagnosis in biological parents.

There are several other adoption studies that find significant correlations between antisocial behavior in adopted-away children and their biological parents, particularly when the child is male. However, the presence of some genetic contribution to some kinds of antisocial behavior is well enough established that this question, in itself, is no longer of much interest. Genetic and environmental factors are both strong. Inquiry has needed to ask more refined questions, such as, for what sort of antisocial traits do the genetic connections matter? DiLalla and Gottesman (1989), for example, note that delinquency (antisocial acts during the adolescent years) has little detectable genetic loading. However, for the subset of individuals who go on to behave in antisocial ways in adulthood, the genetic factors are an important component, along with learning and experience.

Gene–Environment Interaction

The thrust of much of the recent research on the etiology of antisocial behavior is that we must move beyond seeing either genes or environment in isolation. One of the earliest reports to lay out this research paradigm was by Cadoret and colleagues (1983). In carefully reanalyzing the data from three studies on genetic and home environments, they concluded, "The most compelling facet of this analysis is the significance across samples of a Genetic X Environment interaction" (p. 306). They found that it was the combination of genetic background in the presence of adverse family environment that most reliably produced antisocial behavior. A more recent study by Cadoret and his colleagues (1995) similarly found, "Environmental effects and genetic-environmental interaction account for significant variability in adoptee aggressivity, conduct disorder and adult antisocial behavior" (p. 916).

British psychiatrist Michael Rutter (1997) summarized the recent research findings: "The time has come for an explicit focus on the forms of *interplay* between genes and environment" (p. 390, emphasis added). He begins by laying to rest the agenda—in effect for decades—of specifying what proportion of behavioral traits are genetically inherited (heritability) versus what proportion is environmentally influenced. He concludes, "The precise quantification of heritability has little value because it provides no unambiguous implications for theory, policy, or practice" (p. 391). Moreover, like many investigators in behavioral genetics, he dispels the notion that strong genetic influences imply that little can be done environmentally to modify behavior or performance. He points to the fivefold increase in crime rates and the disturbing fact that homicide rates in the United States are many times higher than in any European country to dispel any notion that such behaviors can be adequately accounted for by genetics alone.

Rutter describes three forms of gene-environment correlation: First, in *passive gene-environment correlation*, parental genes, because they influence parental behavior, affect the child and her experience. For example, a sociopathic father will be more likely to abuse or neglect the child, which, in turn, may lead to the antisocial proclivities in the child. Second, in *evocative gene-environment correlation*, the child's or adolescent's genetic loading elicits particular responses from others. For example, it has been demonstrated that infants with difficult temperament are more likely to elicit negative responses from their parents, and older children with difficult temperament are more likely to be the focus of parental criticism and hostility. Third, in *active gene-environment correlation*, the individual's genetic characteristics actively shape the environment she lives within. "There is much evidence that antisocial individuals act in ways that greatly increase the likelihood that they will experience high-risk environments in adult life" (1997, p. 395).

Rutter reviewed research that emphasized the interaction of genetic and environmental factors, for example, the study by Cadoret and colleagues (1995) demonstrating that adoptees at greatest risk for developing conduct disorder are those who have both genetic and environmental liabilities. The practical implications these findings on interaction are that "the alleviation of environmental adversities is most crucial for individuals at genetic risk [because they are most vulnerable]" (Rutter 1997, p. 396).

❖ C H A P T E R   4 ❖

Trajectories in Antisocial Behavior

A great many young people indulge in some antisocial experimentation without ever becoming involved in dangerous or destructive crimes. Researchers have observed that in certain neighborhoods delinquency seems to be almost the norm (Loeber 1990, Moffitt 1993). The vast majority of children and adolescents who engage in such antisocial adventures, however, do not go on to become dangerous or chronic offenders. The courts, the schools, and most parents understand that many young people pass through a phase during which some shoplifting, some fighting, or some vandalism demands a response from family and community—while appreciating the fact that most such youths have it within them (with help) to correct course over the long run.

On the other hand, when a young person engages repeatedly in antisocial acts and then fails to respond to the usual interventions, then at some point it becomes clear that this is more than just dabbling. At that point the primary question for all concerned is: Where is this child headed, and what does he need in order to steer in a healthier direction? The long-term trajectory followed by youths with antisocial behavior patterns can range all the way from a temporary phase of adolescent delinquency (e.g., an episode or two of shoplifting), to repetitive nonviolent offending (a series of burglaries and car thefts), to a chronic mix of violent and nonviolent offending, to lifelong psychopathic character with violent and nonviolent crimes and even murderous preoccupations. Substance abuse often plays a major role in chronic offending, by disinhibiting impulses and by eroding the individual's productive capacities. Outcomes range from recovery from antisocial habits by late adolescence or young adulthood to chronic low-level crime with occasional scrapes with the law and occasional incarceration, to conviction on heinous crimes and incarceration for much or all of one's adult life. In one way or another, discerning what kind of trajectory a youth is following is a major preoccupation of the courts and probation officers and of mental health personnel. Authorities must decide, for example, whether to prosecute on a given charge, whether to seek a waiver of jurisdiction for trial in adult court, whether to seek commitment to a correctional institution, and so on. It also is the most personally gripping concern for families and for schools and other community institutions.

In this enterprise of identifying the types and trajectories of antisocial youth, we are working, developmentally speaking, at midstream. That is, the offender is still a juvenile—a child or adolescent—with years of personality development lying ahead. Only the most deterministic theorist would claim that personality is fully formed by age 12 or 14. However, much personality development has been laid down. The insults to early psychological development have occurred years before, as have the damaging effects, in utero, of neurotoxins and other biological insults. In many cases, by the mid-adolescent years, personality traits and adaptive styles are largely in place, and substantial change can be exceedingly difficult. Habits of antisocial behavior can be deeply ingrained by early adolescence, and several studies have pointed to the persistence of antisocial behavior (e.g., Loeber 1982, 1991). Hence, the task of defining types of antisocial youths and predicting their long-term outcome is on unsure footing. Young people can change, sometimes in startling ways—especially if they get the right help. Yet it also is possible to describe behavioral traits and personality styles that tend to persist for years or even decades.

If, through the study of personality, behavior patterns, and risk factors, we can know with even modest confidence the kind of trajectory a youth is following, then we can have some idea of what to expect. We then are in a better position to know how to protect the public and can specify what kind of interventions provide the most hope. One other benefit accrues from knowing the youth's trajectory. Family and friends can come to terms with the most likely prospects for the youth and can prepare themselves emotionally and in practical ways.

If there is anything that social scientists like to do, it is to classify things. They will expend great effort devising schemes for classifying everything from personality types to categories of misbehavior and mental disorders. The two most recent editions of the *Diagnostic and Statistical Manual* of the American Psychiatric Association (*DSM-III-R* and *DSM-IV*) are so complex that separate books are published to instruct clinicians in how to use the system.

Categories for classifying individuals are always based on large-scale research, and are defined by statistical methods—the most rigorous means of presenting their findings in summary fashion. As experienced clinicians know, however, even the most sophisticated classification schemes fail to capture important qualities of many of the real individuals who appear in our offices. Statistical methods necessarily obscure the unique qualities of the individual in favor of trends that appear across large numbers of cases.

These reservations notwithstanding, some of the personality types and statistics deriving from research in recent years can provide useful clues about what to look for when deciphering the most likely trajectory a youth is on and what to do about it. Being able to identify the delinquent youths who present the greatest long-term risk is especially useful, given that a small proportion of youthful offenders is responsible for the majority of serious crimes.

There are several possible approaches to classifying antisocial individuals. One can begin by classifying only according to personality and behavior, and by setting aside the question of outcomes. David Lykken's (1995) classification scheme follows this course; he identifies nineteen types and subtypes of antisocial personalities. Some of his distinctions may elude the casual observer or policymakers—for example, between the "disaffiliated sociopath" and the "disempathic sociopath." Such differences may be meaningful only to those who must work directly with such individuals. One can also take the opposite approach to classification, and order only according to outcome, deferring the question of the personality types involved. This was Moffitt's (1993) approach, when she posited the distinction between "adolescent limited" types of antisocial youths (where delinquency desists before adulthood) versus "life-course persistent" (where antisocial activities persist well into the adult years).

It is easy, retrospectively, to classify individual trajectories: group A desisted in criminal behavior before adulthood; group B carried on with minor offenses and irresponsibility; and group C got into high gear during adolescence and then persisted in a life of crime and punishment. Such after-the-fact analyses are useful only if they provide clues about what to look for early on. Prospectively, say at age 12 or 13, we want to know what indication would help predict the subsequent trajectory. This search for attributes of the individual, her experience, and her history is a search for risk factors—conditions that are associated with an undesirable outcome. The search for risk factors has been accompanied in recent years by investigation of the opposite—protective strengths. These are the attributes of the individual and her social context that seem to buffer her from the negative effects of adversity. Protective strengths are, of course, most beneficial in the early years.

RISK FACTORS AND PROTECTIVE STRENGTHS

The term *risk factor* is used in somewhat different ways by different writers. The broadest definition of risk factor may be that provided by psychologist Bruce Compas and his colleagues (1995): "Those characteristics of the person or the environment that are associated with an increased probability of maladaptive developmental outcomes" (p. 273). Notice that this definition is neutral with regard to causes. That is, a risk factor can be some attribute that is statistically associated with a poor outcome but that is not presumed to be a cause of that outcome. Poverty and race, for example, can be associated statistically with antisocial outcome; but there is no reason to believe that either one causes crime. However, some risk factors are causally involved in untoward development—neglect and abuse, for example, or the "fearless-impulsive" temperament.

In this midstream endeavor to characterize antisocial individuals and to predict their subsequent behavior, some developmental risk factors are remote in time. Early deprivation and neglect or having an antisocial parent, for example, may have a lot to do with Janie's antisocial development over her 14 years. However, these factors are relatively distant, and they do not help much in delineating her current characteristics, in predicting where she will be a year from now, or in specifying the kind of intervention most likely to benefit her. Of greater relevance in the present are her recent behavioral history, her current personality traits, and her immediate social milieu (family, community, and peers).

Behavioral History

When considering the issue of long-term trajectories, it is well to bear in mind the commonsense precept (borne out scientifically) that the best predictor of behavior in any particular domain is the individual's history of behavior in that domain. Hence, whatever personality factors and risk factors we might identify as useful, we must bear in mind the individual's behavioral history. Confronted with 17-year-old Jason, who has committed several serious assaults over the previous year, we would be wise to expect that he may commit more assaults in the coming months—unless some rather dramatic changes are brought about in his life. Conversely, juveniles with no history of overt aggression by the age of about 16 seldom go on to commit violent assaults.

In this business of predicting antisocial behavior, there is no shortage of causes for humility. There are numerous accounts of juveniles who, with no history of aggressiveness or other obvious risk factors, have unexpectedly committed violence of vast proportions. In a rural community in eastern Washington State in 1996, for example, 14-year-old Barry Loukaitis, with no history of arrest or significant antisocial behavior, went to school with a high-powered rifle and shot three students and a teacher. He may represent that subgroup of adolescents who overcontrol their aggressive impulses, and who act out rarely but sometimes very violently. The converse situation also ought to give us pause—when an individual with a dense history of antisocial acts, along with several other risk factors, dramatically alters course. Such episodes serve as reminders of just how limited is our ability to predict trajectories in individual cases.

Versatility and Early Onset

From the numerous studies that have aimed to characterize and track antisocial youths, two key risk factors have emerged over and over again that distinguish youths more likely to engage in serious offenses and more likely to commit their antisocial ways beyond adolescence. First, it has been recognized at least since 1966, when Lee Robins reported the findings from her massive follow-up study in *Deviant Children Grown Up*, that a *diversity of types of antisocial behavior* is a bad sign (Robins 1978b). Children whose problematic behaviors span several categories of offending—theft, physical aggression, truancy, sexual assault, lying—are more likely to develop serious and chronic offense patterns than children whose antisocial proclivities are restricted to a single category, such as stealing. One report notes a substantially higher risk for juveniles whose crimes span only two categories, aggression and theft. Corresponding to this characterization, Rolf Loeber's (1990) "aggressive/versatile" type is described as typically engaging in "cafeteria-style" offending, involving two or more types of offenses, including violence, property crimes, and drug offenses. He distinguishes this type as showing aggressive *and* concealing problems (e.g., surreptitious theft), frequent hyperactivity, poor social skills, and academic problems.

This most worrisome group of versatile delinquents also shows the second major risk factor that figures prominently in poor prognosis—*early onset of conduct problems*. Children whose conduct problems (not including normal oppositional behavior or argumentativeness) begin early, in the elementary school years, tend not to desist in their antisocial ways before adulthood (Moffitt et al. 1996). Other things being equal, children whose first arrest or police contact occurs by age 11 or 12 are more likely to follow a long-term trajectory of antisocial behavior. It is no surprise that this early-onset feature also figures prominently in Hare's Psychopathy Checklist (Chapter 2). Statistics collected by the Office of Juvenile Justice and Delinquency Prevention place the early-onset factor in bold relief. As shown in Table 4–1, children whose first referral to juvenile court occurs at age 10 or 11 have a 60 to 61 percent probability of returning for subsequent referrals. The probability of such recidivism declines with rising age at first referral, and dramatically so after age 14. Youths whose first referral occurs at age 17 have only a 16 percent chance of returning. Those whose first juvenile court referral occurs at age 10 or 11 seem to

TABLE 4–1. Percent of Juveniles Returned to Court after Each Referral

	Number of Court Referrals							
Age at Referral	1	2	3	4	5	6	7	8
10	61	84	96	97	–	–	–	–
11	60	85	91	92	98	–	–	–
12	59	83	89	97	98	95	98	96
13	57	82	90	93	95	97	96	98
14	53	77	86	91	92	94	96	95
15	45	69	80	84	89	89	91	93
16	33	55	68	73	77	81	82	83
17	16	27	36	41	45	48	50	53

Adapted from Snyder and Sickmund 1995.

comprise a different population from those whose first referral occurs at age 16 or 17.

These two key risk factors—versatility of conduct problems and early onset of antisocial behavior—tend to go together, with some exceptions, of course. When both features are found together, particularly in the presence of frequent offending, they help to identify youths who present a high probability of serious and chronic offending and a diminished promise of positive response to treatment.

The identification of youthful offenders with the worst prognosis for serious and chronic offending is especially salient in light of another set of research findings: It has been found repeatedly and in various locales that a small proportion of youthful offenders account for the majority of serious and violent crimes (Office of Juvenile Justice and Delinquency Prevention 1993). In a Philadelphia study (Wolfgang et al. 1972) it was found that "chronic offenders" (those with five or more police contacts) constituted 18 percent of the cohort of youthful offenders, but these chronic offenders were responsible for 62 percent of all offenses and about two-thirds of all violent offenses! In the National Youth Survey of adolescents aged 12 to 17 (Elliott et al. 1986), the small group of delinquents classified as "serious violent" offenders (5 percent of the cohort of all juveniles at that age) committed an average of 132 delinquent offenses annually.

It should be emphasized that this group of "serious-violent" youthful offenders—the ones who commit the bulk of serious crimes and who persist in their criminal careers well into adulthood—is a distinct minority of juveniles who come to the attention of the police and courts. The majority of youths who are referred to juvenile court never return for another referral. The majority of juveniles incarcerated in detention facilities are incarcerated only once, and only about half of juveniles who are committed to correctional institutions are committed more than once. What these statistics mean is that, despite the high-profile cases of delinquents who return repeatedly, most youths who find their way into trouble with the law learn their lesson one way or another, and they do not come back.

Some of the juveniles who manage not to return to detention or to the institution do so by not getting caught—at least for a long time—and many go forward with a quieter antisocial lifestyle of petty crime and irresponsibility (the profile that might earn a diagnosis of antisocial personality disorder) but without committing the criminal acts that bring a response from police and the courts. But at least some of these non-recidivists learn some lessons about how to get on in life without such intolerable behavior.

Other Risk Factors

Several other risk factors have been identified that help to distinguish the long-term trajectories of antisocial youths. The risk factors identified vary considerably depending on the sample studied and the assumptions of the researchers. Parental uninvolvement and parental criminality raise the odds against an adolescent who has begun a pattern of antisocial behavior. In children, attention deficit/hyperactivity disorder (ADHD), when it occurs *with* conduct problems, raises the odds that the youth will go on to develop further delinquency. In one study in New Zealand, 60 percent of children with ADHD became delinquent by age 13 (Moffitt and Silva 1988). In adolescents with conduct problems, ADHD may make it more difficult to change course. Recent research makes it clear, however, that ADHD and antisocial behavior are two different things. While the two conditions statistically may tend to go together, many children with ADHD never develop antisocial behavior patterns, and the majority of conduct-disordered children and adolescents do not have ADHD. Nonetheless, we must be cognizant of the fact that attention difficulties make it more difficult to succeed in school, which in turn may make a child more likely to associate with a deviant peer group. Children with ADHD are generally more challenging to socialize at home and at school.

The problem of risk factors and long-term outcomes for individual juveniles must be considered more broadly than just the individual and family attributes. The odds that any given juvenile will persist in delinquent habits depends not only on individual qualities and history, but also on the reactions he encounters in his social environment—the response from family, friends, and local institutions such as police and the courts. Many parents are heavily burdened by financial and work demands, unstable relationships and wrecked marriages, and sometimes by their own drug and alcohol problems. Such stressed parents often are unable to provide the level of monitoring and guidance their children and adolescents require. Especially when children enter the teen years and become more independent and secretive about their activities, it often can be easier for parents just not to pay attention. The energy and commitment necessary to confront and "fight" constructively with adolescents can be more than many parents can manage.

Permissiveness/Tolerance

A parallel process occurs in the broader social milieu. In an effort to be helpful to children in trouble, many of our institutions have become permissive and thereby fail to provide young people with normal, expectable feedback and limits on their behavior. In an effort to "meet kids where they're at," schools dramatically lower expectations, and they put up with all manner of destructive and unhealthy behavior. Such a culture of tolerance is in place that many adolescents who desperately need direct and realistic feedback about their behavioral choices come to feel that daily drug abuse, coming to school drunk, and skipping classes on a regular basis are normal and acceptable. The truth is that we do such adolescents no favors by expecting less of them. Such permissiveness can be expected to perpetuate exactly the problems those students arrive with.

The culture of tolerance was elegantly analyzed by Malcolm Gladwell (1996) in *The New Yorker*. Gladwell argued, in an article titled "The Tipping Point," that by tolerating pervasive, low-level delinquency and crime, we unwittingly encourage heavier sorts of criminal activity. Gladwell's argument parallel's the "broken windows" thesis of James Wilson and George Kelling. Their thesis is that if physical evidence of decay is allowed to persist in a neighborhood, then citizens tend to be discouraged and to withdraw— leaving the area to vandals and escalating social decay (Moe and Wilkie 1997). Gladwell demonstrated how the lack of response to small crimes like vandalism can lead to a local epidemic of such crime, then to a general breakdown in social order and respect. In short, normal community standards can be eroded quickly when incipient transgressions are ignored.

We therefore should add another risk factor to the list: a social milieu that is unable or unwilling to provide the delinquent youth with appropriate limits, guidance, and, when needed, confrontation or punishment for antisocial behavior. Other things being equal, a juvenile with a pattern of antisocial behavior is more likely to persist in his antisocial ways, and is more likely to progress to more serious crimes, if he does not encounter firm limits and confrontation from family and community.

PROTECTIVE FACTORS/RESILIENT CHILDREN

Reflecting upon any sort of disorder or pathology, it is perhaps most natural to ask, What causes this troubling behavior? Through countless hours of clinical intervention and decades of research on antisocial behavior, the aim from within this "illness model" was to explain how one factor or another led to the unwanted behavior. But the preoccupation with the causes of problematic behavior obscured a subtler phenomenon—the many children exposed to substantial risk factors who do not display behavioral problems. By the early 1980s it had dawned on many researchers that this quieter drama—the drama of resilient children—warranted serious attention (Rutter 1979, Werner and Smith 1982).

In the midst of the most deleterious circumstances—fractured families, poverty, parental substance abuse and criminality, even abuse and neglect—some children somehow manage to grow up free of the kinds of psychological damage and behavioral problems that we associate with such negative influences. These resilient children are the quieter ones who do not disrupt or skip school, use drugs, or join gangs. They do their homework, look after their siblings (and sometimes their parents), and prepare to be good citizens. Recognizing the existence of this surprisingly successful subgroup led to the sensible question, What is it that enables these children to develop along healthy lines and to avoid the pathologies that befall so many of their peers and even their siblings? This is the search for protective factors and the conditions of resilience.

The study of resilient children promises practical as well as theoretical benefits. Understanding what conditions buffer a child from the effects of adversity will suggest interventions to strengthen those factors in at-risk children. Even in this midstream enterprise to help older children and adolescents change course, knowledge of conditions that enhance resilience carries powerful implications for how best to go about intervening. In addition, a good grasp of protective factors helps to clarify the mechanisms by which adversity leads to negative outcomes. For example, as noted below, violent neighborhoods do not produce violent youths when the family remains strong and healthy.

What we mean by "protective" is some condition or attribute that protects a child from harm when he is exposed to adversity such as abuse or neglect. What is it about the children who grow up in violent neighborhoods and fractured families that enables them not to be derailed in their quest for healthy development? Several attributes associated with stress-resistant outcomes have been identified:

Competence

Competence, a key aspect of intelligence, is seen as "the ability to construct an internal representation of an event . . . so that it can become sufficiently meaningful to be acted upon" (Hauser et al.

1989, p. 113). If a child possesses the cognitive skills to grasp the nature and meaning of events affecting her, then she will be less vulnerable to the damaging effects of those negative conditions (Garmezy et al. 1984). Gaining such cognitive distance from painful or demoralizing events can lessen the need for maladaptive defenses such as acting out (e.g., aggression) or substance abuse. Of course, for youths who have established a pattern of antisocial endeavors, those defenses are already in place, and the quest for insight is of little or no interest. This is why psychotherapy is not often useful with chronically antisocial individuals. Their competence and cognitive skills have been channeled into pursuits other than self-knowledge and social adaptation.

Intelligence

Intelligence is more likely to be beneficial in helping even chronically antisocial youths to achieve a course correction. Low intellectual functioning can be a risk factor for academic failure, deviant peer relations, and involvement in antisocial adventures. Later on, though, for delinquent adolescents and young adults, good intellectual skills can serve as an important adaptive strength, helping the youths to change course, to achieve what theorists call "recovery of function." Other things being equal, it is easier for a boy with good intellectual strengths to finish school and to learn job skills than it is for another youth with much weaker intelligence. This involves the matter of alternatives. A key ingredient in young people moving away from an antisocial lifestyle is skills development, and possessing the requisite intellectual capacities removes one possible impediment.

Locus of Control

Two other personality attributes consistently associated with resilience in children and adolescents are locus of control and self-esteem (Garmezy 1981). Locus of control is the extent to which one feels that she is in charge of her own life and future, versus the extent to which she feels that events happen *to* her and are beyond her control. Researchers Werner and Smith (1982) reported that for children who were not under particular stress or adversity, locus of control and self-esteem made little difference in outcome. However, for the highly stressed group—children from violent, abusive, and unstable backgrounds—the children who succeeded were those who believed that they exercised some control over events in their lives.

Locus of control is an especially sensitive index in the development of antisocial character. One of the most pervasive features of antisocial youths is the attitude that they are not in charge of events they participate in, that these things "just happen." Listening to a chronic offender, it often sounds as if the crime he committed not only just happened, but it happened to him! Most often, the chronically antisocial offender cannot imagine how he could do things differently in order to avoid the untoward outcome (prison, injury, etc.).

Locus of control is such a key personality dimension because irresponsibility for one's actions and obligations lies right at the heart of what we mean by antisocial. The sociopath seems to learn early on not only to deny responsibility but also to think in ways whereby control and efficacy are seen as external to the self. In some cases, denying responsibility has a simple, practical function, that is, getting out of trouble. But the external locus of control is so pervasive in the personalities of many antisocial youths that it appears to represent a long-standing cognitive style, a habitual manner of looking at life and one's own behavior. The sense of self-efficacy—the belief in one's ability to bring about intended effects—is limited to the most immediate aims and wishes, and there is no sense of a future or any investment in being planful. Some children may learn to deny responsibility through association with a deviant peer group or from irresponsible parents, and in such cases denying responsibility can be instrumental. For others, however, it seems to involve defects in cognitive development, in the early, formative experiences Greenspan described, where one learns, through countless interactions with loving parents and others, the most rudimentary connections between affects and wishes, on the one hand, and actions and consequences, on the other.

Self-Esteem

Self-esteem is an important and complex construct. In children, a positive self-concept can mean a willingness to try new things, to risk making mistakes, and to take on ever-greater challenges in academic and social realms. Positive self regard accompanies well-adjusted and healthy individuals at all ages. With antisocial youths, however, what often appears to be self-esteem can be little more than an inflated sense of self-importance along with a dearth of insight into one's real qualities and potential. This is not self-esteem. The 15-year-old delinquent who insists that he'll be playing in the National Basketball Association in a couple years has not built real self-esteem. Instead, what we see here is an inflated but vacuous sense of self that is built upon narcissistic relations with others and, in most cases, modest real skills. This enables the youth to feel good about himself part of the time, but it is an empty confidence. Such means of inflating the sense of one's own value are unstable and are doomed to recurrent and painful disappointments—disappointments that can feel like insults and often lead to rage. Such narcissistic injury is at the heart of such rage reactions that we read were triggered by being "dissed."

Real self-esteem is built on a foundation of accomplishments—success in academics, work skills, social relations, music, art, athletics, and so on. Real self-esteem is seldom flashy or "high." It is built slowly and incrementally from childhood onward on the basis of countless small, normal efforts (Brooks 1991). Its benefits are manifest not in the short term but only in the long-term perspective on individual development. This formulation contrasts with the so-called self-esteem movement, wherein adults attempt to instill self-esteem by saying encouraging things and training the child to think positively about the self. This is not where self-esteem comes from.

Family Strengths/Relationships with Adults

Several family qualities have been associated with positive outcome for children and adolescents who are exposed to significant adversity. It has been found repeatedly that for children growing up in violent neighborhoods and/or in poverty, strict parental supervision has been key in preventing delinquency (Rutter 1979, Wilson 1974). Michael Rutter, in studying extremely troubled family settings, found that the children who managed to hold onto a good relationship with one parent were far more likely to have a healthy outcome. This is similar to Garmezy's findings that in lower-class families the children with positive outcomes were those who were blessed with a "positive identification" figure—one parent they could identify with.

Similar studies have examined the outcome for children growing up in violent neighborhoods. How well such children had adapted was "systematically related to characteristics of the child's home environment" (Cicchetti 1996, p. 315). Researchers Richters and Martinez (1993) reported that it was not just the accumulation of adversities that predicted poor outcome (antisocial behavior), but rather it was when the violence and instability of the neighborhood invaded the family that children's development was derailed. Hence, if the family manages to function well—to protect, nurture, and supervise the children—then the likelihood of antisocial outcome is greatly diminished.

Another factor that can have protective power is when a child or adolescent who is exposed to serious risk factors is somehow able to maintain a positive relationship with at least one healthy adult (Werner and Smith 1992). This may be a parent, but in many cases this is a teacher, a coach, or a grandparent. In the midst of family and community violence, failing schools, and a history of neglect and abuse, some youths are able to make good use of that one key connection to a healthy adult outside the family. Such a positive relationship seems to provide a kind of moral and psychological anchor point, an orienting beacon that helps the youth find her way through the pitfalls and insults that threaten to derail her development.

For many delinquent youths, protective factors may seem to be a matter of opportunities lost in the distant past. Personality traits often appear to be well entrenched by mid-adolescence. Maladaptive defenses such as denial and acting out have become habitual, as have the cognitive styles of external locus of control and a lack of concern for the plight of others. And yet we know that the majority of antisocial youths do correct course, some earlier than others. Hence, our interventions ought to be guided not only by the effort to eliminate the negative influences, but also by the knowledge of the potential protective strengths of intelligence, family integrity, and having one stable adult relationship.

TYPES AND TRAJECTORIES

In an ideal world of psychological research, our ability to distinguish personality types would be so sophisticated and reliable that for any given antisocial individual we could automatically predict his (untreated) developmental trajectory from that point on, and we could specify the particular treatment needed to correct course. At that level of scientific rigor, the personality type would tell us the "trajectory." In the real world, our ability to reliably diagnose types of antisocial character is often weak (usually for lack of valid information), and our capacity to reliably predict a youth's trajectory is a long way off. The principal reason why we cannot predict well, besides the numerous individual factors we cannot see or measure, is that we cannot know for sure what kinds of experience the youth will encounter in the months and years ahead, and we cannot know how she will respond to the opportunities, the challenges, and the setbacks.

A pared-down scheme is offered here, with just four types that capture the most frequently seen configurations of individual attributes and behavioral history. Some less common types will not fit well in this scheme, for example, sex offenders, who will show some of these features and not others. While much finer discriminations among types can be useful for some purposes, in practice the reliability of any scheme for assigning individuals to categories diminishes as the number of categories increases. Frequently we find that a given individual shows qualities that overlap from one type to another. Still, these four types capture the majority of antisocial youths, and they define some of the most salient dimensions along which we would want to characterize antisocial youths. There are, of course, some individuals whose antisocial behavior stems from relatively infrequent conditions, such as abnormal brain electrical functioning (i.e., seizure disorder) or from major psychiatric disorder, but they will be left for consideration in subsequent chapters.

The Delinquent Dabbler

Within the broad range of normal adolescent development, there often is a struggle between identification with social mores versus rebelling and transgressing those norms and expectations. While the vast majority of youths emerge into adulthood with an intact respect for, and identification with, social norms, a good many of those same adolescents make forays into the realm of antisocial activities along the way. Typically such forays involve low-level violations such as vandalism and shoplifting, but more serious crimes can also result. Several conditions may encourage such dabbling—neighborhoods in which a peer group "normalizes" such petty crime, adolescent confusion about where one belongs in the social order, and family conflicts and resentments.

The principal features distinguishing the dabbler from more serious antisocial character are (1) the antisocial behaviors represent a departure from what one would ordinarily expect on the basis of personal history and family/social background; (2) the antisocial behaviors usually begin "late," meaning well into adolescence, instead of being a continuation of conduct problems that began by age 10 or 12; (3) the crimes are usually of a less dangerous kind, rarely involving serious harm to persons; and (4) when caught and confronted, the delinquent dabbler and her family are dismayed, often frantic, and are responsive to intervention (e.g., fully compliant with school sanctions, probation, and community service). The dabbler is not out to hurt or exploit others, and if she causes substantial harm, she will feel genuine remorse and self-recrimination. Her crimes often are of a pointless nature—shoplifting things that she could afford to purchase or things that are not really needed, vandalism of nothing in particular, a senseless provocation leading to a fight.

The late onset and the relatively light quality of the dabbler's transgressions do not mean that such behaviors need not be taken seriously. Indeed, adolescents who experiment with delinquency need, more than anything else, to be met with a decisive response from family and community, including the police and courts. The worst message a dabbler can receive is that her transgressions are more or less acceptable to the community. Adolescents who are struggling with which set of values they will adopt, and where they will end up in the social order, need unambiguous feedback that antisocial actions will not be tolerated. They need concrete feedback about where the limits are and where the lines are drawn, and they should be expected to participate fully in measures designed to help them learn to avoid such problematic actions.

There is always some urgency about helping an adolescent to correct course. Some dabblers find themselves lured more deeply into delinquency by gang affiliations and by the vagaries of drug and alcohol abuse. There is always the possibility that a basically good kid will be associated with deviant peers when a serious crime is committed.

At three o'clock on a sunny afternoon, just after school had let out for the day, a small sedan pulled up alongside the curb near the main walkway leading from the front door of the high school. With windows rolled down, taunts were exchanged between the driver and some kids on the sidewalk. Other students passed by, and still the scene looked pretty normal. As Alicia walked by she saw the barrel of a gun pointing out of the window in her direction. Witnesses reported that she seemed to recognize at least some of the occupants of the car. She reportedly said, with a sneer, "What are you going to do, shoot somebody?" She fell to the ground as the gunshot echoed off the high brick walls of the school building. She was hit by a bullet intended for some rival gang members a few yards down the sidewalk.

Four boys, ranging in age from 14 to 17, were apprehended by police within an hour. All four attended local schools in predominantly middle-class suburbs. Two were known to be gang members. At the time of the shooting, Allen, aged 14, was in the back seat on the driver's side. From information presented in court, it seemed that he was unaware of what was about to happen, or even that a gun was in the car. Allen had a good school record and no history of any police contacts. He avoided drugs and alcohol, and he was thought of as a helpful and promising young man. Some peers reported, however, that he seemed to be "hanging with" some peers lately who were associated with gangs. Some reported that Allen had bragged that he had participated in a burglary.

Allen was in his junior year, talented in science and math, and he expected to attend the university after high school. His family was intact and as stable as most, and there was little reason to believe that he was rejecting the middle-class values of his family and community. But his foray into associating with gang-affiliated peers led him to be a "participant" in a senseless and deadly crime.

The outcome for Allen was unusual for "dabblers." He truly was in the wrong place at the wrong time, and, after enduring prosecution, jail time, and probation, he will be burdened for life with the horror of what he was a party to. The more typical long-term trajectory for dabblers is to leave behind their antisocial experimentation by late adolescence and adulthood. As with all individuals, however, the trajectory ultimately followed depends to a great extent on the response from family and community. Many dabblers learn their lesson from a single arrest, court appearance, probation, and family and treatment interventions. However, dabblers who receive little or no response from family and community are at greater risk for carrying forward with their antisocial ways.

The Neurotic Delinquent

Quite often, youthful offenders are referred for evaluation because a probation officer, a school administrator, or a social worker suspects that there is something more involved in the antisocial behavior than just lack of conscience and identification with delinquent peers. Often there are obvious emotional wounds stemming from loss, neglect, or trauma. Also common are the most blatantly self-defeating behaviors and an astonishing inability to stay out of trouble. Offenses are often pointless and even foolish.

The neurotic delinquent is so named because he is an unhappy youth who suffers from internal conflicts, anxieties, and uncertainties. (There is a related rare subset of violent youths who appear to overcontrol their emotions, especially their anger; such "over-restrained" youths tend to act out less frequently but at times more violently [Tinklenberg et al. 1996].) Almost invariably there is a great deal of anger and resentment. Self-esteem is not high, although temporary "highs" can be obtained through drug use or daring exploits. Some degree of depression is common, which shows up mostly in the form of irritability, disturbed sleep, and a pessimistic or vacuous outlook on the future. Real confidence is lacking. Social skills often are limited, and the delinquent peer group offers ready acceptance to one who might otherwise feel isolated. The process of gravitating toward antisocial endeavors may have begun early, as identification with family and society began to falter by early adolescence. The neurotic delinquent, however, is not free of conscience. Despite the operation of heavy defenses, such youths are capable of empathy and concern for the feelings of others. At times, they may display considerable regret over the hurt they have caused others, and they may genuinely wish to change the direction of their lives. They have the capacity for warm interpersonal relations, although their emotional wounds and the attendant resentments make them wary of trusting others more than superficially.

Twenty minutes out into the suburbs, behind the soundproof door of a psychiatrist's office, parents struggled to understand their child. David, who looked younger than his 16 years, spent most of the time in these sessions sitting with a sullen expression, at times sneeringly hostile to his father and dismissive to his mother. There was no evidence of respect. When pressed for answers, David could describe how he began to associate with gang members, and how he was "jumped in" to gang membership the previous year. He could explain how he came to be in the car the night that shots were fired. But his parents' anguish was unrelieved, for there were no answers to the real question: How is it that David could throw away the values of his family and his education for the dead-end peril of a gang?

David was referred for evaluation by his probation officer. He was in one of the cars involved in gunfire that injured a 15-year-old boy. David was known at school as a capable student—when he applied himself. He also was well known over the past two years for skipping classes, even whole days, and everyone knew he was often high. His grades had fallen from mostly B's to C's and D's as assignments were seldom turned in. He had twice been suspended from school for fighting, and he had been arrested twice over the prior year. The first time was for dealing drugs, but the charges were dropped for some reason. The second arrest was for car theft, and the charges were pending.

David's parents had struggled, too. Following the divorce when David was 7, his father poured himself into his business and a new romantic relationship, and he was largely unavailable to his son. His mother's work and personal life, involving a series of boyfriends, were periodically overwhelming, and she regularly abused alcohol. At one point, when David tried to tell her that his 12-year-old sister was using drugs, his mother replied, "I can't deal with this; just don't tell me about it."

The shooting and its aftermath served as a wrenching wake-up call. For David's parents, nothing could have been more real than how close they came to losing their son, to death or to years in prison. They rallied, but not all at once, and the gains in therapy took several months. David's mother went through a phase of being emotional but unhelpful—one time being furious with David, at another time blaming his father, then blaming herself. Gradually, though, she found her moorings. She began to press David for some answers, and she listened to what he said. She seemed to get some control over her alcohol abuse. For weeks, David's father clung to being angry and denouncing his son's "stupid" choices and irresponsible attitudes. Father and son got stuck in a cycle of angry exchanges. Gradually, the father's defensive hostility gave way to sober reflection on what his son needed from him. He learned that David needed to be pursued and not to be allowed to brush off his parents. He also learned to tolerate some of his son's anger that had accumulated over the years. The balance between mutual respect and honest expression of feelings did not come easily to father or to son.

Probation required that David strictly adhere to the demands of school and his community service work, and that he be accountable for his whereabouts and his schedule. Through the months of incarceration, prosecution, and probation, along with the painful confrontations with parents, David learned how to focus on the day-to-day tasks of education and work, and on the idea that he might have a future.

The principal feature distinguishing the neurotic delinquent is the locus of the conflict. Much of the conflict is internal—between aspirations for a future versus negativism and nihilism; between identification with healthy social values versus rejection and hostility; between needing to be loved and understood versus counterdependency and isolation. Unlike the common sociopathic and psychopathic characters, the neurotic delinquent is powerfully affected by such internal tensions. He has not given up hope of gaining love, self-respect, or a future. As a result, he is often an unhappy and depressed individual. His episodes of hostility and disrespect alternate with periods of self-doubt, anxiety, and depression.

The neurotic delinquent is on perilous footing. On the one hand, his identifications with crime and delinquency are not deep, and he still yearns for connection and hope. On the other hand, the longer he associates with a deviant peer group, and the longer he lets his education slide, the more likely it is that by adulthood an antisocial orientation will be deeply ingrained. For many neurotic delinquents, this is just the trajectory—to an unhappy adulthood marked by occasional crime, self-destructiveness, and substance abuse. As with any individuals who engage in antisocial acts, occasionally a serious crime may result.

For those neurotic delinquents who are fortunate enough to gain a strong and therapeutic response from family and community, a major course correction can result. The majority of such delinquents, however, are not eager to participate in the endeavors they need the most—individual and family therapy, strict compliance with expectations of school and work, and in some cases random drug testing. Often the authority of the juvenile court is needed to compel such endeavors. In those cases where family and community rally vigorously, and where the court or other authority maintain strict oversight, such delinquents can overcome their rejection of society and begin, as David did, to think realistically about their future.

The Common Sociopath

It is the common sociopath who makes up the bulk of the inmates of our detention facilities and correctional institutions and who commits the majority of crimes, wreaking havoc on society. Unlike the neurotic offender, the common sociopath is not troubled much by internal tensions and doubts. He is not particularly unhappy or worried about himself, but only about getting caught for his transgressions or about how to overcome obstacles to his wishes. The conflict is entirely external—between the individual and society. Internal tensions are limited only to concerns about how to avoid punishment and about the best avenues to gratification. Typically, the sociopath feels that he has been treated unfairly. He can earnestly describe the many individuals, from parents and teachers to police officers and judges, who have treated him unjustly. His life-course is often haphazard and frustrating. Often there have been learning difficulties and education has been a struggle; work history usually is sparse especially in juveniles. Interpersonal relations tend to be shallow and unstable, and social skills usually are limited. Conscience is altogether lacking. Rather than feel remorse or self-doubt for his misdeeds, the sociopath generates rationalizations that place the blame on others even for his own behavior. The pain and plight of others is likely to serve only as amusement.

The source of the sociopath's personality attributes lies primarily in the fact that he has not been raised properly. That is, the failure of socialization most often appears to stem from inept parenting—chaotic, neglectful, or abusive family life; harsh and inconsistent discipline (coercive cycles); antisocial modeling of negative behaviors and attitudes; and a failure to nurture prosocial habits or competence in education and social relations. Parents who themselves are poorly socialized often instill in their children the expectation that responsibility for untoward events can be externalized, blamed on others. Locus of control tends to be external, too. Such children grow up feeling that they are not in charge of their own lives, and that they are victims. The sociopath has failed to become a citizen.

The antisocial behaviors of the sociopath can range all the way from a general irresponsibility involving little that is criminal (e.g., in work, finances, and personal relations), to petty crime and episodic violence, to a pattern of serious and violent criminal acts leading to irreversible harm to others. His exploits are often accompanied by drug and alcohol abuse. His propensity for antisocial behavior derives from a general failure of socialization, including poor impulse control, a dearth of conscience and empathy, and a conviction that he is not responsible for the bad things that happen. The majority of sociopaths, however, gradually make some accommodation to the prevailing social order. The mayhem and pain usually subside by middle age. The rate at which sociopaths commit crimes falls off after their twenties; by their forties their crime rate is only a fraction of what it once was (Figure 4–1). Character structure may not change much. But the impulsive and violent acts—those that lead to injury and prison—tend to be reined in. Some sociopathic individuals do make real changes eventually, often after years of a destructive lifestyle, incarceration, and an accumulation of injuries.

Fourteen-year-old Jesse turned up a half-hour late for his appointment, accompanied by his mother and his 12-year-old brother, Jason. No effort had been expended on grooming for the visit to the doc-

FIGURE 4–1. Index Crime Arrests by Age. (Source: FBI Uniform Crime Reports 1996.)

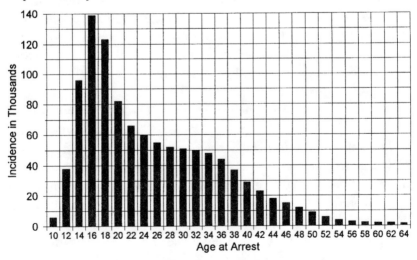

tor. While his mother offered some vague comment about their late-ness, the boys showed no social graces at all, barely acknowledging the examiner—not out of hostility or uncooperativeness, but from a simple lack of social skills. Jason's left eye bore the permanent dis-figurement of being struck by a fork thrown by Jesse three years earlier, and he was partially blind in that eye.

Jesse had run away from home a few months earlier, following an altercation with his stepfather. During the several days he was hiding out with friends in the neighborhood, he terrorized a younger child in a local park by attempting to light the child's coat on fire. A hearing was scheduled on assault charges.

Throughout the interview, Jesse's mother consistently rational-ized Jesse's behavior. She insisted that Jesse was just being funny, that the boy was not really scared, and she had heard that the victim "often makes things up" about his peers. She went so far as to claim that the small lighter Jesse used couldn't really set fire to the kind of coat the boy was wearing. She felt that the police were treat-ing her and Jesse unfairly, and she applied the same kind of reason-ing when discussing Jesse's several previous police contacts—including a reckless burning charge and a fourth-degree assault on his mother. Even when pressed, Jesse's mother seemed incapable of recogniz-ing the personal responsibility Jesse bore for his own actions. His mother's manner of reasoning about these matters was not lost on Jesse. The attitude he displayed toward his early career in sociopa-thy was altogether externalizing. Nothing was his responsibility, and the problem always lay with others. There was nothing he could be doing differently.

Our modern world is full of Jesses. Our society is, as David Lykken put it, turning out sociopaths with factory-like efficiency. The principal reason is inept parenting—parents who, in one way or another, cannot provide their children with a stable and nur-turing upbringing, parents who cannot impart a sound foundation for personality, a capacity for reflection and self-restraint, or a groundwork for interpersonal relations, conscience, and empathy.

Defining an individual as sociopathic does not tell us much about his long-term behavioral trajectory. It does tell us, however, about a personality type that is unlikely to change anytime soon. Even if the criminal acts taper off, the character structure usually remains the same. Shallow and exploitative relations remain the norm, and lower-level antisocial behaviors are typical. Some sociopathic youths like Jesse endure arrests, incarcerations, and injuries, and, by the time they reach adulthood, they learn to avoid the most painful consequences. If they are fortunate enough to have attained a respectable educational level, and if they can learn a skill sufficient to sustain them, then they may avoid chronic criminality, and their sociopathy will be manifest only in noncriminal antisocial behaviors. Many sociopathic individuals, however, persist with their criminal endeavors, at least sporadically. Drug and alcohol abuse are common, as are unstable and violent interpersonal relations.

Because the conflict for sociopaths is external instead of internal, the response to therapeutic intervention is seldom positive. The sociopath, at least when he's being honest, does not believe there's anything wrong with how he conducts himself—with the exception that he may wish to have avoided certain unpleasant consequences. He is not troubled by the harm he has wrought, by the pain others have suffered, or by the trajectory he seems to be following.

Psychopathic Character

A less common but more perilous type of antisocial individual— and the most heavily researched—is the psychopath. While behavioral manifestations can range all the way from episodes of impulsive and petty crime, to sophisticated white-collar crime, to predatory sexual assault and serial murder, the personality structure of psychopaths appears to be stable and chronic. The psychopath can be reliably distinguished using Hare's Psychopathy Checklist (PCL), which, adapted for use with juveniles, reliably identifies psychopaths in a young male population (Forth et al. 1990). Psychopathic character—the fearless-impulsive temperament, the freedom from anxiety and doubt, the charming exterior with the most exploitative motives, the extraordinary ability to focus attention—tends to persist for decades, if not for life. The psychopath is exceptionally difficult to socialize, perhaps because he does not experience the anxiety and fear that plays an important role in regulating behavior and impulse. Underlying these character traits appears to be an inborn, temperamental configuration that is largely stable.

There are good reasons for caution in assigning negative labels to young people. We would like to believe that personality is malleable, at least until adulthood. And yet the evidence suggests that there are young offenders who rightly are termed psychopathic, and we know that they are unlikely to mend their ways. Indeed, the definition of psychopathy, according to Hare's PCL, involves a chronic pattern of conduct problems that begins early. Also, the temperamental qualities are often easily observable and consistently reported by the youth and his family.

The psychopaths we are most likely to encounter are those whose behaviors have gotten them into trouble with police, the courts, school administrators, and other authorities. These are the antisocial children whose conduct problems have brought fear and trembling to the other neighborhood children and to the schools for years. More sophisticated psychopaths—"successful" psychopaths—may elude sanctions for years and may ply their trade in business and politics.

In the early morning hours of an early autumn day, a few miles outside a rural Midwestern town, two boys broke into the farmhouse of an elderly couple to steal some guns and whatever else they could find. When they found the couple sleeping in their bed, they each opened fire into the bedcovers with small-caliber pistols. Wounded and dazed, the man, in his eighties, stumbled to a telephone and called his son. While he desperately shouted, "They're killing us, they have guns," the boys continued to pump round after round into the man until he finally slumped over. A few hours later at the police station, Billy complained in an aggrieved tone to the detective, "The old bastard just wouldn't die; I had to keep firing. . . . The old lady, she kept quiet."

Because he was 15 years old at the time of the double murder, there was a question of whether Billy would be tried in adult criminal court instead of juvenile court. The implications are large. If tried in criminal court, Billy could receive a maximum of life in prison. If tried in juvenile court, he could be incarcerated only until his twenty-first birthday. The question of waiver to adult criminal court necessitated a psychological evaluation to help ascertain maturity level, dangerousness, and amenability to treatment. (These questions derive from the Kent Criteria for waiving jurisdiction from juvenile court to adult court; see Chapter 6.)

To the first question of the evaluation, "Where's home?" Billy needed about ten minutes to explain—how he had recently been staying with friends while his mother was in another city looking for a job, how he had lived with grandparents in the "big city" for a while last year, how he had tried living with his father in Dallas but had left because of conflict with his stepmother, how he had lived on and off with his mother as she endured frequent changes in jobs and residences. Billy had essentially quit school several months before the murders. Records showed, however, that Billy could be a good student when he attended school. Grades over the previous couple of years ranged from A's to F's. Teacher comments ranged from glowing reports about what insightful contributions Billy made in class to reports of harassing other students and showing no respect for authority. He had been suspended three times and expelled once.

Billy had a long record of police contact, with investigations and arrests going back to age 10. There were several instances of violence, toward his mother and her boyfriend, toward peers, and even to a teacher in the sixth grade. There were also burglaries, apparent drug dealing, and an instance of sexual abuse of a child that landed him in corrections (prison) for four months.

Billy was unusually easy to talk with, and he struck up a good rapport. He looked the examiner in the eye and spoke in a frank and straightforward manner, explaining fully and without egocentrism.

He was not evasive and he did not bother to rationalize or minimize his actions. Indeed, he seemed not to be troubled by what he had done. His account of the current murders, as well as that of previous crimes, matched the police accounts.

Billy explained that he was "never afraid of anything," even when he was a young child, and as he was facing perhaps decades in prison, he was concerned but not really afraid. Reports from family indicated that Billy was, as he said, fearless and impulsive, and that boredom was always a bad sign. When he felt bored is when some of the most troubling adventures would be initiated.

Psychological testing revealed solid intellectual strengths. On the standard test of intellectual functioning, every subscale score was in the average range or higher, and there were no areas of particular weakness. One subscale score stood out. Digit Span, which demands that the subject recall increasingly lengthy series of digits—first forward, then backward—is especially sensitive to the ability to pay attention, and is easily disrupted by anxiety. Billy scored far above average on this scale, and well above the mean of his other scores.

A FINAL NOTE ON TRAJECTORIES

A great deal of longitudinal research has been conducted on the developmental pathways of children as they become adolescents, and on adolescents as they become adults. For obvious reasons, though, much less information is available on the long-term outcomes, in later adulthood, for individuals who are antisocial in their youth. We do know some important things, though, for example, that the rate at which antisocial individuals commit crimes falls off considerably by middle age (see Figure 4–1). Does this mean that most offenders, as they traverse the years from adolescence to middle age, alter their personalities? Probably not. Many of the attributes that we see as defining the antisocial personality do not change much despite the decline in serious and violent crimes. For example, the irresponsibility, the lack of empathy, the habitual exploitation—these traits often can persist lifelong, even though overt crimes may disappear from the picture. A few unusual offenders, despite their advancing age, continue to commit crimes, continue to revisit the institutions, and these individuals typically have a short life. Still others, after years of chronic offending and repeated incarceration, make substantial changes not only in their overt behavior but also, more deeply, in their personality functioning. The following case exemplifies the possibilities for individual development and the wished-for "correctional" effects of incarceration.

Jimmy J. did not fit the picture of him I had in mind. I was expecting to meet the man whose criminal career began at age 12, whose rap sheet of arrests and convictions was several pages long by 21 (including two stays in juvenile corrections), and whose crime wave persisted well in adulthood, resulting in three commitments to the state prison. Jimmy J. used a variety of drugs; he had begun drinking alcohol by age 11, and he was a full-blown alcoholic by 14, complete with blackouts. He often committed burglaries just to get money for drugs. He was twice convicted of driving while intoxicated, and once for a hit-and-run accident while drunk that injured a young mother. He had spent a total of eight years locked up by the age of 32 and he had shown no sign of remorse or of learning anything from all the punishment and pain. He was just the kind of chronic offender that many reasonable citizens want to see locked up for good. As I walked into the waiting room, I expected to meet a hardened criminal.

My preconceived notions about this client were dashed within minutes. Here was a middle-aged African-American gentleman whose demeanor and personality violated all the expectations. Jimmy J. was not tough or imposing, nor was he slick or polished. There was no effort to impress, only to convey things truthfully. He displayed the demeanor of one who has made peace with himself and his past and who considers realistically the prospects for the future. He related with frankness the trajectory he had followed and the bad choices he had made. There was not a hint of placing blame on others. Instead, he looked at himself with the full, painful weight of the wasted years and lost opportunities. Yet he also showed a capacity for forgiveness toward himself and kindness toward others. He explained with humility the works he hoped he could do in the years ahead—the volunteer work with prison inmates and with young men in trouble with the law. This was something he knew a lot about.

Jimmy J. explained that for twenty-five years nothing had made any difference in the way he lived his life. Coming from a violent home with alcoholic parents, young Jimmy began early to fail academically and to associate with rough kids from similar backgrounds. The school failure, the numerous fights and expulsions, the long string of crimes—all were liberally smoothed by abuse of alcohol and drugs. Nothing made a difference until the age of 36. On his third imprisonment, and after numerous efforts by would-be helpers, Jimmy J. had what he termed "a change of spirit." He took up the spirit and intent of Alcoholics Anonymous, and he began to help others in prison. Religion became an important force in his life for the first time. His commitment to a religious lifestyle provided a moral foundation around which his other values and sense of self coalesced. He worked with several volunteer organizations over the eight years since that time, many of them with a religious basis. He managed not to be rigid in his thinking or critical of others whose beliefs were different from his. At his last release from prison, at age 37, Jimmy J. married and had remained so ever since.

With the assistance of a vocational counselor, Jimmy J. had sought a full-scale psychological evaluation. It seems that he had been barred from working with youthful offenders—the work where he felt he had the most to offer—because of his criminal background. He had been free of any and all antisocial behavior for nine years. After years of effort, the state had granted a "Final Discharge Restoring Civil Rights." Still, the rules were the rules, and he was unable to work with juveniles. A formal evaluation by a psychologist might help persuade the authorities.

In many states today, Jimmy J. would be incarcerated for life under the new "Three Strikes" statutes. But there are some crucial lessons in Jimmy J.'s case and others like him. First, the long-term outcome in some very dismal cases can change dramatically for the better by middle age. Indeed, Jimmy J. represented just the kind of outcome we would hope for when "corrections" actually works. For, not only did Jimmy J. cease his antisocial lifestyle, he actually accomplished substantial personality change. Hence, it may be premature or even foolish to give up entirely on some chronic offenders, at least before middle age. Second, such long-term change probably does require substantial rehabilitative efforts and time locked up. It is doubtful that Jimmy J. would have mended his ways without the repeated incarcerations along with the opportunities to improve himself.

THE PREDICTION OF VIOLENT BEHAVIOR

The prediction of violence occupies a particularly sensitive position at the intersection of the behavioral sciences and law. Despite considerable dissension and debate about its scientific merits, clinicians are frequently called upon, in a wide variety of settings, to predict who will and who will not behave violently. In forensic settings, formal evaluations regularly express judgments regarding the likelihood of dangerous behavior in the future, and the courts rely on expert testimony regarding dangerousness in a variety of civil and criminal matters. For example, juvenile courts often solicit psychologists' judgments about a youth's level of danger to the community as well as her "amenability to treatment." Parole boards often rely on clinical judgment of potential risk to the community. Psychiatrists' opinion about a patient's danger to self or others figure prominently in civil commitment of the mentally ill. Even in purely clinical practice, the matter of predicting violence makes an appearance. In the California Supreme Court's decision in *Tarasoff v. Regents of the University of California* (1976), the precedent was established that mental health professionals have a duty to protect third parties from their patients' potential violence. The duty to warn a third party of potential violence obtains whenever the therapist knew or should have known, that "a patient poses a serious danger of violence to others" (*Tarasoff* 1976, p. 345). Hence, even psychotherapists with no training in predicting violence must be alert and responsive to matters of potential violence in their clients. The prediction of violence also gained special significance in recent years, in relation to the findings that a small proportion of offenders commit the vast majority of serious crimes (e.g., Wolfgang et al. 1972).

The Crystal Ball

For a long time, the expertise of psychiatrists and psychologists to predict violence went largely unchallenged, and countless life-affecting decisions were made on the basis of their opinions. Then, beginning in the late 1970s a series of controlled studies and reports began to rock the boat. As John Monahan (1984) put it, "Dark clouds began to form in our crystal balls" (p. 10). As an example, in 1979 a study was published in the respected *Journal of Consulting and Clinical Psychology* (Quinsey and Maguire 1979) comparing the ability of psychiatrists and school teachers to predict dangerous behavior in a sample of mentally ill offenders. It was found that the level of interjudge agreement was no better for the psychiatrists, and that these experts' predictions were no better than those of the teachers! Two years later, in his influential monograph that reviewed numerous research studies, Monahan (1981) concluded that clinicians cannot accurately predict violent behavior in most circumstances. Some studies found that psychiatric experts' predictions were not much better than chance. Several writers reached the conclusion that clinicians' ability to predict violence is so poor as to render such judgments untrustworthy and misleading. Some went so far as to insist that making such predictions was unethical, because of the lack of a sound scientific basis (Grisso and Appelbaum 1992). Psychiatrists and psychologists, according to this reasoning, should not be making such judgments at all, especially when they involve depriving individuals of their civil rights, as in civil commitment of the mentally ill. From this body of discouraging research findings and professional soul searching, the authority of clinicians to predict violent behavior was dealt a setback, and it has yet to recover (Miller and Morris 1988).

The prediction of violent behavior at first appears deceptively simple. It might seem just a matter of collecting the most reliable predictor variables, such as history of violence and personality type, then combining these variables to yield a violence "prediction quotient" of some kind. Of course, in practice it is never so straightforward. For one thing, the framework for the prediction problem varies greatly. In one case, a clinician may be asked in court for the likelihood that a given delinquent will behave violently in the coming years; in another case, the problem involves discriminating which individuals from a large pool of offenders are most likely or are least likely to reoffend.

The Base-Rate Problem

The most basic reason why, with all our research data and clinical experience, we cannot accurately predict violent behavior involves the base-rate problem. The behaviors of interest (violent acts) occur very infrequently in most populations; that is, their base rate is low. Our ability to accurately identify which individuals will or will not engage in a certain behavior diminishes as the prevalence of that behavior approaches zero.

For example, suppose you know from past research that, on average, about three high school students out of a hundred will commit a serious act of violence during any given year. Suppose that you want to predict which students in your school will act violently so they can be enrolled in a violence prevention program. In this case, assuming the absence of a bona fide crystal ball, the most accurate prediction you could make would be to predict "none." That way, you would be accurate 97 percent of the time— an impressive record, indeed. The trouble, of course, is that you would fail to identify the violent kids, and the principal will not be impressed. Your predictive efforts, despite their high level of "accuracy," are for naught.

Now suppose that you cannot afford to miss all of the potentially violent kids because violence is a growing problem in your school district. Hence, it is important to score as many "hits" as possible. You must change your strategy so as to identify as many as possible of these potentially violent kids. But now, because the science of behavioral prediction is rather weak, in order to score more "hits" (true positives), you also wrongly identify as violent several kids who are not violent (false positives). This mathematical problem is illustrated in Figure 4–2, where the "hit rate" is plotted as a function of the false-positive rate, or "cost." The dotted line represents the relation of hit rate to cost if we know nothing about the individual students—their history, personalities, attitudes—and selected students randomly. The curved line, with better-than-random prediction, plots the relation of hit rate to cost *with* the salient information on

FIGURE 4–2. Successful "hit rate" versus cost (false positives)

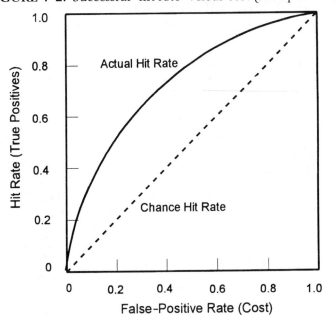

individual students. Ideally, our receiver operator characteristics (ROC) curve, described below, would hug the left side of the graph, yielding high hit rates with few false positives.

Now back to your task of identifying potentially violent students. By insisting on identifying more of the truly violent students, you have snared fifteen students out of 100 who meet your criteria as potentially violent. You start getting calls from indignant parents. Your false-positive error rate has climbed as you strive to identify more of the violent students, that is, as you have used a bigger net. You could go even further if necessary: if you felt it was essential not to miss any of the potentially violent students, you might further expand your criteria, this time until you identify, say, sixty students out of every hundred. By then you probably would be identifying most of the true positives, but you would have created other troubles. At some point you have to decide where to draw the line between failing to identify violent students and misidentifying many students as violent who are not.

Where you draw the line depends on how serious you judge one type of error versus the other. It would mean one thing if a false positive meant that some nonviolent students would unnecessarily be subjected to a three-hour "educational package," but it would mean quite something else if your false positives meant depriving individuals of their civil rights or imposing unwanted and intrusive treatments. The cost of misidentifying violent youths must be weighed against the opposite error—failing to identify violent youths. There may be times where failing to identify potentially violent youths will have little practical loss, for example, where there is little or no violence or where there are no useful interventions anyway. But there are many circumstances where the identification of potentially violent youths is of urgent concern to the community. The best that social science can do in that case is to outline the mathematical trade-off between "hits" versus false alarms, and, of course, to employ the best possible judgment and data in making the predictions. The ultimate decision of where to draw the line between the two is not a scientific decision; it is a political one, and it will turn on factors that cannot be measured.

Clinical Versus Actuarial Prediction

A major axis in the debate over prediction of violence involves the distinction between clinical and actuarial prediction. Until clinicians' crystal balls were found to be clouded in the late 1970s, the vast majority of such predictions were based on the doctor's clinical judgment—the personalized, sometimes idiosyncratic, methods of each individual clinician for understanding the subject's personality and behavior. Such clinical judgment could be quite sophisticated, taking into account the subject's behavioral history, psychological test data, and other important factors. But it often relied heavily on intuition and "clinical sense"—more art than science. It is this kind of prediction that we now know is not very good.

The alternative to clinical prediction is actuarial prediction. Actuarial prediction involves statistical combinations of objectively determined predictive factors. The best known example of actuarial prediction is that used by insurance companies to set premium rates. For example, in setting auto insurance rates, the company takes into account objective variables such as the driver's age, the type of car, and the incidence rate of accidents in the pertinent locale. Individual factors that can be objectively determined (e.g., the driver's number of previous accidents) can be used if they are shown to strengthen the prediction of the behaviors of interest. In just about every study comparing actuarial to clinical prediction of violent behavior, actuarial methods have prevailed (Dawes 1979, Gottfredson and Gottfredson 1988). Clinicians' intuition and judgment, when not informed by more objective research data (e.g., base rates), are notoriously unreliable.

Considerable research has explored actuarial methods for predicting violent behavior. For example, the Violence Risk Assessment Guide (Harris et al. 1993, Rice and Harris 1995) incorporates Hare's PCL-R items, along with other items such as school maladjustment and parental separation to predict violent reoffending (see also Menzies et al. 1982).

In assessing the predictive power of such methods, there has been a long-standing pitfall: any given method's accuracy appears to vary depending on the base rate of the behavior in the population under study, and depending on the selection ratio (the proportion of individuals one chooses to identify and the types of errors one is more inclined to live with). A consensus has formed in recent years that the best method for reporting the accuracy of a predictive method is through the awkwardly named "receiver operator characteristics" (ROC) methodology, often used in assessing diagnostic methods in clinical medicine (Swets 1988, Zweig and Campbell 1993). ROC analysis, applied to any given assessment method, boils down to the kind of simple graph shown in Figure 4–2 that plots hit rate against false positive rate. With such an ROC plot, one can see immediately the cost entailed in identifying any proportion of successful hits. ROC analysis also allows the computation of the method's "improvement over chance" in predicting violence. Douglas Mossman (1994) used ROC methods to reanalyze fifty-eight previously published data sets of violence prediction. One of the major benefits of ROC analysis has been that these newer analyses, because they more reliably measure the accuracy of predictive methods, have shown that predictions of violence by clinicians are actually better than had been reported in earlier research. Mossman (1994) concluded, "Clinicians are able to distinguish violent from nonviolent patients with a modest, better than chance level of accuracy" (p. 790). Better, but hardly a ringing endorsement.

What does all this research tell us about the prediction of violent behavior in real-life settings? After all, the vast majority of instances where a clinician is called upon to make some prognosis do not take place in the context of large controlled studies and ROC analysis. In predicting whether a given individual will act violently in the future, one must pay attention to the lessons from the past twenty years of research on violence prediction: First and foremost, a measure of humility is always in order, because even with the most sophisticated prediction methods and/or with long experience, there are many incorrect predictions—most often of the "false alarm" type. This means that one must acknowledge occasionally what most professionals are loath to admit, that a judgment about the likelihood of violence sometimes cannot be made with a reasonable degree of confidence (Litwack 1985, Litwack et al. 1993). For example, in the case of a youth who has committed a severe act of violence but who has no history of antisocial behavior, there are no base-rate data available, so no confident prediction can be rendered. Second, one must not rely solely on clinical judgment and impressions; rather, predictions must take account of actuarial data. For example, an effort must be made to ascertain base rates of violence for populations with the attributes of the individual(s) in question. Third, a history of violence (especially a recent history) is the best single predictor of future violence. Fourth, other actuarial factors must be taken into account, such as age (violence risk diminishes with age), gender (males are more often violent than females), and current mental illness. For example, a young man with a history of violence, who also has an untreated paranoid disorder might well be considered at high risk (Blomhoff et al. 1990). Fifth, one's prediction need not be posited in a yes-no format. Often, the best one can do is to render an opinion that states a general range of most likely outcomes, and not try to pin it down more exactly.

Psychiatric Disorders and Antisocial Behavior

Any foray into the realm of antisocial offenses and the persons who commit them soon comes upon the matter of psychiatric disorders. Psychiatry has already staked a claim in this area, by defining configurations of antisocial behavior as psychiatric disorders, principally in the form of conduct disorder and antisocial personality disorder. These diagnoses, however, consist of purely descriptive behavioral labels, and they do not express much about the individual's psychological attributes (Vitiello and Jensen 1995). The focus in this chapter is on the *other* kind of psychiatric disorder, the kind in which there are unwanted disruptions in the individual's cognitive, emotional, or behavioral functioning, the kind in which the individual is unable to control in normal ways his perception, reasoning, mood, or activity level. Of particular interest are the relationships between common psychiatric disorders and antisocial behavior. How might we understand the presence of aggression and irresponsibility in an adolescent who suffers from depression, from posttraumatic stress disorder (PTSD), or from attention deficit disorder? The confluence of antisocial behavior and psychiatric disorder also raises thorny issues of responsibility for criminal or delinquent behavior. Considering delinquent acts by youths with mental disease or defect, at what point along the continuum of psychiatric severity do we attribute the crime to disease instead of to volition?

A wide variety of psychiatric disorders can be found in the typical juvenile detention facility or correctional institution, and in far higher proportions than in the general population of young people. The psychiatric disorders that turn up in this population include not only the so-called externalizing problems such as aggression and theft, but also internalizing problems like depression and anxiety (Armistead et al. 1992). The distinction between internalizing and externalizing problems derives from psychologist Thomas Achenbach's extensive studies on the assessment of behavior problems in children. Factor analysis of large data sets consistently turned up these two overarching factors, or types of problems. Authoritative estimates suggest that the prevalence of diagnosable psychiatric conditions among incarcerated youths, not including conduct disorder (e.g., depression, attention deficit/hyperactivity disorder, PTSD, etc.), ranges from 25 to 40 percent, and a sizable proportion of such youths suffer from more than one such condition. California studies have found from 16 to 32 percent of violent incarcerated youth meet diagnostic criteria for PTSD alone (Steiner and Huckaby 1989, Steiner et al. 1997), with the more violent subjects more likely to suffer this disorder. Substance abuse disorders abound in this population—from about half to two thirds of individuals (Haapasalo and Hamalainen 1996).

Even in community settings the prevalence of psychiatric disorders among antisocial youth is substantial. One of the commonest tales heard by juvenile probation counselors is that the boy in their charge "was diagnosed with attention deficit disorder," or "he really has depression," or "is mentally retarded and didn't know that what he did was a crime." Some of these reports of psychiatric illness may be self-serving or defensive, and a measure of skepticism often is in order. Still, there is a sizable subgroup of antisocial youths who show bona fide psychiatric illness along with their delinquent habits. If we take the diagnosis of conduct disorder as the first psychiatric label, then the appearance of a second psychiatric condition such as depression generates comorbidity—the simultaneous presence of two or more diagnosable conditions.

Several kinds of relationship are logically possible between a youth's antisocial habits and her comorbid psychiatric condition. First, the antisocial behaviors and their sequelae might be the *cause* of the psychiatric condition or they may contribute to that condition. A string of delinquent offenses and arrests, or occasionally even a single incident, can profoundly disrupt family relations and can imperil one's academic and occupational future. It is not uncommon to see incarcerated youths suffering depression over the course that their life seems to be taking, involving the realization of lost opportunities, fractured relationships, and diminished hopes. Also, an antisocial lifestyle carries considerable risk for physical and psychological trauma and loss. Delinquent youths, by virtue of their peer groups and pursuits, frequently are themselves the victims of violence, or they may witness violence and death in peers. The symptoms of PTSD are common, including anxiety attacks, depression, nightmares, and dissociative episodes (see below). There even are instances in which a delinquent youth suffers posttrauma symptoms stemming from the violence he perpetrated upon others (Steiner et al. 1997).

The second kind of comorbid relationship is that the psychiatric condition might *cause* the antisocial behavior or contribute significantly to it. The question of a defendant's mental condition at the time of an alleged offense involves just this sort of issue: Was the defendant "insane" at the time of the offense? Did the defendant, because of mental illness, lack the "legal capacity" to commit the alleged crime? More commonly, though, before a youth ever comes before the court for a serious crime, the question arises whether a psychiatric condition might be to some degree responsible for the untoward behaviors. "Is it the ADHD that leads the boy to engage in shoplifting?" Or, "Could it be depression that makes her so irritable that she gets into many fights?"

The prospect of a psychiatric condition causing or contributing to antisocial behavior readily becomes quite complex. Some psychiatric disorders might lead directly to behaviors that transgress social norms. For example, bipolar disorder can, in rare instances, transform an otherwise well-socialized young man into an unpredictable and frightening aggressor. In other cases, though, the psychiatric disorder may contribute to the problem in more subtle ways. For example, although ADHD is a different disorder from antisocial behavior or conduct disorder, ADHD often involves poor impulse control, and poor impulse control makes antisocial actions more likely. In this case the psychiatric disorder, while it is not the cause of the offensive act, contributes to the likelihood of transgressions. Taking a developmental perspective, ADHD makes it more difficult for a child to be socialized, more difficult to succeed in school, and more likely to identify with a deviant peer group—all of which contribute to antisocial learning and behavioral habits, and to the self-definition the child evolves over the years. Identity—one's internal definition of self—can readily coalesce around negative, angry behavior patterns and oppositional interactions with authority.

The third logical relation involving comorbid psychiatric conditions is that there may be no causal relation or substantial contribution between the antisocial behavior and the psychiatric disorder. The delinquent just happens to be afflicted with depression or an anxiety disorder or attention deficit. In human development, though, as in ecology, "everything is hitched to everything else" in one way or another. In some cases where an antisocial adolescent "just happens" to also be afflicted with recurrent depression we find yet another logical relation: the psychiatric disorder may stem from events and conditions that also contribute to the development of antisocial behaviors. The delinquency and the depression both may stem from the same set of developmental insults. Children who are chronically neglected and abused by irresponsible adults may develop antisocial attitudes *and* suffer from depression as a result of their mistreatment. The relationships can become even more complex: neglected and abused children may develop antisocial attitudes and a deviant peer group, and may then develop a substance abuse disorder, which, in turn, contributes further to antisocial involvement. The elements in a cause-and-effect diagram readily become a tangled web of associations.

Several psychiatric disorders frequently complicate the assessment and treatment of antisocial youths. This chapter reviews the most prevalent of these comorbid conditions, with particular attention to the relationship between the psychiatric condition and the patterns of offensive behavior.

In cases involving global neurologic dysfunction and developmental delay, such as pervasive developmental disorder and autism, the assessment and treatment follows primarily from the psychiatric condition, and in most cases the unwanted behaviors are best considered as secondary. It also is true, however, that individuals with mental retardation and some forms of neurologic dysfunction are capable of developing planful antisocial habits. Youths with mild mental retardation, for example, are capable of planning and carrying out destructive and dangerous behaviors, and they often are held responsible for their acts by the courts. A 15-year-old boy with an IQ of 65 set a fire out of anger at the staff at his group home. The fire did extensive damage and nearly killed several residents. In such cases the juvenile court must decide, usually with the assistance of a clinician, whether the youth had "legal capacity" to commit the crime, that is, whether he possessed the capacity to form the mental state of intent (*mens rea*) to carry out the crime. In this case, despite his functioning intellectually around the first percentile, the boy was able to understand the likely consequences of setting such a fire, and he chose to do it anyway, out of anger.

ATTENTION DEFICIT DISORDER

Of all the skills necessary to successfully traverse childhood in modern society, none is more crucial than the ability to pay attention. There are other cognitive functions the failure of which will surely lead to disability—the processes of perception, memory, and logical reasoning, for example. But the cognitive skill whose deficiency most frequently turns childhood into a wearying trial for parents and child alike is the ability to hold still, to pay attention, and to plan ahead.

The capacity to focus and sustain one's attention on a single topic is exquisitely sensitive to disruption, and it is not just attention deficit disorder (ADD) that leads to impairment. Attention can also be seriously disrupted by anxiety, depression, and other cognitive, emotional, and even medical conditions (Cantwell 1996). This is why diagnosis of ADD can be difficult and why careful assessment is important. A child who cannot sit still and follow a class discussion might suffer from ADD. She also may be worried about painful events at home or over the uncertainty about her future, she may suffer an anxiety disorder, or she may be depressed. With ADD currently being such a popular explanation for children's troubles, it is too often the first and only hypothesis. There is a tendency to overdiagnose ADD at the expense of considering other troubling conditions.

The need to be able to pay close attention and to sustain that focus is surely a universal value, an asset in societies even quite different from our own. However, there are two aspects of our modern society that make attention the focus of such intense concern currently. First, as society becomes increasingly dependent on complex technologies, academic success is becoming nearly indispensable for advancement in most occupations. There are fewer comfortable niches in society for those unable to master algebra or to follow a sequence of steps in a technical manual. Second, the world we have constructed for our children is extraordinarily taxing on the human child's capacity to focus and sustain attention. The everyday life of the American child—that is, the daily onrush of stimuli, transitions, and myriad choices—could not have been better designed to undermine calm and deliberative attention and learning. As psychiatrists Arnold and Jensen (1995) put it, "As the environment becomes more complex and demanding, more children may be encountered who exhibit the symptoms [of ADHD] . . . not necessarily because the biology is changing, but because biological attentional capacities are increasingly overwhelmed in modern society" (p. 2300).

Competition for the child's attention has never been more intense. Children's attention is not safe even in school. This one institutional setting devoted to nurturing attention, reflection, and learning is now being invaded by society's chief attention-grabbing institution—advertisers. Many public schools, chronically underfunded, feel compelled to accept advertising in the halls and the lunchrooms in order to pay for basic necessities of education. The most ominous development in recent years has been the success of Madison Avenue's commercial, in-school program, Channel One, developed by advertising entrepreneur Chris Whittle and now owned by Primedia. It has been enormously successful by Madison Avenue standards, reaching over eight million students (about 40 percent of America's high school students) and amassing large profits. Channel One is best described by its own marketing materials to advertisers: "Channel One even penetrates the lightest viewers among teens." In other words, because students are "captive," advertisers can reach even the kids who don't watch much TV. Channel One's success in reaching children is the reason why advertisers like Disney and Warner Brothers are willing to pay up to $200,000 per 30-second commercial. The product of Channel One is student attention, which is sold to advertisers; the provision of educational content is a pretense for capturing the real commodity—the hearts and minds of young consumers. The eminent educator Neil Postman (1995) wrote in his book *The End of Education*, "Approximately ten thousand schools have accepted the offer made by Christopher Whittle to include, daily, two minutes of commercial messages in the curriculum—the first time, to my knowledge, that an advertiser has employed the power of the state to force anyone to watch commercials" (p. 35). Channel One contracts with schools to require students to watch a 12-minute daily program along with 2 minutes of advertising. Fortunately, colonization of schools is being resisted in many locales, but as yet only New York State has succeeded in banning commercial TV in public schools. Given all these developments, it should come as no surprise that attention and its deficiencies have become such a focus of concern nationwide.

The majority of children manage well enough with the social and educational institutions we provide them, and attention deficit is not a clinical problem for most. But for the countless children who are more vulnerable, for those with natural difficulties with attention, this floridly stimulating, hypercompetitive milieu makes it all the more difficult to sustain attention and to learn.

It has long been recognized that there is a small proportion of children whose capacity to sustain attention is so seriously and chronically impaired that they earn the designation of suffering from ADD. The most severely afflicted of these individuals probably would be perceived as deficient in almost any society and in any era. What we today diagnose as attention deficit/hyperactivity disorder (ADHD) has been designated by a variety of labels, and these labels have emphasized different aspects of the disorder. Until about 1980, diagnoses emphasized overactivity and impulsivity with the terms *hyperkinesis* and *hyperactive*. For a while such children were labeled as suffering "minimal brain dysfunction" (MBD)—a reference to the observation that overactivity and impulsivity occurred frequently in children who had suffered encephalitis in the epidemic of 1917 and 1918. The diagnostic label MBD, therefore, carried the etiologic implication of (minimal) brain damage leading to such overactivity.

In the 1980 edition of the *DSM* (*DSM-III*), the diagnostic label shifted to express the newer emphasis on inattention as the most salient attribute of the disorder. The new label was attention deficit disorder (ADD), and it was recognized that ADD could occur with or without hyperactivity. The emphasis on inattention acknowledges that it is this attribute that has the greatest long-term impact on academic progress, social learning, and overall adjustment.

The current diagnosis in *DSM-IV* (American Psychiatric Association 1994), attention deficit/hyperactivity disorder (ADHD), brings the hyperactive-impulsive dimension back into the title.

ADHD can be diagnosed in three basic forms: (1) ADHD, combined type, in which both inattention and hyperactivity are present; (2) ADHD, predominantly inattentive type, in which inattention is present but not hyperactivity; and (3) ADHD, predominantly hyperactive-inattentive type, in which hyperactivity-impulsivity is present, but not inattention. There are nine criteria (abbreviated here) for inattention, at least six of which must be present to diagnose that attribute. The criteria include difficulty sustaining attention, seems not to listen, difficulty organizing tasks and activities, and loses things. There are nine criteria for hyperactivity-impulsivity, again, at least six of which must be present to diagnose that attribute. The criteria include fidgets, leaves seat, runs about or climbs excessively, blurts out answers, and difficulty waiting turn.

In addition to the above criteria for inattention and hyperactivity-impulsivity, the diagnosis of ADHD requires that some symptoms be present before the age of 7 years (early onset); impairment must be evident in two or more settings, such as at home *and* at school (pervasiveness); and there must be clinically significant impairment in social, academic, or occupational functioning (severity). In addition, the clinician must ensure that other conditions such as anxiety or depression are not causing the disruption in attention or the hyperactivity. Because parents or a teacher can be biased, and because the child's behavior can shift dramatically from one setting to another or from one adult to another, diagnosis must involve multiple sources of information. A common tale is about the ADHD child who, upon entering the doctor's office, sits calmly, attends keenly, and expresses himself well, only to resume the vexing hyperactivity as soon as he is back in the car.

Several rating scales are available to aid in systematically gathering adult observers' perceptions of the child's inattentiveness and hyperactivity. These are simple instruments with limited interrater reliability, and they are generally ineffective in detecting the inattentive form of ADHD when there is no hyperactivity (more common in girls). Also, they are subject to considerable bias, for example, in a parent or a teacher whose frustration level has her dangling at the end of her tether. Despite their shortcomings, such rating scales are easily administered to multiple sources, and if employed cautiously they can provide the clinician with useful data on adults' perceptions of the child in various settings (e.g., home versus school).

There is no single psychological test or set of tests that is definitive of ADHD. However, there are patterns of scores on some cognitive tests that commonly occur in ADHD children and adults. For example, two factor scores on the Wechsler Intelligence Scale for Children (WISC-III) (see Chapter 7) are sensitive to the ability to sustain attention—distractibility and processing speed—each of which is poorer in ADHD children.

In recent years, some computerized continuous performance tests (CPTs) have been extensively researched to aid in the diagnosis of ADHD and related conditions in children and adults. The CPTs present the subject with a computer screen (or similar format) response task that assesses inattentiveness (failing to react to a target stimulus), impulsivity (reacting impulsively to the wrong stimulus), and reaction time—all of which can be precisely measured. By comparing the subject's performance along these variables to the performance of known ADHD children of the same age and to non-ADHD children, the clinician is provided valuable data on the actual cognitive capacities. The CPTs have been criticized because they cannot definitively diagnose ADHD (American Academy of Child and Adolescent Psychiatry 1997). In past years, claims may have exaggerated their promise as diagnostic tools. However, when taken as one data source among others, they generate reliable and highly salient data about the child's cognitive abilities, all of which strengthens the diagnostic process. CPTs have also been found useful in monitoring the effects of medications. By contrasting two sets of CPT data on the same patient, the efficacy of medication in controlling ADHD symptoms can be more accurately assessed.

The prevalence of ADHD varies considerably depending on the criteria used to identify the disorder and the setting for the study. Current best estimates are that from 3 to 5 percent of American schoolchildren meet *DSM-IV* criteria. ADHD is more prevalent in boys than in girls, but again the ratios vary, ranging from 3 to 1 to about 9 to 1 (Arnold and Jensen 1995, Cantwell 1996). The primarily inattentive type of ADHD is more often diagnosed in girls.

The etiology of ADHD is not well understood, although it is generally accepted that the disorder stems from some form(s) of neurologic abnormality. It appears unlikely that there is a single causative pathology that might account for all cases of the disorder. Rather, there may be multiple etiologic factors leading to the final common pathway of symptoms we call ADHD. Hence, two different cases of ADHD might have different causes, and even within a single case there may be more than one factor at work. Some twin and genetics research has suggested that ADHD may be "better viewed as the extreme of a behavior that varies genetically throughout the entire population rather than as a disorder with discrete determinants" (Levy et al. 1997, p. 737). This view implies that ADHD should not be seen as a discrete disease entity, but rather as the extreme end of natural variation.

Genetic factors are one clearly established contributing cause of ADHD (Goodman and Stevenson 1989a,b, Sherman et al. 1997), and adoption studies support the (partial) heritability of ADHD. First-degree relatives of individuals with ADHD are several times more likely to have ADHD than are the relatives of non-ADHD individuals, and there is a fivefold increase in the rate of ADHD among full siblings of individuals with ADHD as compared to their half-siblings (Arnold and Jensen 1995). The concordance rate for ADHD is consistently found to be higher for identical twins than for dizygotic twins, for example, 51 percent versus 33 percent (Goodman and Stevenson 1989a) and heritability has been estimated from .55 to .92.

Insults to the brain appear to play a role in some cases of ADHD, for example, in some cases of brain trauma, in some forms of neurotoxicity, and in the neurologic compromises stemming from some infectious diseases. Attention deficit symptoms are a regular feature of children who were exposed to alcohol in utero (Nanson and Hiscock 1990, O'Malley 1994).

Psychosocial stresses can generate a clinical picture that re-
sembles ADHD, and such stresses can play a major role in the
management and treatment of the disorder. There is clinical evidence that early losses and severe maternal deprivation can lead to
ADHD symptoms (Arnold and Jensen 1995). John Bowlby, in his
classic *Forty-Four Juvenile Thieves* (1944), described ADHD-like
symptoms in children who suffered severe early deprivation.
Stanley Greenspan (1997) also observes that the capacity to remain calm and pay attention derives from a secure and active
emotional engagement with loving caregivers. Hence, there are
some children with ADHD-like symptoms whose difficulties stem
largely from early neglect, loss, or abuse.

There have been theories about ADHD being caused by inges-
tion of refined sugar, by food additives or food coloring, or by the
need for large amounts of special vitamins. However, none of these
theories has received scientific support.

Michael Rutter's account of the passive gene-environment correlation, described in Chapter 3, applies in the development of
ADHD. We know that symptoms of ADHD can be considerably
worsened by stress, by unstructured settings, and by overly complex demands. In contrast, providing a highly structured, safe, and
consistent environment can suppress the most troubling aspects of
ADHD. However, because of shared genetic material, the child
with ADHD is more likely than other children to have parents with
particular difficulty in providing that calm and organized setting.
In some cases, therefore, the ADHD child is growing up in a home
that is unusually chaotic and unstructured. All of which means that
the child who is most in need of a structured and calm setting is
the least likely to get it.

Much has been learned in recent years about the natural history
of ADHD. The most obvious impact of the disorder is on the child's
functioning at school. While many ADHD children possess average or better intelligence, the difficulty with sustained attention
and organization make schoolwork extraordinarily challenging—a
problem than tends to deepen over the years as academic demands
become more complex. The approach to tasks is often haphazard,

and there is a failure to complete independent work. The toll on self-esteem can be enormous, and it is common to see the development of oppositionality and other behavior problems, as conflict with parents and teachers spiral. The ADHD child not only is impulsive and readily acts out, but he is at risk for rejecting academic values and identifying with deviant peers. Some ADHD children seem to develop a self-image that is thoroughly negative. Feelings of resentment and anger are common, and the idea that one is a "bad kid" often develops.

For a long time it was believed that children outgrew their attention deficit disorder by adolescence or adulthood. It now is understood that about half of children with ADHD continue to show symptoms of the disorder during adolescence and even later. In many cases, the overactivity diminishes, but problems with attention and organization tend to persist. The problems that are secondary to ADHD—low self-esteem, peer rejection, oppositionality—often persist for years. The long-term trajectory for severe cases of ADHD is discouraging, frequently involving the persistence of learning difficulties and the development of comorbid conditions of oppositional defiant disorder, conduct disorder and substance abuse disorders (Biederman et al. 1996b, 1997, Thompson et al. 1996). In recent years it has been recognized that ADHD children are at increased risk for the development of mood disorders, depression, and bipolar disorder (Biederman et al. 1996a). The recognition of such dismal outcomes highlights the importance of early identification and treatment. If a child can be helped to enjoy some success in school and to avoid the most egregious behaviors that alienate peers and teachers, then some of the damaging effects of the disorder can be prevented.

For ADHD that is unaccompanied by comorbid conditions, there are two effective treatment strategies, behavioral management and psychopharmacology. Behavior management means primarily the provision of highly structured settings with minimal disruptions and distractions and very clear behavioral contingencies. Parent management training effectively reduces the child's disruptive behaviors and helps the child to better focus on tasks. School-focused interventions involve providing structured classroom, in which the child sits in the front, to minimize distractions, with well-organized and predictable schedules. Again, contingency management is helpful as are daily report cards (for immediate feedback). Many ADHD children need not only the usual treatments but also adjunctive help such as counseling and social skills training.

The principal pharmacologic treatment involves stimulant medications, and these are helpful in the majority of cases. The most common stimulants in use are Ritalin (methylphenidate), dextroamphetamine, and Cylert (pemoline). Approximately two-thirds of children with ADHD have a positive response to stimulants on the first try. When a positive response is not forthcoming, a different stimulant may be tried. Each of the stimulant medications can cause side effects such as decreased appetite, insomnia, stomachache, and irritability; however, most such side effects disappear before long. The severity of side effects is related to dosage. Growth suppression is one possible result, but this does not occur in a large proportion of cases.

The combination of psychosocial and medical treatments is emphasized by many researchers. One study showed that a low dose of Ritalin in conjunction with parent training and school consultation yielded the same results as a high dose of the medication alone (Arnold and Jensen 1995). Other research has shown that children treated for several years with the multimodal approach did better than children treated only with the stimulant medication, including having only half the delinquency rate (Arnold and Jensen 1995).

Other medications can be useful in the treatment of ADHD, often along with stimulants. These include the antidepressants, including the older tricyclics such as imipramine and desipramine and the newer selective serotonin reuptake inhibitors (SSRIs) such as Prozac and Zoloft. The SSRIs are preferred because of fewer side effects and medical risks. Other agents are used for specific purposes, such as clonidine for children who develop tics or insomnia on stimulants.

Antisocial character (e.g., conduct disorder and antisocial personality disorder) and ADHD are different disorders. The vast majority of children with ADHD do not become antisocial as adults, and a large proportion of adult antisocial characters did not have ADHD as children. However, ADHD, particularly when it includes hyperactivity, is a risk factor for the development of antisocial behavior. About half or more of children with ADHD develop oppositional defiant disorder (ODD) (Biederman et al. 1996b), and of those with ODD, many develop the more serious conduct disorder (see also Farrington et al. 1990). The exact proportions vary considerably depending on the methods and the setting for the research.

The causal relationship between antisocial behavior and ADHD stems from the developmental impact that ADHD has on key processes of socialization. Many of the traits that we associate with a well-socialized citizen—conscientiousness, planfulness, self-control, respect, and empathy for others—are the very psychological traits whose development is impacted by ADHD and its secondary symptoms. The struggles in school can rapidly lead to rejection of academic values, resentment toward normative society, and an angry, negative identity. Identification with a deviant peer group is commonplace, and substance abuse during the adolescent years often follows. All of this puts children and adolescents at increased risk for the development of antisocial habits. Moreover, children who really have ADHD are at risk, for genetic reasons, of having one or both parents who are similarly disorganized, or worse. Such parents, if they too have ADHD, may be unable to provide their child with the structured and stable environment he needs, and there is an increased risk for antisocial attitudes and traits that will be transmitted to the child.

POSTTRAUMATIC STRESS DISORDER

More than any other human attribute, it is the capacity for flexible adaptation that sets us apart from the other species. Yet those same biological and psychological mechanisms that enable human beings to adapt to such a wide range of circumstances and adversity also can be overwhelmed by extraordinary stress. Experiences of terror, violence, or abuse that cannot be assimilated into the individual's personal and emotional life often remain frozen in time, imposing a tyranny of intrusive, frightening recollection, anxiety-driven efforts at avoidance, and emotional numbing. The methods devised by trauma survivors to elude those intrusions and the accompanying emotions can set in motion a downward spiral of self-destructive behaviors and an impoverished, even deadened existence.

What we today know as posttraumatic stress disorder (PTSD) was described as early as the ancient Greeks. Shakespeare provided an account of several of the symptoms of PTSD in *Henry IV, Part I*, when Lady Percy speaks to her husband, Hotspur:

> Tell me sweet lord, what is't that takes from thee
> Thy stomach, pleasure and thy golden sleep?
> Why dost thou bend thine eyes upon the earth,
> And start so often when thou sit'st alone?
> Why hast thou lost the fresh blood in thy cheeks . . .
> And in thy face strange motions have appear'd,
> Such as we see when men restrain their breath
> On some great sudden haste.
> O, what portents are these?

Psychiatry has had an ambivalent relationship to the conditions stemming from traumatic experience. Key insights into the nature and course of PTSD have been gained, then forgotten, then rediscovered yet again. This cycle of amnesia and rediscovery has been repeated several times over the past century (van der Kolk et al. 1996b). Most recently, with the vast accumulation of clinical case studies and controlled research on combat veterans and abuse victims, PTSD finally was officially recognized as a psychiatric disorder by the American Psychiatric Association in 1980.

Psychiatry's troubled relationship with PTSD stems from two closely related aspects of the disorder. First, it has been difficult to accept that profound psychic turmoil could result from external events, that is, from reality. Freud at first accepted psychiatrist

Pierre Janet's thesis that many hysterical patients' disorders were the result of actual abuse (Breuer and Freud 1895, van der Kolk et al. 1996a). But Freud eventually abandoned the so-called seduction theory and instead insisted that such disorders were the result of internal conflict over repressed infantile sexuality. Psychiatry followed Freud, and Janet's rigorous research on traumatic memories was lost for decades.

The second reason why it has been difficult to hold on to hard-won insights about traumatic conditions is the painfulness of acknowledging man's inhumanity to man. Psychiatry, no matter how scientific, is embedded in the fabric of its social-historical period, and society is often in a state of denial about the most disturbing moral matters. Researchers on domestic violence, rape-trauma syndrome, and child sexual abuse fought an uphill battle for years to focus attention on the prevalence and effects of such trauma (Herman 1981, 1992, van der Kolk et al. 1996a). For example, as late as 1980 the *Comprehensive Textbook of Psychiatry* (Kaplan et al. 1980) claimed that the prevalence of incest was less than one in a million!

At the heart of PTSD is the inability to integrate traumatic experience(s) into one's personal history and emotional life, with the result that the emotions associated with the trauma take on a life of their own. Normally, in the aftermath of terrifying or painful experience, virtually anyone will experience intrusive recall and preoccupation with the disturbing events. This processing of events, painful as it may be, serves adaptive functions, by facilitating learning from events, planning how to avoid them in the future, and, perhaps most important, by gradually accepting what has happened. Such recollecting, over time, diminishes the emotional power of the events and eventually allows the trauma to become an accepted, if painful, aspect of one's personal history.

In PTSD, however, the replaying of traumatic memories does not lead to expanded calm and acceptance. Instead, the recollections set off increased levels of emotional and physiological distress. That distress, in turn, lends greater potency to the memories that become increasingly intrusive and beyond the control of the individual. Psychiatrist Bessel van der Kolk, a leading scholar on PTSD, describes the process thus: "Repetitive exposure etches [traumatic memories] more and more powerfully into the brain. These biological (mal)adaptations ultimately form the underpinnings of the remaining PTSD symptoms: problems with arousal, attention, and stimulus discrimination" (van der Kolk and McFarlane 1996, p. 8). In the normal processing of experience, memories change and fade over time. In PTSD, traumatic memories often are relived years and even decades later with the same vividness and emotional intensity as if they were contemporary experiences.

The repeated and uncontrolled intrusion of disturbing memories creates a sense of being haunted and terrorized, no longer in charge of one's own mind and body. Persons with PTSD typically attempt to organize their thoughts and activities around avoiding situations and stimuli that might trigger such disturbing intrusions. The frequently used defense mechanism of dissociation involves disconnecting the conscious mind from unwanted thoughts and feelings. Dissociation can involve forgetting periods of time that include the traumatic events and processes (amnesia), episodic feelings of unreality as if in a dream (derealization), and feelings of being detached from or outside of one's body (depersonalization), and it can result in emotional numbing and a general impoverishment of daily experience. In severe cases, such as in survivors of the Holocaust and concentration camps, that sense of numbing and disconnection can bring a pervasive feeling of deadness and an acceptance of death and annihilation. The feeling of deadness and estrangement from life was well described by Charles Frazier for his protagonist, Inman, in his Civil War novel, *Cold Mountain*:

> His spirit, he feared, had been blasted away so that he had become lonesome and estranged from all around him as a sad old heron standing pointless watch in the mudflats of a pond lacking frogs. It seemed a poor swap to find that the only way one might keep from fearing death was to act numb and set apart as if dead already, with nothing much left of yourself but a hut of bones. [p. 16]

The defense mechanism of dissociation finds its ultimate expression in the related condition, multiple personality disorder, now called dissociative identity disorder (DID). This is a relatively rare and chronic condition involving a fragmentation of the self into separate identities (Putnam 1989). The best evidence suggests that such fragmentation occurs early in life as a result of severe and repetitive trauma and abuse. Separate ego states are utilized by the individual to contain and to keep apart different aspects of normal and traumatic memories. DID is difficult to diagnose because of the often bewildering symptom picture, but it is increasingly well understood and diagnostic guidelines are now available (e.g., in the *DSM-IV*; also see Lewis 1996). Research has shown that DID is more prevalent among incarcerated youths than in the general population (Putnam 1989).

The key role of physiological processes in PTSD has been recognized at least since Janet (1919) explained that extreme states of physiological arousal block the normal integration of traumatic memories. Psychiatrist Abram Kardiner (1941), whose studies of combat veterans prefigured psychiatry's modern conceptions of PTSD, labeled the disorder "physioneurosis" to denote the chronic physiological states of hyperarousal, irritability, and anxiety. Several biological systems have been found to play important roles in the development and maintenance of the symptoms of PTSD—adrenal hormones (adrenaline and noradrenaline) and their effect on autonomic states (measured by skin conductance, heart rate, blood pressure); neurohormonal effects involving norepinephrine, serotonin, and other neurotransmitters; neuroanatomical effects (e.g., decreased hippocampus volume, decreased activity of Broca's area during exposure to trauma-associated stimuli); and even immunological effects (van der Kolk 1996). Studies such as these have documented the biological substrate for some of the more chronic psychological symptoms of PTSD—the inability to make sense of emotional experience and to use emotions as personal signals, the failure of emotions to organize memories, the repeated intrusion of unaltered memories, and the dismaying tendency to experience emotions as unexpressible physical states (termed "body memories").

PTSD is the one disorder (and its brief form, acute stress disorder) in *DSM-IV* that is defined by its external cause. Six criteria (abbreviated here) are required for the *DSM-IV* diagnosis of PTSD: (1) the patient must have experienced at least one trauma or life-threatening event that involved actual or threatened death or serious injury to self or others, and his response involved fear, helplessness, or horror; (2) the patient suffers persistent re-experiencing of the traumatic event—intrusive recollections (flashbacks), nightmares, acting or feeling as if the event were recurring, intense distress or physiologic reactivity when exposed to cues that are associated with the trauma; (3) persistent avoidance of stimuli associated with the trauma and a general numbing of responsiveness— efforts to avoid thoughts and feelings associated with the trauma, amnesia for the event, diminished interest in normal activities, feelings of detachment from others, constricted affect, and a foreshortened future; (4) physiological hyperarousal—insomnia, diminished concentration, hypervigilance, exaggerated startle response, and irritability or anger outbursts; (5) duration of the symptoms must exceed one month; and (6) there must be clinically significant distress or impairment in normal functioning (interpersonal relations, work, school).

For several of these criteria, the responses of children and adolescents may not fit the adult picture. For example, in response to trauma, a child's reaction may involve disorganized or agitated behavior, and a child may show only partial symptomatology (Pfefferbaum 1997). The *DSM-IV* also includes the designation of PTSD with delayed onset. This is reserved for individuals whose symptom onset is more than six months after the traumatic event. The diagnostic criteria for acute stress disorder are similar to those for PTSD; however, the duration is less than one month.

Epidemiological studies show, not surprisingly, that the prevalence of PTSD varies widely according to the population studied. Some studies of the general population suggest a lifetime prevalence (the proportion of individuals who will suffer the condition at some point in a lifetime) of about 1 to 3 percent. However, the National Vietnam Veterans Readjustment Study found PTSD rates of 30 percent for Vietnam veterans (Davidson 1995). Studies of concentration camp survivors, despite using somewhat different criteria, appear to show probable PTSD rates as high as 85 percent.

PTSD often does not present at first as PTSD, but via masked presentations or in the form of "secondary elaborations" (Matsakis 1994). These presentations derive from the numerous ways that persons with PTSD evolve in order to cope with the cycles of intrusion and avoidance. Also, many traumatized individuals may fail to report the traumatic experience(s) out of shame about the event or because of amnesia for that period of time. Because of these factors, PTSD often is not the first psychiatric diagnosis a patient receives. Typically the initial diagnosis is alcohol abuse, depression, panic disorder, or some other condition.

Just how puzzling a symptom picture can be generated by PTSD was demonstrated by the following case.

At 48, Mr. W., an electrical engineer, lived a stable and comfortable lifestyle. He was a widower with one grown child, lived alone, and had worked productively for nine years for a local communications firm. He was referred by his attorney after a sixth arrest for shoplifting. He had no other history of antisocial behavior, and he had a good record during eight years in the Navy when he was younger. Mr. W. repeatedly attempted to steal items he had no particular use for or interest in. His efforts were clumsy, and he was easily apprehended by security personnel. He had no explanation for these transgressions, except to say that his memory was poor for the period of time while in the stores, and that he felt overwhelming shame and humiliation upon being apprehended. Mr. W. was referred by his attorney, who believed that "something just isn't right with this guy."

Mr. W. was found to be an ingenuous and articulate gentleman who was dismayed by his own episodes of shoplifting. He had no explanation or excuse for his behavior, and he blamed no one but himself. He worried that yet another arrest and prosecution could cost him his job in the electronics industry. At the age of 26, his wife of two years had committed suicide by shooting herself in the presence of him and their young child. The couple had been arguing for several weeks over a difficult decision involving military transfer. Mr. W. anguished that the suicide was perhaps his fault. He suffered typical PTSD symptoms for several years, then was treated through the Veterans Administration. However, a few months after the flashbacks and numbing began to abate, he was first arrested for shoplifting. What ensued is sometimes termed a "repetition compulsion," meaning a compulsion to repeat some behavior again and again, in this case the drama of shame and humiliation.

One of the commonest initial symptom presentations in PTSD is substance abuse. Trauma survivors frequently develop the habit of "self-medicating" with alcohol or drugs, whereupon addiction often becomes a major problem in its own right. One study (Ellason et al. 1996) found that 69 of 106 patients in a chemical dependency treatment unit reported histories of physical and/or sexual abuse, and 26 percent met full criteria for PTSD. Other compulsive and self-damaging habits are common in PTSD—compulsive gambling, eating disorders such as anorexia nervosa and bulimia nervosa, self-mutilating behaviors, panic disorder, and even psychotic symptoms. Another presentation that sometimes masks PTSD (or overlaps with it) is borderline personality disorder (BPD) (Gunderson and Sabo 1993). A substantial research literature has developed in recent years exploring the overlap of symptoms and etiology between BPD and PTSD; see Gunderson and Sabo 1993, Sabo 1997, Bleiberg 1994, and Lonie 1993. The studies of Judith Herman (1992) and others have shown that the majority of adult women diagnosed with BPD were sexually abused as children. Many of the familiar symptoms of BPD—unstable and intense emotions, self-destructiveness, a diffuse sense of self—are also common in PTSD (Sabo 1997).

Van der Kolk posits as a major symptom of PTSD (one not included in the *DSM-IV* definition of the disorder) the "compulsive reexposure" to trauma. In this category, he includes harm to others, for example, unexpected violent reactions, domestic violence, and physical and sexual abuse; repeatedly exposing oneself to danger or degradation (e.g., prostitution); overt self-destructiveness (suicide attempts, self-cutting); and revictimization—the tendency of trauma victims to put themselves in harm's way. Prominent in these categories of reexposure are various forms of delinquent and criminal behavior—violence, abuse, and exploitation of others.

One frequent occurrence in the development of PTSD is the compounding of the original trauma—termed "secondary wounding." This occurs when the persons or institutions to whom the victim turns for assistance or protection disbelieve the victim's account, blame the victim, or deny the victim needed assistance or protection (Matsakis 1994). Secondary wounding takes many forms. There is no end of accounts of child physical or sexual abuse wherein the child's report to the mother or other caregiver was disbelieved or the child was punished for making such a report. Rape victims sometimes are blamed for the assault. Many traumatized Vietnam veterans returned from the war to rebukes from elements of the society that sent them to war in the first place.

Several factors appear to be implicated in how the victim responds to trauma, that is, in whether the effects of overwhelming experience will be overcome, with a return to health and stability, or whether there will develop the cycle of intrusive recollections and avoidance, physiologic hyperarousal, and numbing. First and foremost is the severity and duration of the traumatic experience (Davidson 1995).

Studies have repeatedly found that, given sufficient stress, preexisting personality style and psychological state are largely irrelevant in determining who gets PTSD and who does not. In studies of combat-related PTSD, "The critical variable in the development of PTSD was the degree of exposure to combat" (Matsakis 1994, p. 17). PTSD does not appear to develop because of some weakness or inferiority in the individual, but is the consequence of overwhelming stress. Repeated trauma is especially likely to result in the rekindling of physiological reactions and intrusive recall. Repetitive traumatic experiences are believed to be responsible for

the most serious form of dissociation, that is, in multiple personality disorder (Putnam 1989), now termed dissociative identity
disorder.

Another factor implicated in whether trauma leads to PTSD is
the degree to which the trauma undermines the individual's self-
image and worldview, her sense of stability and safety in the world.
One account described a woman who had been raped and who,
with the help of family and her therapist, seemed to be on her way
to recovery. Then, several weeks after the assault she learned that
her assailant had murdered another of his victims. She suffered an
immediate escalation of symptoms, to full-blown PTSD.

A personal assault is more likely to shatter the victim's trust in
her fellow human beings and in society than are incidents of natural disaster, which are more easily accepted as accidents of fate. In
a recent California study of incarcerated youths (Steiner et al.
1997), many had symptoms of PTSD, stemming from incidents of
interpersonal violence, but none of the 85 youths mentioned the
natural disasters that had recently horrified millions of Califor-
nians—the Los Angeles earthquake or the Oakland firestorm.
Another critical factor is social support. Individuals who enjoy a
stable set of strong interpersonal bonds are more likely to bounce
back from trauma, while those who are more isolated have fewer
resources with which to respond to a traumatic crisis.

The relationship between PTSD and antisocial behavior can
follow each of the possible forms outlined at the beginning of this
chapter: antisocial behavior can lead to traumatic experience and
PTSD; the hyperarousal of PTSD can at least contribute to antisocial acts (e.g., interpersonal violence); antisocial behavior and PTSD
can coexist without one being the cause of the other; and antisocial behavior and PTSD can both stem from antecedent experiences of violence, abuse, and neglect.

Clinicians working in detention and juvenile corrections facilities frequently encounter youths who have been traumatized as a
direct result of their antisocial endeavors and their association with
violent peers. Such youths relate witnessing a peer being killed or
a brother injured, and they often relate their own experience of

being assaulted, shot, or otherwise terrorized, often in the course of some antisocial pursuits. Individuals can even suffer PTSD as a result of their own violent acts. A 16-year-old boy seen in detention suffered from intrusive memories, insomnia, and dissociative episodes two months after he participated in a senseless double murder.

The vast majority of PTSD sufferers do not become antisocial. Rather, they tend to be anxious, wary, and depressed. However, the physiological states associated with PTSD, and the habits evolved to cope with those symptoms, can contribute to violent and antisocial behaviors in some cases. The hypervigilance and adrenaline "rush" can precipitate an unexpectedly violent response from one who momentarily feels startled or threatened. A severe liability in chronic PTSD is the inability to accurately "read" emotional and interpersonal cues. Hence, a PTSD victim may readily misread social cues as possibly threatening. In the adrenaline-driven state of "fight or flight," reflection is short-circuited, and the individual may react directly from stimulus to response without cognitive mediation.

A 36-year-old cabdriver with no history of antisocial behavior had been assaulted in the previous year. The attack had required ongoing medical attention over several months. His PTSD had not been diagnosed at the time of another incident. While waiting at a stoplight, he was angrily berated by a driver in the next car for some perceived driving infraction. After the tirade went on for perhaps 20 seconds, the cabdriver, without plan or forethought (and entirely out of character), jumped from the cab and assaulted the other driver, grabbing the man's head through the open window, leaving the other driver scratched and badly shaken. The cabdriver was dismayed at his own behavior; he lost his license to drive a cab, was prosecuted for assault, and was referred for clinical evaluation. It turned out that he had suffered not only from "fight or flight" reactions and other forms of hyperarousal, but he also had experienced the opposite reaction: just a month prior, in a late-night incident involving physical threats from two apparently drug-affected men (a situation in which he normally would have felt highly vigilant and cautious) he "froze" and for several minutes felt numb and disconnected from his body and surroundings.

Matsakis (1994) explains that such reactions are mediated by, among other things, the adrenal hormones. The "fight or flight" response stems primarily from adrenaline, while the "frozen" reaction probably stems from the secretion of noradrenaline.

Taking the cabdriver's reaction as an example of PTSD-induced violent behavior, it is not difficult to imagine the possible behavioral effects of repeated traumatic experience and threats on young people. For many youths, the experience of being traumatized (often repeatedly) is compounded by the threats of violence and degradation in everyday life—often resulting from their own choices about peers and activities.

A large proportion of antisocial youths report incidents of trauma in their lives before they initiated antisocial acts and before incarceration. As noted above, PTSD can contribute to antisocial behaviors. However, it also appears that the same patterns of violence, abuse, and neglect that generate symptoms of PTSD in children also undermines socialization, making antisocial development more likely. In the California study, the majority of youths incarcerated for violent crimes reported childhood incidents of trauma, often within the family.

In practice with real individuals, these lines of association and causality between antisocial behavior and traumatic experience are heavily interwoven. The following case typifies the complex web of trauma, psychopathology, and antisocial character.

During his fourth stay in detention in two years, 15-year-old Alonzo's public defender told him that there was not much hope of avoiding commitment to juvenile corrections, to "the institution," for his part in an assault that left another boy partially paralyzed. Alonzo claimed not to belong to a gang, but he associated with gang members and he frequently found himself involved in violence and crime. He had been expelled from several schools for fighting, and his rap sheet listed several arrests related to physical violence. He was known to family and friends to have a quick temper and to be "jumpy" all the time.

Evaluation revealed that Alonzo had been unable to sleep normally, probably for several years. He frequently woke up in a sweat, feeling frightened; he was subject to disturbing, often distorted, images of (witnessing) his uncle being shot in the face three years earlier during a drug deal. He suffered anxiety attacks and bouts of depression. Especially when incarcerated, he tried to mask these feelings of vulnerability. Jail is no place to be feeling weak, injured, and vulnerable! While on the outside, he avoided feelings of dread and depression by consuming alcohol and other drugs, but also by plunging himself into high-risk pursuits of burglaries, car jacking, and drug dealing. He had a long history of misreading others' intentions and reacting violently, often with disastrous results.

Alonzo's developmental history was replete with the kinds of instability and mistreatment that are often associated with antisocial development—an antisocial father who was incarcerated much of Alonzo's life, a mother with a serious alcohol problem, mother's boyfriends moving in and out of the home, and one such boyfriend who violently assaulted Alonzo several times when his mother was away. Young Alonzo's deep sense of insecurity and dread severely diminished his capacity to pay attention in school, and academic failure loomed as early as the elementary school years. He began to abuse alcohol (at home) by the fourth grade. The escalation of unpredictable violent attacks was well under way by age 10. By 11 or 12, this young boy was deeply entrenched in a lifestyle almost certain to lead to school failure, social chaos, and eventually prison.

Alonzo quite possibly would have developed an antisocial character even in the absence of actual traumatic experience. He was neglected and mistreated, he had several role models for antisocial attitudes and behavior, and he shared genetic material with antisocial parents. However, like so many incarcerated juveniles, Alonzo's traumatic experiences and his means of coping with them surely contributed to school failure and to anger dyscontrol. His posttrauma reactions placed another obstacle in the way of rehabilitation.

MOOD DISORDERS

Mood disorders encompass several psychiatric conditions that are characterized primarily by pathological extremes of mood, but also include distinct sets of physiological, cognitive, and behavioral symptoms. Such conditions were termed affective disorders in the past, to denote the outward expression of emotion; however, the term *mood disorder* more accurately conveys the subjective emotional state at the heart of the disorder. The two broad types of mood disorders are depression and bipolar disorder (formerly manic-depressive illness). The various forms of depression constitute the most frequently diagnosed psychiatric disorders.

Each of the familiar features of depression and bipolar disorder were well described by the ancient Greeks. Hippocrates described melancholia (depression) as consisting of, "an aversion to food, despondency, sleeplessness, irritability, [and] restlessness" (quoted in Akiskal 1995, p. 1068). The modern classification scheme (*DSM-IV*) includes two primary types of depression—major depression and dysthymia. Major depression is a severe and acute form of depression, disabling in its effects, while dysthymia is a less severe but more chronic condition. Diagnosis of major depression requires, during the same two-week period, five or more symptoms from the group: depressed mood (in children and adolescents this can be irritability), markedly diminished interest or pleasure in activities, weight loss or diminished appetite, disturbed sleep (insomnia or hypersomnia), psychomotor agitation or retardation, loss of energy, feelings of worthlessness, impaired concentration, and thoughts of death.

The less severe but more common form of depression, dysthymia, requires for its diagnosis a depressed mood most of the time (without long periods free of depression) for at least two years (only one year is required in the case of children and adolescents), and two or more of six symptoms—poor appetite, insomnia, lethargy, low self-esteem, impaired concentration, and feelings of worthlessness. In addition, the disorder cannot result from other disorders such as major depression or bipolar disorder, and it must cause clinically significant impairment in functioning (school, work, or interpersonal relations).

Both major depression and dysthymia are well known to occur in children and adolescents, although the symptom picture may vary from that of adults. For example, considerable irritability and oppositionality ("hard-to-live-with" kids) are a more common expression of depressive disorder in children. Children and adolescents are more likely to cope with feelings of depression by provoking conflict or by "stirring the pot." Young people are less likely to present the classic picture of lethargy and gloom associated with adult depressive disorders. Substance abuse is another common avenue for trying to cope with negative feelings and thoughts. In sum, depression in young people can underlie a host of other behavioral disturbances, making careful assessment essential.

The lifetime prevalence of major depression is estimated to be approximately 10 to 25 percent for women and just 5 to 12 percent for men, and the figures of dysthymia are estimated to be about 6 percent, again with women suffering the disorder about twice as frequently as men. The reasons for the gender differences are unclear, but may relate to biological and/or cultural differences. There are data suggesting that the prevalence of depressive disorders is increasing in Western countries, and that the onset of depression may be earlier (Earls 1989). Similar findings of escalating prevalence are being reported for bipolar disorder (Geller and Luby 1997). Again, the reasons for these trends remain unclear, but the increases in prevalence have occurred during the same time frame as the increases in antisocial character.

Numerous research programs have investigated the experiential factors and the genetic/biological correlates of depression. There is a well-established genetic contribution to depressive disorders. For example, twin studies show that the concordance rate for major depression is roughly .28 to .42 for dizygotic (fraternal) twins versus . 48 to .53 for monozygotic (identical) twins. These and other studies confirm that genetic background is important, perhaps amounting to a vulnerability or predisposition to the development of depression. At the same time, however, Merikangas and Kupfer (1995) state that "the moderate degree of concordance between biological parents and their adopted-away offspring suggest that common environmental factors also contribute to the expression of the mood disorders" (p. 1109). Research has repeatedly demonstrated a connection between negative life events and the development of depressive disorders. Social factors such as high levels of stress, social disarray, loss of a loved one, and unemployment can contribute to the development of depression. For some, depression occurs with much less environmental stress than others would require for development of depression. It is possible that some individuals' genetic makeup is such that they can develop depression without external causes, while others will avoid depression even under extreme stress.

Bipolar disorder, according to the *DSM-IV*, can take many forms. However, the essential feature in a typical case—officially termed bipolar type I—is the presence of one or more manic episodes. A manic episode is defined by the presence of a period of "abnormally and persistently elevated, expansive or irritable mood," lasting at least one week. During that period of expansiveness, there must be three or more of the following symptoms: inflated self-esteem or grandiose thinking, decreased need for sleep, being more talkative than usual, having a flight of ideas or feeling that thoughts are racing, and increased goal-directed activity or agitation. These symptoms cannot be better accounted for by another disorder, and the manic state must cause marked impairment in functioning (American Psychiatric Association 1994). For the diagnosis of bipolar disorder there may be single or recurrent manic episodes in combination with single, recurrent, or absent major depressive episodes. In addition, there is a diagnosis of a "mixed" episode, meaning a period of time in which criteria are met for *both* major depression and manic episode during at least a one-week period.

Another variant of bipolar disorder is termed bipolar type II. This disorder involves recurrent major depression in addition to hypomanic episodes—defined as a less severe form of mania— "not severe enough to cause marked impairment" (American Psychiatric Association 1994). Bipolar II requires that there never has been a true manic episode. Yet another variant is termed cyclothymic disorder, described as "an attenuated bipolar disorder" and involving alternating short cycles of subsyndromal depression and hypomania.

The lifetime prevalence of bipolar disorder is estimated to be from 0.4 to 1.6 percent, and, as opposed to depressive disorders, there are no significant gender differences. The genetic contribution to bipolar disorder appears to be stronger than that for major depression. Studies estimate the concordance for bipolar disorder for dizygotic twins to range from 0 to 24 percent, while the concordance for monozygotic twins ranged from .33 to .93, all of which suggests that genetic predisposition plays a strong role in the development of bipolar disorder. Still, there is not full genetic concordance, and the possible role of learning and other experiential factors remains unclear.

The relationships between antisocial behaviors and mood disorders are complex. In the case of bipolar disorder, it appears unlikely that the antisocial patterns of behavior cause the mood disorder because, although some forms of stress might play a role in the initiation of a manic or mixed state, the disorder seems to be largely biological in origin. The more common pathway from antisocial behavior to bipolar disorder is this: that bipolar disorder must be controlled by medications (lithium, valproic acid, etc.), and individuals prone to an antisocial lifestyle are also prone not to comply with medical directives. Being on the run from home, being careless and impulsive, being disrespectful of authorities—all these things make noncompliance with prescribed medications more likely.

Researchers in Boston have discovered some association of conduct disorder (CD) with possible bipolar disorder (Biederman et al. 1997). Geller and Luby (1997) report a 22 percent rate of conduct disorder among bipolar children and 18 percent among bipolar adolescents. Such comorbidity probably arises from the overlap of key features—the impulsivity and high energy and the grandiose thinking. The researchers did not speculate on how many of the CD youths would still show antisocial symptoms when the bipolar disorder is well controlled. Also, University of Louisville psychiatrist Sheryl Schneider and colleagues (1996) reviewed six studies that found substantial comorbidity of conduct disorder with bipolar disorder. (See also Kovacs and Pollock 1995 and Biederman and colleagues 1997 for comorbidity of bipolar disorder with conduct disorder.) Each of these studies establishes rates of comorbidity, but they do not clarify the causal mechanisms or directions.

The causal pathway can also go from bipolar disorder to antisocial behavior. This is infrequent, but the onset of a manic episode can propel a young person into extraordinarily impulsive and even antisocial activities. A mixed state, involving elements of both depression and mania, can lead to a highly agitated, even aggressive state, particularly if conflict and aggression are familiar behavioral expressions in the individual's life. In the case where bipolar disorder brings a delusional or paranoid belief, there is the possibility of the patient acting out aggressively in response to some imagined threat. In such cases it is imperative to initiate medical treatment as soon as possible. Reasoning with a bipolar patient in a manic or mixed state is not productive.

Depression is common among antisocial youths. As with PTSD, the antisocial habits can lead directly to profound loss, pain, and alienation—all of which can bring depression. Paradoxically, we would want to see some dysphoria—some anxiety, depression, or shame—in an individual being held responsible for antisocial behavior. He *should* feel badly about his deeds and the cost to him and others of his misadventures. Indeed, it is a bad sign when a youth being incarcerated for crimes shows no regrets and no worry, and no wish to have done things differently.

Depressive disorders also can underlie some antisocial patterns of behavior, particularly in children and adolescents. Irritability and agitation can be expressions of depression. By itself, depression will not be the cause of a serious and chronic delinquent career, but it can contribute to agitation and dyscontrol, and it can complicate the efforts of youths and their families. The following case exemplifies how depression can drive some antisocial tendencies such as truancy, family conflict, and aggressiveness.

Just past his sixteenth birthday, Larry was nominally in the eleventh grade. But because of skipping classes over the previous year and because of suspensions for verbal abuse of teachers and for threatening behaviors, he had lost credits and would not graduate with his class. Learning difficulties had been evident since elementary school, but he had managed somehow to pass each grade. A diagnosis of ADHD had led to treatment with stimulant medications with equivocal results, and only a few months earlier he had been on extremely high doses of Ritalin (80 mg/day). Conflict with his mother had led to several extended stays with his grandparents, as she feared that one of their battles would escalate to serious violence. The police had already been to the house twice, but no arrests were made so far.

When they were together, Larry and his mother fought incessantly and pointlessly. Larry blamed all his woes on her (with no mention of his absent father), and she readily generated incendiary comments about her son. When she left the room, however, Larry was able to describe more frankly the years of frustration in school and the toll it had taken on his self-esteem. He explained, "I try to get kids to leave school with me. That's because the frustration in school gets me down. But I don't care if I'm stupid." He went on to describe just how negatively his self-image had formed around his learning difficulties. He related that he expected that "after high school, there's nothing for me. I'll have bad jobs and a bad life . . . I expect that I'll be a bum on the streets." While he blamed his mother for his proximal difficulties (restricted Friday night), he could recognize that he used her as a scapegoat, and he felt some remorse over his mistreatment of her. Mental status examination revealed that Larry experienced several of the physiological signs of depression—insomnia, poor concentration, and poor appetite—and these had worsened in recent months, making him more prone to fly off the handle and less able to complete his schoolwork. In addition, his irritable, hard-to-live-with demeanor was accompanied by a gloomy attitude he seldom discussed. He often thought, "If someone was to kill me that would be okay" (passive suicidality).

Years of frustration in school, along with the absence of his father and chronic conflict with his mother, had led to depression. While the gloom and pessimism were evident at times, what Larry's mother and teachers were more likely to see was his irritable and hostile presentation, an angry and disrespectful boy who might be headed for deeper forms of delinquency and school failure. A combination of antidepressant medications and individual and family therapies helped Larry to alter his course over the ensuing months. With improved sleep and diminished agitation, Larry could more readily attend to schoolwork and he was more able to work with his mother and teachers instead of against them. The battles were not over, but they were more often productive.

PSYCHOTIC DISORDERS

The term *psychotic* refers to a marked failure of reality testing, that is, some severe lapse in the ability to discern what is real versus what is imagined or feared, or in the ability to think logically about real things and processes. There are two broad classes of psychotic symptoms: formal thought disorder, referring to the form of one's thought processes, whether they be logical, coherent, and goal-directed; and psychotic content of one's perceptions (hallucinations) and beliefs (delusions). Some psychotic symptoms are well circumscribed, wherein much of the individual's thinking and behavior remain unaffected. For example, in delusional disorder the patient suffers a distinct delusional belief. A delusion is defined as a false belief that is rigidly held, a belief that is not swayed by incontrovertible evidence to the contrary. Delusional disorder is relatively uncommon, but exact prevalence estimates are made difficult by the nature of the disorder. Such individuals tend to keep their beliefs to themselves and they usually do not come to the attention of law enforcement or mental health professionals. Outside the concerns related to the delusion, the patient thinks and functions normally. A woman may hold a delusional belief in her husband's infidelity—despite every evidence to the contrary—yet she can function normally in her job and in the care of her children. At the other extreme, psychotic symptoms are not circumscribed, such as in schizophrenia. There, the psychotic disorder, including formal thought disorder and delusions and hallucination, may pervade and impair most of the patient's cognitive and interpersonal functioning.

Psychotic symptoms can occur in a wide variety of psychiatric and medical conditions. Some psychiatric disorders involve psychotic symptoms by definition, such as in delusional disorder and schizophrenia. Other conditions may involve psychotic symptoms in some cases and not in others. For example, major depression can include formal thought disorder, delusions, or hallucinations, but these features are not necessary for its diagnosis. Similarly, in its extreme form, mania can include psychosis and can be indistinguishable from schizophrenia.

The vast majority of individuals with psychotic symptoms present no substantial risk to others. Instead, they are most often unhappy, reclusive, and sometimes eccentric characters. In some cases, though, there is a potential for aggressive behaviors. The most frequent target of violence is the self, and suicide rates are high among chronically psychotic persons. However, some psychotic symptoms, because they lead the person to misread others' intentions, can bring about a violent reaction. Paranoid disorders, for example, can predispose the individual to fearing for his safety, and unpredictable violence occasionally is the result. Such behaviors usually are not part of a broader antisocial behavior pattern, but rather isolated incidents that should be understood in their proper psychiatric context. The following case is a good example of a powerful psychiatric disorder driving a profoundly aggressive act.

In a small coastal town in Maine, 16-year-old Jerry seemed to be gradually more withdrawn from his family as summer progressed. He began to act in perplexing ways, staying up all night, issuing peculiar and threatening statements to his sister and mother, then failing to turn up for dinner and even for bed at night. He had adopted an intimidating manner, and no one challenged him. His family seemed to just stay out of his way, hoping that the odd behaviors would just go away. One morning when his father was away, he stalked his mother with a large kitchen knife. When she saw the knife and tried to flee, Jerry chased after her and stabbed her to death. His sister came upon the scene, then fled to a car where she barely escaped Jerry's knife. Jerry was hospitalized, then diagnosed with paranoid schizophrenia, and spent the next three years in psychiatric hospitals. He had been under the delusion that his mother and sister were part of some complex plot to kill him and dismember his body, and his only hope was to kill them first.

Among antisocial youth, the presence of a thought disorder can immensely complicate the task of containing the untoward behaviors and steering the individual in more acceptable directions. Although the rate of psychotic disorders among incarcerated youths is higher than in the general population, psychotic disorder and antisocial behavior are very different conditions and they do not tend to go together. However, an antisocial individual who also happens to suffer a psychotic disorder can be expected to be especially refractory to efforts to alter his behavioral proclivities—until the psychosis is controlled by medications and psychosocial treatments. Psychosis in an antisocial individual also can be expected to increase the risk of violent or dangerous behavior.

PERSONALITY DISORDERS

Since the nineteenth century psychiatrists have described personality types that were judged to be socially maladaptive. Philippe Pinel, for example, reported individuals whose thinking and behavior, while not truly psychotic, was seriously disturbed and tended to remain disturbed in the same fashion over time. This paralleled Pritchard's account of antisocial individuals who suffered what he termed "moral insanity"—another relatively stable condition with far-reaching implications for behavior and social relations. Pierre Janet, and later Freud, described the psychological traits of hysteria—what we today label histrionic personality disorder. These various accounts described not a clinical syndrome (e.g., depression, anxiety) that afflicts the individual, but some features that seem to be integrated within the personality itself. Personality disorder is, to some degree, "built in" to the personality.

The 1980 edition of the *DSM* (*DSM-III*) placed the personality disorders on a separate axis from other clinical disorders, thereby assuring that attention to the symptoms associated with axis I disorders would be complemented by attention to enduring personality traits. Personality disorder is defined in *DSM-IV* as, "An enduring pattern of inner experience and behavior that deviates markedly from the expectations of the individual's culture. This pattern is manifested in two (or more) of the following areas." The *DSM-IV* goes on to list potential areas of such deviation: cognition, affectivity (emotion range, intensity, appropriateness, etc.), interpersonal functioning, and impulse control. It also specifies that the maladaptive pattern must be "inflexible and pervasive across a broad range of personal and social situations," and that it must lead to "clinically significant distress or impairment."

The matter of personality disorders carries one into a realm in which the distinctions between health and illness are inherently unclear. Whether a particular behavior pattern is judged to be significantly deviant depends heavily on the norms of her society. As psychiatrists John Gunderson and Katharine Phillips (1995) put it, "Whether persons are considered to have personality disorders depends on whether their personality traits are noxious to the society in which they live" (p. 1425).

Epidemiological studies suggest that the prevalence of personality disorders may be as high as 10 to 13 percent in the general population. Hence, one does not need to be very deviant to earn a personality disorder diagnosis. Prevalence rates are higher in low socioeconomic groups and in disadvantaged communities and in families that are particularly chaotic or dysfunctional.

Personality disorders immeasurably complicate the treatment of other clinical syndromes. The success rates for treatment of depression, for example, are far poorer when a personality disorder is present. They also render far more difficult the assessment and treatment of antisocial youth and adults.

The most prevalent personality disorder among antisocial adults is antisocial personality disorder (ASPD) (see Chapter 2 for definition and criteria). ASPD cannot, by *DSM* criteria, be diagnosed before the age of 18. This is because of the strong pejorative implications of the diagnosis. That is, we would hope that a young person, despite numerous antisocial behaviors, might still turn around by adulthood, and indeed the majority of conduct disordered adolescents do not go on to warrant an ASPD diagnosis in adulthood. The same pattern of antisocial behaviors before the age of 18 warrants a diagnosis of conduct disorder. Because of the strong continuity in behavior patterns from adolescence to adulthood among truly antisocial individuals, the diagnosis of ASP requires that the individual met criteria of conduct disorder before age 15.

The most prevalent personality disorder among antisocial youth, not surprisingly, is the one with the greatest similarity in overt behavioral features. Diagnostic criteria for borderline personality disorder (BPD) include inappropriate and intense anger, impulsivity, unstable and intense interpersonal relationships, frantic efforts to avoid real or imagined abandonment, identity disturbance (unstable self-image), recurrent suicidal behaviors, gestures or threats, or self-mutilation. (The case of Justin, in Chapter 6, describes an antisocial adolescent with BPD.) BPD in clinical settings is more commonly diagnosed among females. However, among the population of juveniles involved in the juvenile justice system, BPD is commonly seen among both males and females. Such severe personality disorder deepens the difficulties in treating such youths, for not only must the treatment staff work with the antisocial habits and attitudes, but now there is a psychiatric dimension to deal with—the inexplicable fluctuations of mood, the dismaying self-destructiveness, the dramatic instability in interpersonal relations, and, perhaps above all, the chaotic relationships between the youths and the staff.

RESPONSIBILITY AND PSYCHIATRIC DISORDERS

Aunt Elaine had occupied a special place in the extended family. She was much loved for her prized desserts and appreciated by all for the spirit she brought to family gatherings and celebrations. At 42, she had no children of her own, but had an easy, reassuring manner with her three siblings' six children. It was known by the adults, however, that for about two years Elaine had some odd ideas about a conspiracy of some sort. She seemed to have grown more tense and distant. She was always vague about her beliefs, but the tone of urgency was unmistakable. Efforts to dissuade such ideas were for naught, and she took the suggestion of seeing a psychiatrist as an insult. Her husband finally had moved out and, most alarming of all, he reported that Elaine revealed that her sister's husband, Robert, was part of the conspiracy. In fact, she had avoided seeing Robert for some months, often making oblique hostile remarks about him. Outside the context of her unusual beliefs, Elaine functioned normally—at work, with the children, and managing the house.

At nine o'clock on a Saturday evening, when she knew her sister and two children were away, Elaine let herself into their home and surprised Robert in his living room. She was armed with a hunting knife, some rope, and a Bic lighter. Threatening to stab him if uncooperative, Elaine attempted to tie Robert to a chair. She explained that she intended to extract a confession from him, by torture if necessary. She clearly believed that Robert knew all about her reasons for this assault. While she attempted to tie him to the chair, Robert broke free and ran from the house. Elaine was apprehended about 20 minutes later at her home. She was calm and cooperative with the police, and she acknowledged every aspect of the assault, justifying her behavior with the claim that she "required" a confession from her brother-in-law conspirator.

In her 42 years, Elaine had never been the object of concern by law enforcement authorities. She explained every detail of her plans and intentions to police investigators and to the forensic (psychologist) examiner—to extract a confession from Robert about his involvement in the conspiracy, then to reveal this to the extended family—all with the aim of eliminating some unexplained peril. Elaine presented a clear case of delusional disorder (formerly termed paranoid disorder), a psychotic condition that entails the presence of a delusional belief in an individual whose functioning was normal outside the context of the delusion.

Elaine's defense in court involved the claim of insanity, the legal term for a psychotic condition that rendered the individual not responsible for the acts in question. There was general consensus among psychiatric experts on each side about the diagnosis; however, they disagreed about whether her disorder rendered her not guilty by reason of insanity. It fell to the jury to decide this difficult question, and their deliberations dragged on for three long days.

Elaine's trial exemplified the dilemma of assigning responsibility for offenses when the individual's behavior was affected by what is designated in legal terminology as a mental disease or defect. On the one hand, common sense tells us that individuals are responsible for their own actions, and the last thing we would wish is to encourage the evasion of such responsibility. On the other hand, the court's moral authority rests upon a premise of fairness. The court's authority would be undermined, as a judge once put it, "if drooling idiots are treated as if they were responsible defendants" (Gutheil 1995, p. 2763). Besides the insanity defense, most states also recognize a *diminished capacity* defense. For most offenses, it must be shown that the defendant acted with "a guilty mind," termed *mens rea*—meaning, roughly, that he knew what he was doing and he did what he intended. First-degree murder, for example, requires premeditation. The effects of intoxication or a mental disorder, however, might be shown to prove the lack of specific intent.

The insanity defense, as it currently is codified in most jurisdictions, stems from the M'Naghten Rule. In England in 1843, Daniel M'Naghten, who had suffered from persecutory delusions for several years, attempted to assassinate the prime minister. When M'Naghten was found insane and thereby not guilty, a public uproar resulted in the House of Lords' posing a series of questions for the judiciary, which elicited a definition of insanity as a defense against criminal responsibility. According to these guidelines, an individual is not guilty if, because of a mental disease or defect (psychosis or mental retardation), (1) he did not know the nature and quality of the alleged act(s), or (2) he did not know that it was wrong.

The insanity defense periodically is assailed by the public and professionals alike, usually following a not-guilty verdict that appear to unjustly absolve some individual from responsibility for a crime. In practice, however, the insanity defense seldom succeeds, for two reasons. First, juries usually take a conservative approach to the matter of relieving individuals of responsibility for their acts. Second, the wording of the instructions to the jury (about conditions that must be met for a finding of not guilty by reason of insanity) make it very difficult to establish that the individual did not understand the nature and quality of the acts or their wrongfulness. In the case outlined above, Elaine finally was found guilty. Despite her clearly suffering from a psychotic disorder, and despite the obvious fact that the offense stemmed from delusional thinking, the jury could not conclude that she was unable to appreciate the wrongfulness of her deeds. She had, in fact, fled to home after the assault, suggesting that she knew that she might be in trouble (i.e., that she had transgressed). Hence, a psychotic individual was imprisoned, probably for several years.

Questions of criminal responsibility address only one part of the meaning of responsibility, that is, whether society will insist that the individual be held responsible for his acts. The other component is whether or not the individual is "able to answer for his conduct and obligation" (*Merriam Webster Collegiate Dictionary, 10th Ed.* 1993). This aspect of the definition is less a social and legal matter than a psychological one. In the case of Elaine, although her attorneys argued that she should not be held responsible for the assault because of her mental illness, Elaine herself took full responsibility for her acts. While she did not want to go to prison, she acknowledged her deeds and her intentions, and did not externalize responsibility. Elaine's internal locus of control contrasts with the typical configuration in antisocial individuals. In various ways, antisocial youths usually disavow responsibility for their untoward actions. They demonstrate an external locus of control, insisting that the origin of their misbehaviors is anywhere but within themselves.

Society is occasionally confronted with a tragically violent crime by an individual whose behavior is neither motivated by comprehensible antisocial aims (e.g., revenge, rage, money, pride), nor the result of obvious mental illness. In such cases, as when a young girl murders a neighbor child for no apparent reason, it is perhaps the most natural conclusion that "she must have been crazy." The insanity defense is readily pulled into such trials, as this can be the only plausible defense. The following case exemplifies the insanity defense in a particularly shocking triple murder.

THE INSANITY DEFENSE IN A TRIPLE MURDER

February 2nd was the coldest day of the 1995–96 winter in Moses Lake, a town of 16,000 in eastern Washington State. The school day at Frontier Junior High was scheduled to start two hours late because of the cold, but 14-year-old Barry Loukaitis did not arrive on time for class. Instead, Barry left his home later in the morning.

He was dressed in unusual garb—a long black coat and a black Stetson hat—and walked with a stiff gait the mile or so to school, over the frozen, snowy ground. Witnesses later testified that Barry had looked odd, but they thought perhaps his stiff gait was due to the cold and the extra clothing.

Classes were under way as Barry walked down the deserted hallways. As he turned and walked through the door into his algebra class, he raised a lever-action high-powered rifle from under his long coat and began firing, first at a student, then another, then at the teacher, then at another student. A long standoff ensued, during which Barry arranged students in the back of the room. He positioned himself in a corner where police snipers could not easily target him. A heroic teacher slipped into the room and tried to negotiate and reason with Barry. Finally, with police swarming all over the school, the teacher rushed Barry, pinning him against the wall, from where police could enter and disarm him.

Barry was known to be a good student, earning mostly A's and B's, and he was responsible for his work and respectful of teachers. He had no history of any kind of behavioral trouble. There was no aggression or acting out of any kind, and he never used drugs or alcohol. Barry had not been very social, but he always had a few friends. In retrospect, some peers and teachers noted that Barry had seemed more irritable and angry in the weeks prior to the shootings, but no one had any clue that he would carry out a scheme of multiple murder. A Stephen King novel, *Rage*, found among Barry's things, closely parallels the actual sequence of events that Barry carried out on February 2nd. It never was determined exactly what role the novel played in the actual planning and execution of the murders, but the parallels were striking.

Barry Loukaitis presented just the kind of case where common sense would dictate that severe mental disorder surely was the root of the problem. Indeed, a psychiatrist hired by Barry's attorney concluded that he suffered from bipolar disorder and that he was delusional at the time of the crime. One would want to believe that such a crime could only have been carried out by one in a psychotic state. No substantial motive for the shootings could be discerned, even after months of interviews and mountains of testimony. Eventually a second psychiatrist concurred with the first psychiatrist in the diagnosis of psychotic bipolar disorder, but neither of these experts could specify any verifiable or objective evidence in support of their diagnosis. A psychologist and a psychiatrist hired by the court conducted extensive evaluations, including a full psychological test battery, and concluded that although Barry suffered some depression in the weeks prior to the shootings, there was no evidence for bipolar disorder or psychosis of any kind. They had to acknowledge that they had no explanation for Barry's behavior, but they were confident that he was not legally insane at the time of the shootings.

Barry represents that class of rare, violent individuals who seem to over-control aggressive emotions (Tinklenberg et al. 1996). But this descriptive classification provides little by way of explanation. Because of the seriousness of the offense, jurisdiction over the case was waived to adult criminal court. Then, nineteen months after the shootings that staggered the small community, a jury rejected the insanity plea and convicted Barry. At the age of 16, Barry Loukaitis was sentenced to life in prison without the possibility of parole.

❖ C H A P T E R   6 ❖

The Role of Evaluation

Assessment of children and adolescents is a regular part of everyday life—at school, at home, and in the neighborhood. Teachers constantly monitor children's progress in academics, in peer relations, and in social skills. The pediatrician checks physical development and makes note of social-emotional progress or delay. Competent parents routinely track the child's evolving behavioral and emotional characteristics as well as interpersonal skills.

When a child's behavior in any of these arenas deviates much from the norm, parents, teachers, and doctors intuitively understand that any number of factors might be at work. A child's pattern of aggressive peer interactions, for example, will trigger various hypotheses. This behavior might be seen as (1) "just a phase he's going through"; (2) an expression of the emotional strain of the parents' divorce; (3) an alarming, early indication of coercive, antisocial habits; (4) an angry response to mistreatment and neglect by parents; or (5) an expression of frustration over learning in school.

In most cases, these informal assessments by parents, teachers, and others are sufficient. The hypotheses generated by such assessments guide interventions. The child's work load at school may be adjusted or extra help may be arranged. Divorcing parents might realize that their child's emotional needs have been put aside for too long. Adults may coordinate their efforts to set clearer behavioral limits and define consequences for unacceptable behavior. When interventions are seen to be helpful and the unwanted behaviors recede, hypotheses are confirmed. The adults believe they have learned something about the child, something that can be applied to other situations in the future.

For a minority of children and adolescents, however, the antisocial habits persist or worsen. Parents and school staff look more deeply into the child's current circumstances or personal history that might contribute to the problems without finding a "handle" on the behavior. At some point, when the disturbing behaviors are not responding to the usual interventions (limit-setting, punishment, guidance, counseling), and when the adults are running out of ideas, then a more formal, psychological evaluation may be in order.

The majority of youths who develop antisocial habits never become the subject of a formal, clinical evaluation. Often, it is perfectly obvious what is the source of misbehavior (e.g., neglect and/or abuse), and the options for intervention or treatment may be sparse, anyway. Hence, the practical value of evaluation is limited. In these cases, there may be little that the adults can do beyond imposing the usual sanctions (e.g., school suspension), keeping themselves and those in their charge out of harm's way, and hoping for improvement. The youth's behavior may take its course until authorities such as the police and the courts are compelled to intervene. Moreover, when systematic professional intervention is not available, the clinical model never presents itself as an option. In many cases, however, the emergence of antisocial behavior is puzzling and the options for intervention need to be sorted out.

The aim of formal, comprehensive evaluation of youths with antisocial behavior is to understand the nature and source of the untoward behaviors and to guide intervention along the most promising avenues. A corollary aim is to delineate the problems and interventions in a way that facilitates coordination of efforts by the persons and agencies involved. Nothing ensures failure in dealing with problematic adolescent behavior like adults working at cross purposes. The term *comprehensive* implies two features in the evaluation: first, that the alarming behaviors be accounted for within a broad psychobiological context, including assessment in the cognitive/intellectual, emotional, interpersonal, and biological/medical spheres; and second, that the antisocial behaviors be understood in a developmental framework. Some evaluations have more circumscribed or forensic purposes, for example, to determine whether or not an individual is competent to stand trial or whether he possesses the "legal capacity" to commit an alleged crime; but these are less common and are predicated upon legally delineated aims. Competency to stand trial and legal capacity are discussed at the end of the chapter.

A developmental approach situates behaviors in relation to the developmental tasks appropriate to the age, and in relation to the youth's level of mastery or frustration over those tasks. For example, we can sometimes trace a child's oppositionality and negativism to mounting frustration in school, stemming from learning difficulties or attention deficit. Similarly, an adolescent's normal, developmental need to form an identity, along with poor social skills and difficulty being accepted, can lead to associating with a deviant peer group and initiating the formation of a negative identity. For many unhappy, alienated adolescents, it feels preferable to develop an identity that stands in opposition, in conflict with normative society, than to have no identity at all, no sense of belonging.

The developmental approach to evaluation overcomes the liabilities of a "snapshot" view of the individual—an image of the individual frozen in time, with no history and no future, just a collection of current observable attributes. A diagnostic label, by itself, is seldom useful because it tells us little more than we knew in the first place. When a misbehaving youth is referred for evaluation, it is because we are already concerned about those behaviors. Several of the more common diagnoses of antisocial youths—conduct disorder, oppositional defiant disorder, antisocial personality disorder—are little more than labels attached to the patterns of unwanted behaviors. Instead of a diagnostic snapshot, therefore, we should be looking for a fuller explanations of how the behaviors of interest fit into the youth's personal development—the kinds of stresses he is subjected to, his intellectual or emotional limitations, his prospects for education and work, and his level of family support.

Even in cases where there is a psychiatric disorder such as attention deficit/hyperactivity disorder (ADHD) or depression, diagnosis alone is of limited value. This is because antisocial behaviors are seldom the direct result of psychiatric disorder. Rather, as described in Chapter 5, the relationship between antisocial behaviors and psychiatric conditions is often highly complex and difficult to disentangle. Hence, when ADHD is diagnosed, effective treatment (e.g., with stimulant medication) may make it easier for the youth to restrain impulses, but seldom will such clinical treatments eliminate the antisocial habits. Evaluation must still delineate the ways in which the ADHD relates to the alarming behaviors, and it must give some account of how, for this child, at this time, the impulsivity led to these kinds of antisocial acts. In addition, it must specify the most promising treatment program for the whole child or adolescent—including somatic therapies when indicated (e.g., medications), psychosocial treatments (behavior management, counseling, family therapy), and other kinds of nonclinical interventions, such as change of living arrangement, altered school program, or directives from the court.

In the endeavor to understand the nature and source of antisocial behaviors, and to specify the most promising interventions, substantial information must be gathered from three domains: (1) the objective view—the actual behaviors of concern and their configuration within the life and world of the youth; (2) the subjective point of view of the youth himself and all that it reveals about his personality and prospects; and (3) the psychological profile of the individual, including cognitive, emotional, and interpersonal functioning and any clinical (psychiatric) syndromes or personality disorders.

A comprehensive evaluation must also take into account the medical conditions that might impact the youth's behavior in direct or indirect ways. A physical examination—sometimes even a neurological examination—is usually prudent. Occasionally, for example, an abnormal electroencephalogram (EEG) in a highly impulsive youth leads to a trial of anticonvulsant medication, which can reduce the frequency and severity of outbursts. Also, the youth's current legal circumstances must be taken into account. A boy who for the first time is facing a serious criminal charge may experience situational anxiety and therefore be highly defensive. Contrariwise, some individuals in trouble with the law may be prone to exaggerate whatever psychological distress they feel in an effort to diminish their own responsibility (malingering). In the extreme, we occasionally see some charged individuals virtually fabricating mental illness in order to support an insanity defense.

THE BEHAVIORS: THEIR NATURE AND TRAJECTORY

The foundation upon which all other aspects of assessment rest is a thorough understanding of the actual behaviors of concern. This is the objective behavioral aspect of evaluation. All of the information gathered in the course of evaluation ultimately must be applied in the effort to understand the behaviors that occasioned concern in the first place. It is essential, therefore, to gain an accurate profile of the actual antisocial behaviors, the history and context of these behaviors, as well as the responses and interventions of others.

In the same way that the justice system classifies types of crimes and their severity, clinical evaluation must determine exactly what kinds of antisocial behaviors have occurred. If there was an assault, was it premeditated, or was it impulsive or provoked? Was a weapon involved, and if so, what kind, and where did he get it? Was the victim a stranger, an acquaintance, or family member? Did the youth commit the assault alone or in the presence of others, and did there appear to be a motive or goal? It makes a world of difference to society (and to the evaluator) whether a young boy is in the habit of breaking into unoccupied cars in the middle of the night to steal whatever items he can finds, versus whether he participates in car jacking, involving confrontation of drivers, stealing the car, and delivering it to a middleman who sells it to a "chop shop." The question of whether or not the boy confronts his victims has important prognostic value, because the willingness to confront or assault one's victims augers badly for future violence.

The next objective aspect of antisocial behaviors is their temporal configuration, that is, their frequency, duration, and onset. Common sense tells us that a girl who participates in a single burglary with some delinquent peers at the age of 16 is probably on a different trajectory from a girl who, by the same age, has participated in two dozen such break-ins, who has developed considerable skill, and who has a well-developed network of associates. It is essential to know how often a youth participates in antisocial behaviors. Frequent antisocial endeavors suggest that such behaviors have become integrated into the youth's lifestyle and attitudes, whereas infrequent antisocial acts may signal occasional acting out of conflicts with family or authority.

A key objective aspect of antisocial behavior is its onset. Children whose delinquent careers begin by age 10 or 11 usually are on a different trajectory from those whose acting out begins in mid-adolescence. When trouble was evident by such an early age, what kind of behaviors were they? Another prognostically potent variable, described in Chapter 4, is the versatility of the youth's antisocial behavior. We need to know whether antisocial behaviors span several categories (shoplifting, burglary, assault, sexual assault) or the youth has a problem just in getting into fights or just engaging in shoplifting. High versatility augers poorly for future antisocial habits.

It is crucial to delineate just how the antisocial behaviors are situated within the broad context of the youth's social world. To what extent do the antisocial acts mirror the behavior of other youths in the same school and community? Is this normative antisocial behavior in his neighborhood (e.g., fighting or drug use)? Has the youth selected for friends peers who support antisocial attitudes and behaviors? Or, does the youth have friends who do well in school, behave respectfully, and stay out of trouble? What of the youth's family background: Do parents or others in the home model antisocial attitudes, or are they alarmed by such untoward actions? Is there a family history of violence, of theft, of incarceration? What role models is the youth likely to identify with? Are prosocial behaviors rewarded in the family or in the peer group? Is progress in school and work valued?

A key aspect of the social world of antisocial youth is the reaction of others to the antisocial behaviors. Have signs of trouble mobilized parents and/or extended family, and if so, have parents acted competently? Have the adults sought out help and resources? Have the adults conveyed, right from the beginning, that such destructive behaviors are unacceptable? Have they backed up their warnings, and are they willing and able to fight constructively with the adolescent? Have they meant what they said, or have their words dissipated in a fog of vacillation and uncertainty? Are parents burned out? Are parents resigned that their daughter is following a pathway to incarceration and commitment? Another aspect of the response from others is: What has been tried? Beginning with the smaller antisocial acts, how have school, parents, and community reacted? What sanctions have been applied, and how has the girl responded?

Each of these objective aspects of a youth's antisocial behaviors must be understood alongside the subjective perspective of the youth himself.

SELF-APPRAISAL: THE VIEW FROM WITHIN

Once we have an adequate account of the objective aspects of a youth's antisocial behaviors, the next most informative set of information comes from appraisal of the youth's own perspective on his untoward behaviors. The first concern, one that often jumps right out at the examiner and others, is the extent to which the youth acknowledges the problematic behaviors versus the extent of minimization and denial. Some delinquent youths will argue—often convincingly and at great length—over the extent and seriousness of their actions. Even when convicted of multiple instances of certain crimes, a boy will argue endlessly over the details, the charges, the others who were responsible, and who was really at fault. This kind of arguing serves the psychological purpose of deferring the time when he must accept personal responsibility for his choices and his actions. At the other extreme, some antisocial individuals forthrightly acknowledge the poor choices they have made and the offenses they have committed. Such offenders often report a dismal history of mishaps and misbehavior. They may feel motivated to do things differently in the future or they may feel powerless to change course. This matter of avoiding versus accepting responsibility relates to the overarching factor in self-appraisal—locus of control. This is a cognitive dimension that powerfully prefigures every discussion and reflection upon one's problem behaviors.

Locus of control is the extent to which one experiences the events and processes in one's life as stemming from one's own choices and efforts, versus experiencing events as "just happening" or as happening "to me." Many individuals speak as if even their own behaviors are determined from outside the self. Hence, there is little sense of self-directed action. The connections seem never to have formed between thinking about one's needs and wishes, one's planning, and the actions that are undertaken. Locus of control is not just matter of intelligence. Some perfectly intelligent antisocial individuals habitually display an external locus of control, often using their intellectual skills to argue for conclusions favorable to their case and surely convincing themselves along the way.

An external locus of control carries a considerable liability for the individual prone to antisocial behavior. Because personal events and behaviors are experienced as originating outside the self, there is no basis for self-correction. If one consistently looks outside the self for the causes of trouble, then one will never come to terms with the part one plays in such events. One will never learn to alter attitudes and change course. Also, when one's untoward attitudes and behaviors have led to serious antisocial offenses, treatment can gain no foothold. There is no foundation for a treatment alliance when the delinquent cannot consider how her own choices and actions have brought her to such unhappy circumstances.

For some chronically antisocial individuals, the external locus of control is so deeply ingrained that they feel that *they* are the victims. Listening to such individuals tell their story, there often is an overriding air of being aggrieved, as if *they* are the victim of all these unhappy events. When giving their personal history, such individuals frequently recount a long series of conflictual relationships with teachers, parents, police officers, judges, probation officers—all of whom have treated them unfairly. The sense of being mistreated, the feeling that life is unfair, permeates experiences so throughly that it is impossible to draw attention to the choices and transgressions that have led to the crisis, which ensures that real insight into experience and behavior will remain weak. This incapacity for insight is one reason why traditional counseling and psychotherapy is generally ineffective with antisocial youths.

Locus of control relates directly to how the individual feels about his own transgressions. Feeling remorseful about one's mistakes and the harm they have wrought is a key ingredient in bringing about positive change. But one can hardly feel remorseful over one's misdeeds if one does not feel responsible for one's choices. There can be no motivation to change if all these unhappy circumstances are somebody else's fault, hence, the familiar experience with a chronically antisocial youth that since he cannot truly understand that he has been doing anything wrong, there can be little motivation for doing anything differently in the future—other than to try harder not to get caught. Antisocial youths, particularly those whose experience includes repeated encounters with authorities, often are skilled at generating the *appearance* of motivation for change. Many delinquent youths have been discharged from institutions and appear to have made substantial changes, but within a short time they reoffend and end up right back in the institution.

The capacity to observe the self—the observing ego—often is weakly developed in antisocial youths. This deficient cognitive skill regularly accompanies the defensive purpose of denial and evasion of responsibility. Needless to say, youths who lack the ability to reflect upon their own internal processes will be hard pressed to grasp the connections between emotion and thought, on the one hand, and impulse and behavior, on the other. Similarly, individuals who lack the capacity to observe the self usually have only the weakest conception of a future. They have only a snapshot view of life. Ideas about the future are grandiose and unrealistic, with no appreciation of the real endeavors one would need to undertake in order to approach one's ideals. Lacking the ability to realistically appraise the self, there is little capacity to plan out a sequence of efforts that might lead toward one's goals.

The subjective perspective of the individual reveals key aspects of psychological functioning, especially those related to locus of control, insight and remorse, and the motivation to change. Systematic assessment of the several components of psychological functioning is indispensable in accounting for antisocial behaviors and in charting the most promising interventions.

PSYCHOLOGICAL PROFILE

A full account of an individual's antisocial behavior and how it relates to his personal trajectory and prospects for the future requires a psychological profile that addresses and integrates each of the three major areas of personal functioning—(1) intellectual/cognitive capabilities and liabilities, (2) emotional life and personality style, and (3) the quality and development of interpersonal relations. Evaluation must also address the personality attributes of adaptive skills, characteristic defense mechanisms (coping strategies, response to stress), and the presence of any psychiatric conditions.

A good grasp of intellectual strengths and weaknesses is useful in making sense of the youth's response to learning and his identification with school and work. Consider Henry who, over the seventh and eighth grades, has missed numerous classes in order to hang out at a local mall where he and some peers had been banned for incidents of shoplifting.

Henry's performance in school had been shaky since the early grades, but it had been unclear how much of this was attitude and how much was intellectual deficit. Formal evaluation was never performed because Henry always seemed to be just getting by, and he did not qualify for evaluation or special services through the school district. Formal testing revealed deep deficits in Henry's intellectual strengths, with an IQ well below average (Full-Scale IQ = 78) and with particular difficulty learning and retaining new verbal information. Achievement testing confirmed the toll that his deficits had taken: Henry was now about three grades behind in many academic areas, including reading. These test findings, along with lengthy interviews with Henry and his father, revealed that Henry had been mightily frustrated for several years in school. Rather than react to these difficulties by asking for more help or by becoming anxious and depressed over it, he had chosen the alternate response—to simply reject the pursuit in which he felt he could not succeed. Henry finally expressed just how painful and frustrating school had been. He could then say that he wished school were easier for him, and he really did want to finish school and be able to have a decent job in life. It turned out that Henry's antisocial activities were secondary to his rejection of school. He was not skipping school in order to associate with antisocial peers. He was associating with antisocial peers as a convenient way to avoid the frustration of school.

The opposite kind of intellectual test findings can have important implications as well. When we find solid intellectual strengths in a girl who is rejecting school, then we know we must look elsewhere for an explanation of her rejection of academic and work values.

The personality profile must be sufficiently rich and detailed to help account for salient behavior patterns, to estimate the likelihood of future behavioral difficulties, and to anticipate the prospects for treatment. A personality profile draws the interconnections among individual attributes, including characteristic emotional states and affect management, typical defense mechanisms and coping style, and the quality of interpersonal relations. For example, an individual who characteristically relies upon externalization when stressed (projection) is likely to respond with a paranoid style, becoming anxious and distrustful and rigid in his thinking. Psychological treatment is often unproductive in such cases. An individual who has "disconnected" from emotional needs, whose relationships are shallow and exploitative, will feel little need to alter course other than for instrumental purposes. In contrast, an individual whose personal style when under stress is to examine the self or to turn to others for help is a better bet in psychological treatment and more likely to alter maladaptive behaviors. It goes without saying that the quality of one's interpersonal relations depends heavily on one's styles of coping and adapting. Turning to others for help could be a case of healthy, reciprocal relationships, or it might be an instance of parasitic relations in which others are seen to exist only to meet one's immediate needs. Personality patterns that are seriously maladaptive or harmful to others may be diagnosed as a personality disorder (borderline, schizoid, etc.).

One other feature that psychological assessment must address is the presence or absence of a clinical syndrome, that is, a bona fide psychiatric disorder. Interviews, mental status examination, and psychological testing all can help to determine the presence of thought disorder, mood disorder, delusional disorder, attention deficit disorder, or other psychiatric conditions, which, if present, must be treated as part of any approach to altering antisocial behavior patterns.

COMPONENTS OF PSYCHOLOGICAL EVALUATION

The endeavors that go under the title "psychological evaluation" are many and varied. The composition and extensiveness of evaluation depend on the resources that are available, the questions posed by the referring person or agency, and the orientation of the examiner. Some evaluations have circumscribed purposes, such as an evaluation to determine a defendant's competency to stand trial. However, when there is a need for comprehensive evaluation of antisocial youths, the aim is always the same—to provide a developmental understanding of the unwanted behavior patterns and to delineate the most promising interventions by assessment of the three broad domains outlined above—the objective (behavioral) view, the subjective point of view, and the psychological profile.

There are three principal sources of information in psychological evaluation—the hard data of written reports such as court documents, school records, and clinical records; interviews with the youth and significant others (i.e., parents); and psychological testing. In special circumstances, other sources of data are useful, for example, the staff observation of a youth in detention, or the verbal report of teachers, school administrators, and probation counselors.

Hard Data

Antisocial youth (for that matter, most youths) are unreliable sources of information about their own behavior; particularly in the evaluation of antisocial individuals, self-report is always suspect (Gacono and Meloy 1994). There is, therefore, no component of psychological evaluation that is more crucial than a reliable set of factual information on the individual's personal, academic, and behavioral history. Such hard data usually come in the form or written reports prepared by school staff (e.g., school psychologist, teachers), by court personnel, by doctors, therapists, and others. (It is well to bear in mind, of course, that even carefully prepared reports from the court, from school personnel, and from doctors are subject to inaccuracy, omissions, and sometimes falsehood. Such reports, however, generally provide a reliable framework within which to begin inquiry.) Also, in most cases parents are able to provide information about their child's early development, school progress, social development, and behavioral history. Such factual information is indispensable because it provides a framework within which to conduct the inquiry, and it specifies the actual behaviors that need to be accounted for.

Nowhere in the psychologist's armamentarium is there a mental x-ray. Even the most sophisticated psychological tests can be meaningfully interpreted only in relation to actual behaviors and the individual's perspective on those behaviors. Proper psychological evaluation relies on a triangulation among data sources—a pattern analysis. The meaning of one data set depends on its relation to other sets of information. Ultimately, a psychological analysis integrates the behavioral history with the subjective perspective and the personality profile in a way that accounts for the observed behaviors and specifies the most promising treatments.

The hard data that are needed go beyond just the information about a youth's offensive behavior. In sorting out the developmental factors leading to antisocial behavior, it is important to have reliable information on academic performance, grade reports, behavioral reports from school, academic achievement scores, and medical reports. Moreover, such factual data about academic performance relate directly to a youth's prospects for the future. It is far easier for a delinquent to make use of treatment and stay out of trouble if he can read and write competently, if he can succeed in at least some parts of school, and if he possesses some work skills. In many cases, the youth himself is the least reliable informant about these key questions.

While an evaluator could conduct interviews according to a routine protocol, without paying much attention to behavioral and academic history, such evaluation risks accomplishing little more than muddying the waters. In interviews and mental status examinations, the most productive queries are those that press the youth to explain his choices and to account for his behaviors. Only then do we observe crucial features of his personality style, for example, about his defensive style: Does he deny or minimize (denial)? Does he blame someone else (externalization) or provide digressive and misleading excuses (evasive)? Does he seriously insist that such things never really occurred (possible thought disorder)? Does he blandly acknowledge the facts, but show no real concern (detachment)? Does he acknowledge the behaviors, but charm the examiner into believing such things could never happen again (psychopathic)? Does he appear to show real remorse, for example, anguish about the hurt he has brought to his family? Does he show signs of struggling to understand or to alter his behavior?

Hard data also provide the best antidote to clinical arrogance. It is all too easy, solely on the basis of test data, to generate clinical narratives about an individual's psychological profile. But unless the test data are brought to bear upon the messy and often confusing array of actual behaviors, these findings amount to little more than formulaic excerpts from textbooks or from computer-generated narratives. Documents labeled "Psychological Report" have been observed to issue from accredited psychiatric hospitals that were nothing more than Minnesota Multiphasic Personality Inventory (MMPI) narratives mixed with the psychologist's speculations—all without reference to the youth's behavioral profile or history. Such productions may be conditioned upon budget cuts or managed care pressures, but whatever the reason, such "evaluations" do a disservice to the youth and to the mental health professions.

Once the hard data of a youth's personal, academic, and behavioral history is adequately grasped, then a meaningful interview and mental status examination can be conducted. The mental status exam is a component of the clinical interview. Some clinicians conduct a separate, formal mental status exam, while for others the mental status and the clinical interview are intermixed.

Clinical Interview

The clinical interview is the most important single source of information about the individual being evaluated. It is in the clinical interview that the youth can tell his own story, providing facts, sequences of events, and reasons. It is here that the youth's subjective experience can be accessed, where the examiner can observe his personal style of piecing together his own worldview, his self-image, his style of responding to stress.

Generating all this useful information in the interview presupposes a reasonable degree of cooperation and honesty on the part of the individual. Threats to this enterprise vary according to the attitude the youth takes toward the evaluation itself. At one (less common) extreme are youths who view the evaluation as an opportunity to learn something useful about themselves. Some have worked with counselors or doctors in the past. They may be open and eager to understand themselves in ways that will help them change course for the better. At the other (more common) extreme are youths who view a psychological evaluation as just another way to manipulate and control them. If they cooperate at all, it is minimal compliance where brief, uninformative answers and "I don't know" are the norm. The possibility of misleading or even fabricated responses makes it essential that some hard data on the youth's history be used for cross-validation. Somewhere in between these extremes of attitudes are situated the bulk of antisocial youths who are referred for evaluation—youths who may be guarded or suspicious, afraid they might be labeled "crazy," but who also harbor some curiosity about themselves, their past, and their future. Usually, after the interview is under way for a while, the youth relaxes to some degree and participates adequately.

Going into the clinical interview, there are several domains of functioning that the examiner needs information about. First, and often most crucial, is the youth's family relations and family history. It essential to gather data on parents, stepparents, siblings, and step-siblings, including their current whereabouts and occupations. Equally informative are accounts of their behaviors, the type of relationships they have had with the interviewee, and the reasons for various transitions in their lives. For example, it is well to know that a 16-year-old half-brother moved out of the home when the client was 8 years old. But there often is a rich story behind that move. Only on further inquiry might the examiner learn that the older boy was kicked out after the discovery that he had been sexually touching a younger half-sister. When a father was reported to have left the state a few years ago, it is important to know why, as best as the client understands. Was it to take a better job, to avoid child support payments, or to join a girlfriend?

Following an account of the facts, it is well to know what these events mean personally to the young client. If a boy's father left the state years earlier, does the boy miss his father? Is he angry about the abandonment, or does he cover up all such emotions with bland detachment? Is he bland about being let down by the most important people in his life, yet seeking vengeance on authority in other forms? Does he take it out on his mother, his teachers, his stepfather?

Closely related to the matter of family relations is the quality of the youth's interpersonal relations. The pivotal question here is the extent to which those relationships are stable, healthy, and reciprocal (i.e., with mutual give and take) versus unstable, exploitative, and shallow. Youths who show the capacity for at least some healthy interpersonal relations will be more likely to learn and work productively in the years ahead. Youths who cannot appreciate the perspective of other persons (egocentrism), who cannot respect the feelings of others (empathy), or consider the consequences of their actions for others are more likely to drop out of school or work, and they are more likely to repeat their offensive behaviors.

Education is the principal job and responsibility of young people. As such, the nature and history of the youth's involvement in school is central to understanding his overall development, including the emergence of antisocial behavior. Hence, the interview must account, again, for the objective and subjective aspects of the youth's academic endeavors. It is important to understand the youth's actual learning experience. Was learning easy or at least within

normal limits? Were there serious frustrations that eventually alienated him from the whole enterprise of school? Were there areas of
special interests or skill? How did the youngster fit in with peers?
Was there a comfortable social niche, a sense of where she be-
longed and felt at ease, or was it always a struggle to fit in? Regarding problem behaviors: we must know not only how many
times the youth was suspended, but why. What were the actual
behaviors, and why was the youth engaging in them? Was there
a shift in attitude toward school and learning at some point? Were
there always behavior troubles in school or did they emerge in
adolescence? If there were missed classes or whole days of unex-
cused absences, where was the student, what was she doing, and
with whom? What were the parents' responses (when they finally
learned)? With regard to the youth's future, it is crucial to assess
the current attitude and beliefs about learning and school. Is there
hope of further academic or skills progress? What kind of assistance might the youth need in order to resume forward progress?
Academic and intellectual testing can be useful in this context,
but the youth's attitude can set limits on the progress we can hope
for.

Related to the matter of academic strengths is the youth's broader
range of skills and interests. Some children who feel forever out of
place in traditional school settings demonstrate considerable skill
in other arenas, for example, in mechanical endeavors, in sports,
or in hobbies. The capacity to apply oneself consistently to some
focused pursuit, whether it be mathematics, ballet, or bicycle repair, and to endure the normal frustrations and the incremental
progress, is an ego strength that builds self-esteem and encourages
identification with the healthy values of learning and work. One
of the commonest observations among youths with substantial
histories of antisocial behavior is a remarkable lack of any real skills,
academic or otherwise. Inquiry into how such youths have spent
their time through the adolescent years reveals mostly "hanging out"
with peers, watching TV, and playing video games—all passive
endeavors. For such youths, the effort to develop a job skill, for
instance, is an entirely new experience, and it can be difficult to

follow through with work commitments or to stick out the tiresome days of training and work needed to hold a job.

Does the client have the ability to tolerate normal frustrations in work or learning? Kernberg (1975) describes what he terms "nonspecific manifestations of ego weakness" including, for example, poor frustration tolerance and poor anxiety tolerance. There are several other ego strengths the evaluator must ascertain: the ability to plan a sequence of steps, and to keep these in mind while moving from one step to the next; the ability to tolerate delay of gratification (e.g., sex, food, revenge); the ability to constrain impulses (sex, aggression); the ability to make use of others' ideas and guidance; the ability to tolerate some anxiety without acting out or other maladaptive defenses. The sum of such ego strengths corresponds roughly with what is meant by personal maturity or personality resources. None of these ego strengths is innate, though some individuals may have an easier time than others in developing such resources. Rather, these personal strengths need to be learned incrementally—built through countless day-to-day experiences with sequences of ideas and plans, efforts and consequences, and discussion and reflection.

Throughout the clinical interview and mental status exam, the youth is revealing his own subjective "take" on his personal history, his behavior, and his prospects for the future. The two factors of interest in this subjective realm are (1) the extent of realistic self-appraisal—insight, and (2) the degree to which the individual feels distressed by his own harmful actions—remorse. The capacity to observe the self—to realistically appraise one's attributes and behavior, to track oneself over time, and to relate events to emotions, emotions to actions, and actions to consequences—is the basis of insight. Insight varies to some degree with intelligence. Intellectually limited youths often find it more difficult to understand the relationships among emotions, actions, and events. However, insight and intelligence are not the same thing. Some intelligent antisocial youths endlessly fail to appreciate the role they play in their own travails, and some antisocial youths with low IQs are able to understand their own actions perfectly well.

The level of insight a youth shows about himself and his personal history is of great importance to those who must deal with him. Individuals with insight into their own behavior are in a good position to accept responsibility for their actions and to make use of help to change their ways.

When offensive acts have been committed, there is pain and loss, regret and anxiety. When reckoning with the offender, society does not want to be alone in feeling the pain and regret. The judge in her courtroom, the property owners, the victim and her family, and the media are all on the lookout for indications that the offender, too, feels bad about his misdeeds. Nothing is quite so vexing to victims and to society as an offender who caused harm but seems not to care. The presence or absence of remorse is frequently cited as a factor in making decisions about sanctions, punishments, and treatments. Psychologically, remorse is an emotional force that motivates the individual to change her behavior. Where there is no remorse, the motivation for change is minimal or nonexistent.

The Mental Status Examination

A psychological or psychiatric evaluation should, in every case, include a formal assessment of the client's current mental and emotional functioning—apart from whatever might be learned from the client's explanations of personal events and family history. The mental status examination (MSE) is sometimes added as a more structured component of the interview, while some examiners prefer to glean the data for the MSE from queries intermixed throughout the interview. In their excellent text, *Using DSM-IV: A Clinician's Guide to Psychiatric Diagnosis*, psychiatrists LaBruzza and Mendez-Villarrubia (1994) include a clear exposition on how they prefer to mix the MSE questions throughout the interview, rather than to pose a more formal, perhaps artificial, set of questions. The MSE should give the examiner a good overall picture of the client's psychological status by addressing several areas of current functioning: (1) the client's general appearance and self-presentation (neat and clean, or disheveled); (2) level of alertness and orientation (is she wide awake and does she know where she is and why she is there?); (3) level of cooperation (attitude toward the examiner and the process; is this a valid assessment?); (4) affect (flexible and responsive, or flat and detached); (5) communication quality (level of rapport; egocentric, constricted, or guarded quality); (6) thought quality, as expressed in speech and communication (are thoughts clear and goal-directed, or tangential and peculiar?); (7) level of insight into current situation (i.e., does she appreciate the situation realistically); and, unless a more formal appraisal of intellectual strengths is to be conducted, (8) a general impression of intelligence.

Besides these questions about cognitive, affective, and communicative functioning during the interview, the examiner must inquire more broadly about the client's current functioning and symptomatology: Are there recent indications of mood disorder (disturbed sleep, depressed mood, racing thoughts, etc.), dissociative disorder (derealization, out-of-body sensations, etc.); anxiety disorder such as posttraumatic stress disorder (PTSD), or psychosis (hallucinations, delusions)?

Just about every aspect of personal functioning that is assessed in the MSE can be powerfully affected (usually negatively) by the use of drugs or alcohol. Mood can be altered by current or recent drug/alcohol use; motivation can be eroded by the chronic abuse of marijuana; even psychosis can result from drug use and withdrawal. Hence, the MSE must also inquire into drug and alcohol abuse, both current and recent. Substance abuse is implicated in a large proportion of delinquent acts, primarily because drugs often work as disinhibitors, weakening the normal internal constraints upon behavior. In addition, involvement in the culture of drug use and drug dealing can be directly involved in antisocial endeavors, for example, to earn money for drugs by conducting burglaries.

Psychological Testing

For just about every mental capacity or trait believed to be important in the understanding of human behavior, there is a psychological test (more often, several) to measure it. Currently, there are thousands of tests in print, with the number growing every year. Psychological testing has become a considerable growth industry, with numerous companies marketing their instruments with slick advertisements and often rather expansive claims. All of this has come about because psychological testing, when carefully applied, *can* generate valuable insights about individuals' personality and behavioral traits, and it can help to guide intervention.

A psychological test is a method for the assessment of some mental ability or trait through the use of a standard stimulus set and a standardized scoring protocol. Within this definition, there is great variation among psychological tests, ranging from simple behavior rating scales that can be filled out by a parent in a few minutes, to rigorous actuarial-based self-report tests of psychopathology, to elaborate computerized apparatuses for stimulus presentation and response recording.

Despite the considerable sophistication of many psychological tests, most of what is gleaned about individuals from testing can, in principle, be gained in other ways—through observation, history-taking, and interviews. Psychological tests, after all, operate on the basis of carefully selected samples of behavior, that is, the performance of the client during the test. Analysis of test data aims to generalize to the broader domains of functioning in the patient's life. While the MMPI may tell us that our client appears to be paranoid, what we really want to know is how he functions in real interpersonal contexts. Because real life is fraught with confounding conditions and forces, and because we often cannot observe client behavior in a natural setting, tests can be an efficient way to derive meaningful information, or at least to generate hypotheses. Also, some tests isolate specific cognitive and behavioral functions that in real life are usually heavily confounded with other, concurrent processes of thought and behavior. This is especially true in neuropsychological testing and in the computerized tests of attentional strengths.

The psychological tests that are useful in understanding a youth's antisocial behavior and in specifying the most promising interventions can be subsumed under two broad categories—tests of intellectual/cognitive functioning and tests of personality traits and psychopathology. In addition to these traditional psychological tests, there are numerous behavior rating scales, such as Thomas Achenbach's Child Behavior Checklist (Achenbach and Edelbrock 1983). These are valuable research tools but they generate information that often is better gleaned directly from parents and teachers and from observation.

The one test that is specific to antisocial proclivities, and that does not fit neatly into the categories of psychological tests, is Hare's Psychopathy Checklist–Revised (PCL-R) (Forth et al. 1990). This simple scale, because of its psychometric strength and its capacity to reliably distinguish psychopathic individuals, has greatly advanced research on antisocial character and is valuable in forensic settings. The PCL-R is not widely used in general clinical practice, however, because in many settings it can be difficult to be sure that one has access to accurate information on the patient's history. The antisocial individual typically cannot be relied on to provide such information.

Intellectual/Cognitive Functioning

Intelligence is a modern idea, one that appears deceptively simple. The concept of intellectual strengths as a separate dimension of personal functioning did not emerge until the end of the nineteenth century, and the first crude scale for measuring intelligence was not available until 1905. The nature of intelligence and how best to measure it has been the subject of considerable debate. There are numerous skills and capacities that make up what we mean by intelligence, for example, the verbal skills of vocabulary and abstract reasoning, and the nonverbal skills of visual-spatial problem solving, eye-hand coordination, and speed.

The fact that intelligence is composed of many separate abilities lies at the heart of the major debate over the nature of intelligence. Because the various skills tend to correlate, that is, individuals who are strong in one domain tend also to be strong in other skills, there seems to be a unitary factor in intelligence, which Charles Spearman calls g (for "general"). It was the idea of g that led to the concept of an overall intelligence quotient (IQ). There were several stages in conceptualization and scoring leading to the present-day IQ. In an earlier stage the formulation of mental age divided by chronological age yielded the IQ. Currently, IQ scores do not rely on a mental age but are derived directly from comparison of the subject's scores to age-indexed norms. Edward Thorndike and other researchers rejected the idea of a unitary factor in intelligence, and instead emphasized a number of independent, specific abilities. This debate over how best to conceive of intelligence continues to the present day, for example, in Howard Gardner's (1983) theory of multiple intelligences.

The healthy debate over the nature of intelligence balances a disturbing countertrend—the reification of the construct itself. This involves the tendency to think of intelligence as a real, measurable quantity existing independent of our theories and assessment methods. In fact, the opposite is the case. Intelligence is a theoretical construct, and it is always in the process of being reshaped, redefined, and challenged yet again, which gives rise to the ironic quip that intelligence is what intelligence tests measure.

At first glance, intellectual strengths and weaknesses may seem largely irrelevant to the matter of behavior problems. We know, for example, that antisocial habits can emerge in children and adolescents of any intellectual level, and that IQ is no predictor of the success or failure of socialization. Moreover, IQ is no predictor of psychiatric disorders. Some medical insurance companies in recent years have refused to fund assessment of intellectual functioning on the reasoning that IQ does not relate to problem behaviors or to psychiatric conditions. They claim that intelligence is an educational concern. Such reasoning, however, misses the point that for any individual the intellectual, emotional, and interpersonal domains all function as an integrated whole. We can no more understand a youth's psychological development and behavior without a grasp of her intellectual functioning than we could understand physical development without some grasp of metabolism.

Intelligence is the psychological construct upon which was developed the early science of psychometrics—study of the measurement of mental abilities and traits. The studies of educational and psychological researchers led to a sophisticated grasp of various forms of test reliability and validity. These psychometric dimensions, and the mathematics underlying them, have facilitated the development of countless other instruments for assessing mental traits and abilities.

The Stanford-Binet scale was the dominant test of intelligence for many years. However, the most widely researched and applied test for the measurement of intellectual functioning currently is the Wechsler Intelligence Scale for Children, third edition (WISC-III) (Wechsler 1991). The WISC-III consists of ten subscales, each of which taps a different aspect of intelligence. The ten subscales fall into two broad categories—verbal and performance. The verbal subscales consist of intellectual tasks that are more directly related to knowing and reasoning—information, similarities, vocabulary, arithmetic, and comprehension. The performance subscales are tasks that involve a more active effort by the subject—picture completion, coding, picture arrangement, block design, and object assembly. Statistical analyses have repeatedly supported the aggregation of the subscales in the verbal and performance factors. That is, the tasks that involve knowledge and reasoning tend to correlate more among themselves, and the tasks that involve an active effort tend to correlate more among themselves. Some individuals tend to be stronger on the performance tasks, while others are stronger in the verbal tasks. In addition to these ten subscales, there are three supplementary subscales. Digit span, for example, is sensitive to the ability to pay close attention and to briefly screen out extraneous stimuli. As such, it is heavily impacted by attention deficit disorder and by anxiety, and it loads heavily on another factor termed freedom from distractibility.

Intellectual assessment generates data that are useful in several ways in the evaluation of antisocial youth. The first involves the youth's relationship to his principal task throughout the developmental years—education. Within the domain of education, there are two directions in which to look: (1) retrospectively, to understand any obstacles or frustrations that undermine motivation and commitment to school; and (2) prospectively, to assess the youth's prospects for future education and training.

Looking closely at youths with antisocial behavior, we frequently find school failure in the background. How this educational collapse came about and what role it plays in the antisocial behavior is key. There are some children whose learning difficulties have made school frustrating for years. Children with attention deficit disorder, for example, if they do not get the necessary support and treatment, may give up and no longer even picture themselves as successful in school. By the middle school years, identifications can shift away from education and normative social life, and toward deviance, rebellion, and acting out. Substance abuse is common among students who have disinvested in the educational enterprise, and this, in turn, further moves the child into the realm of antisocial attitudes and behaviors.

Testing for intellectual strengths and weaknesses can help to specify the obstacles the child has been struggling with. Contrariwise, in some cases testing can demonstrate that intellectual capacities are not the issue, and that we must look elsewhere to understand the child's withdrawal from educational commitment. For any given individual, the meaning of intelligence test scores depends on their relation to other data—the child's performance in school (e.g., grades, teacher reports) and the child's actual academic achievement. Academic achievement tests, administered by the schools, assess the child's learning in various subject areas as compared to other children of the same age. There are several widely used tests of academic achievement, such as the Comprehensive Test of Basic Skills (CTBS) and the Iowa Test of Basic Skills. These are usually administered by school districts every year or two, and they provide a very rough estimate of how much a child has learned in various subject areas such as reading comprehension and math concepts.

Looking prospectively, intellectual assessment can help to set realistic goals for the child. It can be valuable for an adolescent and his family to know that there are no large intellectual obstacles to academic success, and that if he wants to succeed he can. In contrast, if an adolescent generates a Full-Scale IQ of 82 (below average), then pushing him into college classes, or even into rigorous high school courses, may be setting him up to fail yet again. Large disparities between intellectual potential and actual performance (e.g., on academic achievement tests) can suggest focal deficiencies, such as learning disabilities or attention deficit. Further testing usually can delineate such deficiencies and can generate recommendations for appropriate treatment.

Intellectual and other cognitive tests not only generate IQ scores and define areas of deficit; they also indicate areas of strength. Many youths, especially antisocial youths, show significantly greater strengths in visual-spatial and other performance areas of functioning. Such students may be better suited to training in the building or mechanical trades than to studying English and mathematics. Our modern culture has tended to value verbal intelligence over other forms of intelligence. But the thrust of the multiple-intelligences idea is that different people have different kinds of intelligence, and that true intelligence should not be defined by one kind of intellectual skill rather than another.

Careful application of intellectual testing can also be helpful in identifying psychiatric conditions that can play a role in antisocial behavior. Attention deficit disorder (ADD), for example, must be diagnosed from a convergence of data from several sources—teacher and parent observations and testing for attentional weakness with a continuous performance test (CPT). In addition, two factor scores derived from the WISC-III—freedom from distractability and processing speed—are sensitive to ADD. Relatively low scores on these factors can be suggestive of ADD and indicate the need for more focused testing.

A prominent feature of many psychiatric conditions is an impaired ability to think logically and to express oneself clearly. In some conditions, such as borderline personality disorder, thought disorder remains largely concealed in the ordinary activities of everyday life. Such underlying thought disorder may be evident only under conditions of high stress or toxicity (e.g., drug use) or in the reasoning involved in interpersonal relations. It will not be evident on structured intelligence tests, that is, on tests where questions have relatively straightforward answers. On the other hand, in more malignant forms of thought disorder (e.g., in schizophrenia), the illogical reasoning and peculiarities of expression will be manifest even on a structured intelligence test. Hence, when there is a question of possible thought disorder, it is useful to determine how well the youth can explain abstract relations or provide the reasons behind social conventions, and then to compare his performance on the structured intelligence test to his performance on unstructured projective tests (see below).

Personality and Psychopathology

The largest part of the psychological testing enterprise involves efforts to measure individual personality traits and dimensions of psychopathology. The conceptual demarcation between personality traits and psychopathology is always the subject of reflection and debate. Personality traits that are maladaptive are not necessarily pathological until they cross some threshold. That threshold, in current psychiatric parlance, usually is defined as when they cause clinically significant distress or impairment in functioning. Several hundred instruments of diverse types and levels of sophistication seek to report the degree of an individual's depression, his need for social approval and attention, his tendency toward rigid thinking or paranoid ideation, his thought disorder, and so on. Tests of personality functioning fall roughly into two categories: (1) self-report tests in which the patient's response involves a choice among predetermined answers (fixed format), such as true-false responses to questions about the self (e.g., the MMPI); and (2) projective tests, in which the patient's response does not follow predetermined choices but involves the patient's own mental projection onto the stimulus (e.g., the Rorschach).

There are many self-report tests of personality, some based on specific theories of personality and some relatively theory-free. The most widely applied self-report tests of personality are the two current versions of the Minnesota Multiphasic Personality Inventory (MMPI-A for adolescents; MMPI-2 for adults) and the several forms of clinically sophisticated tests designed by psychologist Theodore Millon, for example, the Millon Adolescent Personality Inventory (MAPI).

The MMPI, first developed nearly a half century ago, involves several hundred true-false statements through which the patient reports on her own experiences, thinking, and emotions. Administration time is roughly one hour. Items address a wide range of personal traits and experiences as well as indications of psychopathology. There are items, for example, that ask about experiences that are known to be associated with psychosis, depression, paranoid thinking, and so on. This seems to be a straightforward strategy of the patient reporting on his own traits and experiences. However, the scoring and interpretation of the MMPI and the Millon scales utilize sophisticated protocols to overcome two potential pitfalls in self-report inventories. First, many individuals tend to portray themselves in a way that deviates significantly from the truth, especially when asked about traits one would not be proud of. Subjects have a strong tendency to minimize or deny problems. Second, some individuals, intentionally or otherwise, portray themselves as more afflicted than they really are. Malingering involves the deliberate exaggeration of symptoms for some external gain (e.g., in civil litigation). Hence, test-taking attitude became the subject of considerable scrutiny and research.

The outcome of concern for the accuracy of self-report inventories has been the use of *validity scales*, which are built into these tests to detect the patient's tendency to minimize problems (defensiveness) or to exaggerate problems (malingering). The validity scales are the first thing an examiner looks at when the patient completes the test, for if the validity scales are highly elevated, then the test is invalidated and the clinical scales cannot be interpreted. The use of validity scales has been a key development in psychological testing because without them the examiner cannot know how seriously to take the findings. Self-report tests lacking validity scales are useless in forensic settings, and they are of limited value in any clinical practice.

The second potential pitfall in interpreting self-report tests like the MMPI is the question of whether items mean what we think they mean. It is an empirical issue as to whether questions that we think relate to paranoid thinking *are* answered in the way we would expect by persons who are paranoid. The recognition that we cannot take at face value the meaning of test items led to the actuarial scaling of the MMPI. Items were selected for the various scales not according to what we believe they mean, but according to how well they actually discriminate a given subgroup of persons (e.g., paranoids). In parallel fashion, the interpretation of the MMPI is based on the similarity of the obtained profile to known subgroups. Thus, we can conclude, for example, "Individuals with this profile tend to be wary, suspicious, and rigid in their thinking. They may be overtly paranoid and the possibility of delusions should be considered."

Paralleling the MMPI and other fixed-format tests of personality are various kinds of projective tests. In projective tests the patient generates her own response to the stimulus. Some examples of projective tests include the Thematic Apperception Test (TAT) and the Rorschach Inkblot Test. In the TAT, the patient is handed a series of large cards with deliberately vague and ambiguous scenes involving people. He is instructed to tell a story about each scene— what is happening, what will be the outcome, what the persons may be thinking and feeling. The TAT and similar tests provide an impetus to fantasy, but with some boundaries that are set by the stimulus picture and the instructions. In the hands of a skilled clinician, the TAT can provide insight into the mental operations of the patient, particularly as they involve interpersonal relations. The TAT has suffered, however, from difficulty in developing a reliable scoring method. Its interpretation tends to rely heavily upon the theoretical orientation and training of the psychologist.

The best-known projective test of personality is the Rorschach Inkblot Test, first published as a psychological test in 1921 by Swiss psychiatrist Herman Rorschach. Rorschach was not the first to study the assessment of personality through the use of inkblots. Alfred Binet, the originator of intelligence testing, and several other researchers explored such methods around the turn of the century. Rorschach's set of ten inkblots, however, rapidly became a standard, and has been the subject of seventy-five years of research and theory and countless applications in clinical settings. The stimulus cards, being just inkblots, provide the patient even less structure and guidance than is provided in the TAT and in similar methods such as sentence completion tests. Hence, the patient is fully at the mercy of his own mental processes as he reports "seeing" something in the card. Since there is truly no "thing" in the stimulus, whatever the subject reports has been projected onto the inkblot.

Because the Rorschach (as with other projective methods) lacks a fixed response format, it was difficult to develop a reliable scoring system, without which the Rorschach—despite a large and devoted following in clinical settings—became the subject of controversy and even scorn within the scientific field of psychometrics. Various scoring systems were in use (Allison et al. 1968), and the interpretation of any given Rorschach protocol often depended on the individual proclivities of the examiner, where he was trained, and by whom. The Rorschach, for many, came to symbolize the rift between the hard-nosed science of modern psychology and the softer, theoretical domain of clinical assessment and intervention.

However, through the efforts of psychologist John Exner, Jr. and many colleagues (Exner 1986, 1991, Exner and Weiner 1982), the Rorschach was given a reliable scoring system, and thus full license to operate in the modern world of scientific inquiry and clinical application. Numerous investigations determined empirically just which scoring methods and criteria were reliable and which scoring categories carried valid and meaningful implications for personality functioning. Over the past two decades, thousands of rigorous, empirical studies have explored the scoring and interpretation of Rorschach responses in individuals from age 6 on up.

The Rorschach, unlike the MMPI and the Millon scales, is not keyed to specific dimensions of psychopathology such as depression, psychopathy, or mania. Instead, it provides information on a wide range of personality variables—the quality of thought organization, emotional life and its modulation, defensive operations, impulses, and interpersonal relations. The Rorschach, because of its unstructured stimuli, is especially sensitive to formal thought disorder. While some patients with thought disorder can conceal such difficulties on structured tests like the WISC-III or even the MMPI, the unstructured stimuli of the Rorschach more readily make such underlying disturbance evident. Because of its format, the Rorschach is far more difficult to fake than are other kinds of tests.

Terrence: Antisocial Behavior with Underlying Psychosis

Right from the start, Terrence, age 15, had seemed to the detention staff to be peculiar in ways that set him apart from the other boys. His emotions seemed odd at times, with inappropriate expressions on his face, and his explanations often were difficult to follow—despite apparently good intelligence. After he spent three weeks in detention, the staff requested a psychological evaluation for him. He was scheduled to spend three more weeks locked up before trial on a charge of second-degree burglary. Because of a history of running away from home, the judge refused to allow him to reside at home.

Terrence had broken into a neighbor's house in the middle of the day by climbing a ladder to a second-story window. The owner surprised Terrence in the house, who then fled by jumping to the ground. He readily acknowledged his crime to the arresting officer, who found Terrence at his home about a half hour later. He told the officer that he had decided to break into the house because he had heard some boys nearby telling him, "Go ahead, get in there and find the money." The local police knew Terrence from previous incidents over the past year—a 911 call from home when Terrence had threatened his mother and stepfather, a shoplifting charge, and several instances of truancy and running away from home.

A review of the records indicated that Terrence, currently in tenth grade, had performed well in school up until ninth grade, when his grades began a steady slide. He had begun missing classes, seldom turned in homework, and was known to smoke marijuana often. Efforts to get him into counseling at school were unsuccessful, and at the time of the burglary Terrence was being considered for placement in an alternative high school with shorter days and greater tolerance for his idiosyncrasies.

His parents reported that Terrence was the product of an apparently normal pregnancy and delivery, and he was a healthy baby, toddler, and preschooler. His parents divorced when Terrence was 9 years old. He had no difficulties with learning in the early grades, but he always was rather shy and preferred to play by himself. There had been conflict at home just the past year, as Terrence had provoked arguments over seemingly trivial matters and had been threatening several times. He refused counseling. The pediatrician assured his mother that this probably was normal adolescent rebellion, and that he would grow out of it. Terrence's biological father had died about two years earlier of a congenital heart ailment. He and Terrence had visited together only about twice each year, and his mother reported that Terrence showed little emotion at his death. Mostly, she reported, Terrence just kept to himself. He had some friends but he seldom seemed motivated in the past year to do things with them. He seemed to be withdrawing.

At the interview, Terrence initially appeared to be alert and cooperative. But within minutes it was apparent that his social skills were more than just deficient. His affect seemed detached from what we were talking about, and there was no feeling of rapport, which usually develops, even with difficult adolescents. Terrence's account of his life circumstances was straightforward. However, when pressed on the reasoning involved in some of his decisions (such as to rob his neighbor's house), his explanations became illogical and disjointed. For example, he would make mutually contradictory statements, yet even when the contradiction was pointed out, he failed to show any concern for the logical impossibility. He also used some odd terms, referring for example, to one endeavor as "chanceful." These responses are possible indications of formal thought disorder. In addition, Terrence acknowledged that he often heard his father or some other man speaking to him. He continued to insist that the voices he heard in the yard the day of the burglary were from real kids, despite the fact that he never actually saw the youths.

The WISC-III generated a Full-Scale IQ of 95 (average), with little scatter among subtests and with only a six-point difference between Verbal and Performance IQs. There were two odd locutions on the WISC-III, but they were not considered strong indications of thought disorder. The MMPI-A protocol was rather unusual in that the validity scales showed both significant defensiveness and a high level of openness and a tendency to be revealing. The clinical scale configuration was impossible to decipher because of significant elevations of five of the clinical scales. Such a pervasive scale elevation can be suggestive of psychopathology in many areas, and it can also be an indication of confusion or an odd test-taking approach. The Rorschach was more definitive. Even a cursory examination of the content reveals psychotic-level disturbances in thinking. His third response, for example, was "A kid's toy that's spinning and it's menstruating." Another response was "A bat with a man's head and he's reaching his wings out to touch out here." Such bizarre combinations of elements and body parts, animate with inanimate, along with an inability to explain such percepts, made clear the severe degree of thought disorder.

Terrence warranted a diagnosis of schizophrenia. He showed both the negative symptoms of apathy, social withdrawal, and flat affect, and the positive symptoms of auditory hallucinations, and formal thought disorder. (Hearing voices is not uncommon among children and adolescents with depression, with ADD, and other nonpsychotic conditions. The pivotal issue is whether the children understand that the voice they hear is just their mind "playing tricks," or whether they believe that someone or some spirit is actually speaking to them. Hearing voices and knowing that it is a process within one's brain is not, by definition, a psychotic symptom. Believing that one is hearing from one's dead grandfather or from the devil does violate reality testing.) As a result of evaluation, Terrence's many transgressions made more sense as the peculiarities of a developing psychotic disorder than the crimes of a truly antisocial youth. Clinical treatment with antipsychotic medications, a highly structured daily routine, and individual and family therapy were initiated.

Justin: An Antisocial Adolescent with Multiple Diagnoses

By the time 16-year-old Justin was jailed to await trial for assaulting a police officer, he had a list of prior police contacts that nearly filled a page—several fourth-degree assaults (striking his mother, kicking his mother's boyfriend, assaulting a boy at school), shoplifting charges, episodes of running away from home, even setting a fire in which a neighbor's garage burned to the ground. He had been incarcerated four times, including a six-month stay in a juvenile corrections institution. In addition, he had amassed a considerable psychiatric history. Twice while in detention he had made apparent suicide attempts by cutting on his arms, once with the broken glass from a light bulb, and detention staff had transferred him to a nearby psychiatric hospital. Justin carried an array of psychiatric diagnoses—depression, ADD, PTSD, intermittent explosive disorder, bipolar disorder, and borderline personality disorder. A panoply of psychiatric medications had been tried, but without clear success. An EEG, used to assess for neurologic abnormalities, was normal, ruling out a neurologically based disorder of impulse.

Justin's educational history did not look much better: impulsive in the early elementary school years, diagnosed with ADD at age 10, and treated with stimulant medication (with questionable results), deepening academic deficits and lack of interest in school, special classes for behavior-disordered children, frequent visits to the principal, and countless suspensions from school.

Justin's mother reported that he was a healthy baby, and that he had no medical conditions. However, she also acknowledged that she drank heavily in the early months of the pregnancy, before she realized she was pregnant. She also reported that a stepfather had been physically abusive to her and to Justin when Justin was 3 to 6 years of age.

In person, Justin was the picture of despair and vengeance indiscriminately directed at self and others. His demeanor toward the examiner was bland and detached, but he was minimally compliant. Someone had told him that if he cooperated with the doctor this might help him in some way. His arms bore prominent scars from self-inflicted cuts. Some of them were fresh, and two of the older scars appeared to have been sutured. He talked freely, with no sign of trying to impress the examiner, of his assaults on himself and others. He explained that the self-cutting felt like relief. The pain of the cut felt better than the awful emptiness or "nothing" feeling he sought to escape. He was unsure if he might kill himself at some point. Justin explained that his father was currently in prison in another state for "bail jumping" and that he hadn't seen him for about a year. He was sure, though, that when his father was released next year, he and his dad would move to Louisiana together to "kick it" and stay out of trouble.

Mental status exam revealed good orientation and sound memory. He suffered from symptoms of depression including insomnia, irritability, depressed mood, and thoughts of suicide. He also showed signs of dissociation—feeling as if in a dream at times and feeling outside of his own body—as well as hyperarousal (exaggerated startle reflex, nightmares, anxiety attacks). He did not recall being abused, but he related that his mother told him that he was beaten by the ex-stepfather. He displayed several signs of magical thinking, for example, that he could "sense" the thoughts of others, that he could tell when his mother was in danger. And, while some of his explanations were tangential and digressive, there were no frank psychotic symptoms, that is, no delusions or hallucinations.

Justin's Full-Scale IQ on the WISC-III was 92 (average), but there was a great deal of scatter among subscale scores. For example, his score on Vocabulary was 12 (above average) while his score on Block Design was just 5 (far below average). As with ADD, his freedom from distractibility score was poor, as was his processing speed. Although his performance on the WISC-III was highly variable, there were no peculiarities or disordered responses that might indicate severe problems in thinking.

Justin produced an MMPI-A of questionable validity: he endorsed a large number of unusual experiences. This can reflect an effort to impress upon the examiner the depth of his plight or it can reflect actual confusion, thought disorder, or serious pathology. Clinical scale elevations suggested depression, anger and resentment, paranoid ideation, and possibly thought disorder. In short, he reported an array of psychopathology that appears to reflect what we knew about Justin. The Rorschach was more revealing, and there was considerable evidence for formal thought disorder. Thus, when the stimuli were unstructured and ambiguous, the quality of Justin's thoughts deteriorated markedly. This combination—no sign of thought disorder on structured tests like the WISC-III and cognitive slippage on the projective tests—is the hallmark of severe personality disorders such as borderline personality.

The array of psychiatric symptomatology Justin presented is being seen with increasing frequency in juvenile correctional settings—patterns of serious antisocial behavior in youths who also meet diagnostic criteria for multiple psychiatric disorders. Many of these disorders overlap. Justin had been abused, and he showed some of the signs of PTSD. But PTSD symptoms and histories of abuse are common in another condition he met the criteria for—borderline personality disorder (BPD). BPD, in turn, involves emotional instability and intense anger as well as self-destructive behavior (depression). Justin's possible ADD also can be mimicked by posttrauma conditions. Abused children often are unable to focus their attention normally, and they frequently are impulsive, aggressive, and generally unmodulated.

In cases like Justin, involving a dense history of antisocial and self-destructive behaviors, along with numerous psychiatric symptoms, it is impossible to disentangle all the strands of pathology. In practice, we often cannot confidently specify which disorder is primary and which is secondary. What is clear, however, is the substantial treatment regimen that will be necessary if he is to overcome even part of the psychopathology. Such youths must be securely held in a highly structured treatment setting that ensures abstinence from drugs and alcohol and the provision of psychiatric and behavioral services. If a youth needs medication to help control impulses and to advance in school, then he must not be running away, he must not be using other drugs, and he must not be exposed to physical assaults or exceptional stresses. He needs a highly predictable program of behavioral contingencies with clear expectations for progressing, for gaining rewards, and for moving forward in life.

EVALUATIONS FOR LEGAL PURPOSES

Some psychological evaluations of antisocial youths are conducted for the purpose of helping to answer legal questions. Forensic evaluations do not carry the clinical aim of understanding the nature and source of a given youth's antisocial behavior, but instead focus narrowly on specific legal issues such as competency to stand trial, legal capacity, and the question of waiver to adult court for trial. Some of the same methods are used, but there is less exploration of personality attributes and personal history. Two of the more common types of juvenile forensic evaluations will be reviewed.

In the legal context, it is well to bear in mind that the examiner (psychologist or psychiatrist) does not make the ultimate decision about legal questions. Instead, the examiner provides relevant information for the trier of fact—the judge or jury. Hence, as Melton (1994) states, evaluators should not offer—nor should courts seek—

conclusory opinions about ultimate legal issues. For example, for the question about competency to stand trial, the examiner might provide the court with salient information about a youth's cognitive and communicative capacities, but would not render a final conclusion about whether or not the defendant is competent. In practice, however, courts do request experts' conclusions about those ultimate issues and examiners often comply.

Competency to Stand Trial

No individual can be tried, convicted, or sentenced for a crime if he is not able to understand the nature of the proceedings against him (trial) and to assist his attorney in the preparation of his defense. This is a fundamental right, guaranteed under the U.S. Constitution (*Drope v. Missouri* 1975). The legal standard for competence to stand trial was delineated in the case *Dusky v. United States* (1960). The pivotal question there was "whether the defendant has sufficient present ability to consult with his lawyer with a reasonable degree of rational understanding—and whether he has a rational as well as factual understanding of the proceedings against him" (p. 402). In adult cases, the issue of competency usually is raised by the defendant's attorney, often after difficulties in communication arise. If the attorney suspects that a mental illness or cognitive limitation exists, she may request that a competency evaluation be performed. When the question of competency arises, the court must decide—after reviewing the clinician's evaluation—whether the defendant lacks the capacity to understand the nature of the proceedings and to assist legal counsel in preparation of the defense.

In general, the courts have found that the threshold for competency is not very high. For example, an individual can be afflicted with a major mental illness and still be found competent, and a defendant can suffer significant cognitive deficits (e.g., mild mental retardation) and still be able sufficiently to assist counsel. In addition, a defendant can be legally insane at the time of an offense and still be competent to stand trial. If, due to mental illness, the defendant is found incompetent, the proceedings must be stayed. However, the defendant may be found competent at a later date if, through treatment or spontaneous improvement, the defendant's mental status is sufficiently improved to meet the standard for competency.

In the case of juveniles, there is an additional factor to consider besides mental disorder or cognitive defect—the developmental line of age and maturity (Grisso 1998). Most courts addressing the issue of competency in juveniles have upheld the *Dusky* standard. However, the age and maturity of the juvenile become significant factors that must be considered along with the question of mental disorder or cognitive limitation (Heilbrun et al. 1996). Presumably, a normal 9-year-old would be less likely to meet criteria for competency than a normal 12-year-old. Add to that developmental consideration the occurrence of cognitive deficits or psychiatric disorder, and the likelihood of legal incompetence rises considerably.

Evaluation for competency to stand trial need not entail elaborate or sophisticated psychological assessment and analysis. The focus is primarily cognitive. Are there cognitive deficits that would preclude the youth's understanding the proceedings or communicating effectively with her attorney? If there are cognitive deficits— for example, a low IQ in a 10-year-old boy—can he understand the purpose of a trial, the role of judge, defense and prosecuting attorney, the meaning of evidence, the possibility of punishment if found guilty? These questions about the mechanics and functioning of the court are often used to test for competency. If there is a mental illness, can the youth, through the use of medications or other treatment, understand and communicate sufficiently for trial to be fair?

Some efforts have been made to develop standardized tests to assess for competency to stand trial (Grisso 1986, Lipsitt et al. 1971). However, an examiner can garner richer data through standard intelligence tests (and subtests) and inquiry that reveals the youth's ability to understand those fundamental structures and processes involved in trial.

Waiver to Adult Court

Almost from its inception, the juvenile courts have had to grapple with the question of where to draw the line beyond which juveniles are sent to adult court for trial. The upper age limit of juvenile court jurisdiction is set by the states. For the majority of states, the upper age limit is 17, but for several states the age limit is 16, and for a few it is 15. The question of whether jurisdiction should be in juvenile court or adult court also turns on the kind of crime the youth is charged with. Depending on the alleged crime, the age of the defendant, and his criminal history, the prosecutor may seek to waive jurisdiction to adult (criminal) court for trial. In cases where the crime is especially violent or dangerous, the juvenile court's premise of "the best interests of the child" takes a back seat to public safety. In many states, legislative mandates automatically transfer to adult court cases involving especially violent crimes such as murder and rape.

Beginning in the 1980s, with the worry about being "soft on crime," the rate at which juveniles were transferred to adult court has escalated. From 1989 to 1993, the number of cases waived to adult court increased by 41 percent (Snyder et al. 1996). The implications of transfer to adult court are enormous for the juvenile and his family and for the community. Once in adult court, there is no longer any presumption of the court acting as the "kind and just parent." The "best interests of the child" is irrelevant. Moreover, sentences can be harsher (though not always). If found guilty in juvenile court, the longest sentence in most cases cannot extend beyond the age of 18 or, in some states, 21. If found guilty in criminal court, however, the sentence could be decades, or life, or even capital punishment. Some states disallow the death penalty before the age of 18, but many do allow it for crimes committed at age 16 or 17. Recently a bill was introduced in the Texas legislature to allow capital punishment down to age 11! Imposition of the death penalty in juvenile cases, however, has been rare, and many death sentences for juveniles have been reversed (Snyder and Sickmund 1995).

The state of Arkansas faced a wrenching dilemma in 1998 when two boys, aged 11 and 13, systematically murdered five middle-school students with high-powered rifles and wounded many others. Under existing Arkansas law, because of their age these boys cannot be waived to adult court for trial. Because the trial must take place in juvenile court, the maximum sentence they could receive if convicted is incarceration until the age of 18, at which time they have to be set free. Because state laws cannot be applied retroactively, there seems little that anyone can do. When they turn 18, these two boys will be free to walk into their local gun store and legally purchase firearms.

Because there is so much at stake in waiver to adult court, the issue frequently becomes highly contentious. A U.S. Supreme Court decision provided a set of guidelines that are applied in determining whether to waive jurisdiction to adult court (that is, in cases not legislatively waived). In 1961, while on probation for other offenses, Morris Kent, 16 at the time, was charged with rape and robbery. The juvenile court judge waived jurisdiction to adult court where Kent was tried, convicted, and sentenced to 30 to 90 years in prison. Kent's lawyer challenged the waiver. After the appeal was turned down by an appellate court, the case was appealed to the Supreme Court. The Court ruled, in *Kent v. United States* (1966), that the waiver had been invalid and stated that Kent was entitled to "the essentials of due process and fair treatment." The Court ruled further that the juvenile court judge should have provided a written statement of the reasons for the waiver.

The Court also provided guidelines for deciding questions of waiver to adult court. These became known as the Kent criteria (Grisso 1998) and include eight factors, such as the seriousness of the charge, whether community safety requires waiver, and the record and previous history of the juvenile. Two of the eight Kent criteria involve matters upon which psychological evaluation directly bears. First is the question of the sophistication and maturity of the juvenile. Juveniles who appear to be more mature and sophisticated in their antisocial ways are more likely to be waived than juveniles who seem more childlike in their demeanor. Second is the prospect for adequate protection for the public and the likelihood of reasonable rehabilitation of the juvenile in currently available services. This involves assessment of the juvenile's antisocial character and other relevant factors (openness to treatment), and a prediction of how likely it is that she will be rehabilitated versus being violent again in the future (always a difficult call).

Treatment of
Antisocial Youth *

The treatment of antisocial behavior is a modern endeavor. As late as the nineteenth century, antisocial individuals were viewed for the most part as innately inferior, as constitutionally defective in the moral faculties. Society's response to such troublesome characters followed from that biblical principle of an eye for an eye—punishment or banishment from society. The aims of punishment were simple—retribution and keeping society safe from the moral defectives (deterrence).

By the early twentieth century, the emergence of modern schools of psychology fueled the development of a whole new set of responses to those who disregard the laws and terrorize the citizenry. Sigmund Freud's psychoanalysis, and earlier investigators such as Pierre Janet, provided new insights into the powerful effects that early experience can have on later behavior. Equally portentous for the matter of antisocial behavior was the development of behavioral psychology—the law of effect and behavioral conditioning. Today, we take for granted the potent and often lasting effects

---

*This chapter was prepared by Lisa Boesky, Ph.D., and Delton Young, Ph.D.

of selective reinforcement and modeling of behaviors. But in the early part of the century it was a revolutionary idea that such forms of conditioning could so radically shape behavior.

Psychiatrist August Aichhorn gave a boost to the clinical principle of "treating" antisocial behavior with the 1925 publication of his classic, *Wayward Youth*. This book described the treatment of what we would today call "neurotic delinquents"—basically unhappy, neglected, and abused kids who were often responsive to a benevolent but firm therapeutic approach. It was recognized that many such delinquents had not been adequately socialized. Other social institutions were also beginning to reflect the newer thinking about the malleability of behavior, including antisocial behavior. The first juvenile court was founded in Chicago in 1899, and by 1925 special courts for children and adolescents had been established in all but two states. (For a rich discussion of the history and current dilemmas of the juvenile court in the United States, see William Ayers 1997.) The juvenile court was envisioned by its founder, Jane Addams, to function as "a kind and just parent." That is, the court would act in the "best interest of the child." The original juvenile court was promoted as a clinic that would "treat" the youngster and "cure the corruption." These reformers believed that by applying the principles of modern social sciences, the roots of delinquency could be discovered and the right interventions could correct the untoward habits. As Ayers (1997) put it, "Influenced by the efficiency of child-study movements, and the growth of modern sociology and psychology, the watchword was treatment, not retribution" (p. 25).

Following from these developments in the early part of the century, most of our institutions now reflect at least the *idea* of treatment and rehabilitation. Today, many delinquents are sent to correctional institutions or to training schools, and we have departments of rehabilitation. Numerous forms of treatment are applied even to the most violent and dangerous young offenders. The most sophisticated methods of psychological research and treatment are brought to bear on the problems of young people who are developing or overcoming their antisocial habits.

The clinical treatment of antisocial behavior, however, is accompanied by a paradox. Doctors and other clinicians treat illness and affliction. Even in the psychiatric realm, psychiatrists and psychologists diagnose and treat afflictions that are almost universally unwelcome by the patient—depression, anxiety, neurosis, and so on. But the majority of antisocial individuals do not feel afflicted. It is society that is afflicted. If there is a conflict, it is not *within* the individual, but *between* the individual and society. In the vast majority of instances of antisocial behavior, the perpetrator knew what he was doing, was at least briefly planful, and meant to do what he did. The diagnoses of conduct disorder, antisocial personality disorder, and oppositional defiant disorder are purely descriptive behavioral labels and do not imply an inability to reason, to plan, or to carry out one's intentions. In some sectors of modern society, therefore, treatment of antisocial offenders is seen as peculiar, especially as society feels increasingly burdened and terrorized by the actions of the few. The emphasis in recent years has backed away from treatment and toward community protection and deterrence (i.e., imprisonment). The special provisions for juveniles have partially eroded. For example, increasing numbers of youth are tried for crimes in adult court, and adult punishments are meted out.*

The traditional medical model of illness and treatment has not, by itself, been very effective in dealing with the antisocial charac-

---

*Between the years 1984 and 1990, the number of cases judicially waived to adult court increased by 78 percent (Office of Juvenile Justice and Delinquency Prevention 1993), and that number continues to climb. Juveniles waived to adult court do not necessarily receive lengthier sentences. Snyder and Sickmund (1995) report that "transferring serious juvenile offenders to the criminal (adult) justice system does not appreciably increase the certainty or severity of sanctions" (p. 156). There are exceptions, however, as in the case of juveniles convicted of murder. If they are convicted of murder in adult court the maximum sentence can be life in prison, whereas if they are convicted in juvenile court, they could be committed to prison only until their twenty-first birthday in most states.

ter, because this disorder is not well accounted for as an affliction within the individual. Treatment methods that focus solely upon individual matters of emotion, personality, and cognition have not fared well. To be effective, treatment programs must move beyond the traditional model of individual illness and treatment to include family, school, community, and other social milieu factors.

There now are comprehensive, community-based treatment programs that are effective with the majority of antisocial youths. Such programs integrate the treatment of individual attributes—attitudes, personality traits, skills, and defenses—with social factors such as family functioning, school support, and community stability.

CLINICAL MYOPIA

Considerable gains have been made in the treatment of the antisocial character. In clinical practice, however, as in most of the behavioral sciences, our perspective is limited by our methods and by our training. In the case of antisocial behavior, perhaps more than any other "disorder," the problem behaviors can be fully understood only in a broad social and political context. A clinical focus solely on the individual delinquent—while it is a practical place to begin—will miss some of the most potent factors directly implicated in antisocial behaviors.

Perhaps the most glaring example of such societal factors is that involving gun violence. We clinicians can apply our newest methods for treating perpetrators of gun violence; we can treat the family and mobilize resources. We can examine the youth's background and find the neglect, the poor modeling, the violent neighborhood; we can prescribe group treatments, family therapy, perhaps even some medications. We can make some improvements in some cases. But if our aim is to reduce gun violence, then all these clinical measures will be of limited help, because we are not addressing the political and economic factors that contribute directly to the problem.

The rate of murder in the United States is many times higher than in any other Western nation, and the factor that accounts for that wild disparity is the easy availability of handguns. Criminologist Frank Zimring (1995) reported that the rate at which serious assaults occur in the United States is only about 30 percent greater than in England, yet the homicide rate is 530 percent greater! Roughly 80 percent of juvenile homicides involve firearms, the vast majority of them being handguns (FBI 1992). (For a full discussion of the research on handgun violence, see Berkowitz 1994.) In another study, Sloan and colleagues (1988) compared the number of gun-related murders in Seattle and Vancouver, B.C.—two cities that are similar in size, income, and employment levels. What distinguishes the two cities is the availability of handguns. In Seattle handguns are readily available, and in Vancouver there are tight restrictions on handguns. The rate at which citizens were murdered by guns was about five times higher in Seattle. This figure contrasts with the rate of killings involving knives (assumed to be equally available in both cities). The Seattle to Vancouver ratio for knife-related killings was just 3.5 to 3.1. Criminologist Alfred Blumstein (1995) points out that while billions of dollars are spent annually in an attempt to stem the drug trade, almost nothing is spent to stem the trade in illegal handguns.

One of the strongest statistical predictors of antisocial violence is poverty. One researcher, Mike Males, from the University of California, Irvine, goes so far as to argue that poverty, more than any other variable, predicts violent crime in this society at this historical period. He points out that murder rates are always higher when poverty is more prevalent, both geographically and historically. For example, murder rates during the Great Depression skyrocketed, peaking in 1933 at 9.7 murders per 100,000—slightly *higher* than the alarming 1993 peak of 9.5 murders per 100,000 (Ayers 1997). Poverty, by itself, is not a cause of crime. However, in late twentieth century America, poverty exacerbates many of the social and economic conditions that undermine family and community health (see Chapter 8).

There is not much of practical value that a doctor or a teacher or a probation officer can do about such broad social and economic forces beyond the same civic actions that all citizens have available—to speak out, to vote, to try to educate their fellows. Clinicians will treat delinquents and their families; teachers will try to equip young offenders will some of the tools needed to live within society; probation officers and judges will attempt to instill respect for the law and social order. However, there also is a duty to bear in mind the potent effects of fractured communities, of poverty and underfunded schools, of unremitting media violence, and of the easy availability of handguns. As the prominent theorist Alan Kazdin (1994) put it, "It would be an unfortunate consequence . . . if promising interventions inadvertently diverted attention from other factors in society that might be altered on a larger scale in an effort to reduce aggression and antisocial behavior" (p. 376).

Bearing in mind what Kazdin calls the "social matrix in which aggression and violence are accepted" enables us to resist the current pressures toward dehumanization of young offenders. There is no shortage in recent years of newspaper columnists, talk-show hosts, and even social scientists who are willing to whip public opinion into a frenzy over juvenile crime. Hyperbolic images of "wolf pack" kids or "superpredators" distort the problem of antisocial youths into an hysterical and pernicious image (Ayers 1997). This brings us to the crux of the matter: If our clinical approach focuses only upon the individual—his bad attitudes, poor social skills, and perhaps his "bad genes"—and if we fail to note the effects of poverty, of poor schools, and of fractured communities, then we make room for the most pernicious belief of all—that antisocial behaviors are a natural outcome for these (inherently bad) persons. Political and economic factors are let off the hook as we attribute bad outcomes solely to "bad people."

None of this is meant to let the individual offender off the hook, either. The individual must be held fully accountable for his antisocial acts, and blaming the "system" or poverty or media violence only defers coming to terms with his own attitudes and prospects for the future. We know that failing to hold an offender accountable only leads to more trouble. At the same time, however, we also know that for any given community, social and economic conditions can powerfully affect the incidence of criminal behavior. Intellectual honesty demands, therefore, that as we go about holding young offenders accountable and sending them for treatment, we bear in mind the conditions that predispose large numbers of modern youth to engage in antisocial behavior.

TREATMENT BROADLY CONSIDERED

It should be clear now that we cannot adequately understand antisocial behavior without a grasp of the disparate causal factors ranging from genetics and temperament to a host of socialization practices. Similarly, treatment of antisocial behavior cannot be limited to the traditional list of clinical interventions—the various therapies and medications. Effective treatment must be seen in its broadest possible array. Treatment of antisocial behavior is defined, for purposes here, as any planful intervention designed to alter behavior patterns in desirable directions. This would include not only traditional clinical interventions, but also interventions not ordinarily found on a list of clinical treatments—interventions such as police arrest, altered school assignment, prosecution in juvenile court, a stay in juvenile detention, probation, community service, or commitment to a correctional institution. Nonclinical interventions, such as being arrested or being held in detention, can be examined in the same ways that we might study a particular form of psychotherapy or a medication. There is no reason, a priori, to assume that arrest or detention would be a less effective intervention than clinical therapies.

Nonclinical interventions—whether they be school suspension, police arrest, or incarceration—have been built into our social institutions since long before the first psychiatrist came upon the scene. These institutional responses are triggered by behaviors that violate the limits of what each institution can tolerate. Repeated disruption at school leads to suspension. Endangering other students leads to expulsion. Assault or robbery leads to arrest; and repeating such actions leads to lengthy incarceration. No clinician is needed to set these institutional interventions into motion.

The various levels of institutional response define a rough hierarchy of severity in antisocial development. Commitment to a corrections facility, for example, is applied in cases of severe and usually repetitive criminal activity; but such commitment would be inappropriate for a girl whose crime was shoplifting costume jewelry. Similarly, a boy whose antisocial proclivities involve defiance toward teachers might be a good candidate for suspension, but he would not be subjected to expulsion or arrest.

Most clinical interventions, on the other hand, can be appropriately applied at any level of severity of antisocial development. The appropriateness of family therapy, for example, is determined by the resources the family can bring to bear on a youth's behavior and attitudes. Family therapy might be crucial in turning around a 13-year-old girl whose transgressions have not yet led to police involvement, but it might also be key in helping an 18-year-old boy make the transition from an eight-month commitment to corrections (prison) back into the community. Other clinical treatments, such as medications and psychotherapy, similarly can be applied.

EARLY INTERVENTION AND PREVENTION

There is a hierarchy in the depth of a youth's involvement in antisocial behavior, a hierarchy defined by the kinds of institutional interventions his behavior has triggered. This section discusses this hierarchy, along with clinical treatments. Throughout this discussion of treatments, one constant is the importance of early intervention. Antisocial behavior is not something that a child is born with, nor does it spring out of nowhere. Rather, the attitudes and habits that support serious antisocial behavior develop over time, beginning in childhood and deepening through the adolescent years, if left unchecked. The worst thing that can happen is for early habits of aggression or exploitation or dishonesty to go unaddressed. Serious problem behaviors do not occur in random fashion, but are almost always preceded by lighter forms of antisocial behavior (Loeber 1991). It is less important that the response from adults be just right than that there be some response that clearly labels such behavior unacceptable. The importance of early intervention is demonstrated by the research (reviewed in Chapter 4) showing that antisocial careers that begin by age 10 or 12, when left untreated, are far more likely to persist into adulthood (Farrington et al. 1986).

The value of early intervention is underscored by the success of some *prevention* programs—efforts aimed at curbing the development of antisocial habits and behaviors in children who are at risk—even including targeting children in utero, through ongoing assistance to the mother and family (Lally et al. 1988). School-based and family-based prevention programs have repeatedly demonstrated reductions in problem behaviors in long-term follow-up (e.g., Hawkins et al. 1991).

Most Youths Who Engage in Antisocial Behavior Are Never Arrested

A majority of youths engage in some antisocial acts during childhood and adolescence. This might involve bullying a peer, cheating on a test, stealing a candy bar, or trying some marijuana. The majority of such acts are relatively isolated incidents that do not presage an antisocial career, but are better understood as experimentation. In some locales, a pattern of delinquent acts (acts that would be considered a crime if committed by an adult) is almost normative during the adolescent years. Many youths experiment with such misbehavior, then proceed to more productive endeavors. Only a subset of children and adolescents who misbehave in these ways get caught. When a youth is caught by school authorities, by parents, or by others in the community, it usually is after a series of such antisocial acts has been committed. In those cases where a boy has developed a habit of threatening or assaulting peers, where a girl comes to rely on cheating on tests, or where she regularly smokes marijuana between classes, then it is best that these acts trigger some response from adults. In cases where there is no response forthcoming, the youth may read this as implicit approval. When antisocial behavior becomes more than an isolated incident, it is imperative that a response be generated.

By middle childhood, school has become the principal agent for socialization. The expectations increase dramatically during these years for the child to be able to get along with peers, to learn from and be respectful toward teachers and other authority figures, and to strengthen individual skills of self-knowledge, reflection, and self-restraint. The "contract" between parents and schools is for the school to educate the child in academic subjects, but the school staff also promotes the social skills and the self-control of children. In recent years, the expectations placed on the schools have expanded in many cases to include meeting even basic health and nutritional needs. In short, schools have been expected to take over many of the most fundamental functions that used to be performed by parents and others in the child's community.

The school's ability to work effectively with this broad range of expectations is predicated upon a basic level of cooperation by the child and her parents. Antisocial behavior constitutes one of the severest challenges to the school's mission. With well trained teachers and savvy administrators, the school is well positioned to deal with children's antisocial proclivities—up to a point. Basic respect for peers and for authority, normal self-restraint and reflection, social problem-solving skills—all these are matters that schools deal with effectively every day. However, when the antisocial actions exceed the range of skills that the school can educate the child in, when the behaviors undermine the mission of the school and disrupt the education of other children, then some action must be taken to re-align the child and her parents with the mission of the school.

A variety of alternative school assignments are available. Through special education services, for example, many districts operate "behavior disorder" classes—self-contained classrooms with a high teacher–student ratio and specially trained teachers who work closely with parents, doctors, and administrators. Many children and adolescents with behavior problems—some of which may be antisocial—flourish in the high structure and high-attention setting of behavior disorder (BD) or severe behavior disorder (SBD) classrooms. Whereas such difficult children may have been on a downward spiral in a regular classroom, learning little in academics or in social skills, the SBD classroom can provide a setting in which learning can resume and the child can avoid descending further into poor self-esteem and identification with deviant peers.

Alternative high schools and middle schools provide a whole-school setting for older children and adolescents where amended schedules and expectations can allow continued success. Serious antisocial behavior, of course, is no more acceptable in alternative schools than in regular schools. However, many youths whose behavior difficulties involve some antisocial acts can make use of alternative schools to continue their education when they clearly would not have succeeded in regular school. Administrators in alternative schools also are often astute in detecting antisocial attitudes and behaviors that need to be addressed.

Schools often find themselves in a dilemma when a student's antisocial behavior appears to exceed the range of what the school should deal with. At what point do school authorities conclude that a certain behavior is beyond their purview? At what point is it better for the youth to be dealt with by police and courts than by school administrators and parents?

Anthony's seventh grade year had been difficult by any measure. His commitment to schoolwork had fallen off and his grades were failing (despite good intelligence); he had twice been suspended for open defiance and verbal abuse of teachers; and he had apparently initiated a fight with another boy, leading to a third suspension and meetings with the parents. In April, just a half hour after school let out, another middle-school boy returned to the school building, holding his face in his hands, and walked directly to the office. His face was bloody, with bruised and lacerated lips and eyes. He was in tears, and it took awhile before he could relate that Anthony had attacked him on the sidewalk just two blocks from the school. He was dizzy and an aid car was called to take him to the emergency room.

Investigation by school administrators determined that Anthony, angry over the boy's remarks to another peer that day, had punched the boy in the face, then, with the boy on the sidewalk, had kicked him several times in the head and face. The incident was handled by school authorities because it occurred on the way to or from school grounds; the police were never contacted. Anthony was put on "emergency expulsion" and was then suspended for a total of 11 days. A few weeks later, Anthony was arrested at a video arcade, jailed at the detention hall, and charged with second-degree assault for attacking another boy with a heavy stick. The prosecutor wondered aloud whether Anthony might have been better off being arrested and charged with the assault on the boy near school. As it turned out over ensuing months, Anthony did respond to the larger authority of the juvenile court. He ceased his pattern of indulging his anger and attacking others.

The majority of young people whose misbehavior leads to adult sanctions (e.g., by school, by parents) are never arrested. This is for the good reason that those lesser sanctions are often sufficient. If parents must take off days from work in order to supervise their child during his suspension from school, they become highly motivated to modify the boy's behavior. Parents may find ways to work together more vigorously than previously. Meetings with the school may yield clearer sets of limits and consequences, and parents may be more vigilant about enforcement this time around. The grounding, the loss of privileges, the parents' scorn—all these can amount to a considerable force for many youths who have been dabbling in antisocial behaviors.

Most Juveniles Who Are Arrested Are Never Arrested Again

The majority of antisocial behaviors are handled informally by family, school staff, neighbors, and others, and for the most part such interventions help the child to become more responsible and respectful. When a youth's behaviors exceed the capacity of such informal mechanisms, when danger to self or others is apparent, then arrest can be the result. When a youth is arrested, he is confronted not by some adults he already knows, adults who presumably love and care for him, but rather by the impersonal agents of society at large—the police. This can represent a profound step for many youths and their families. The appearance of a police officer at the door is a clear signal that events have become serious. Whatever minimization and denial the parents may have indulged in often evaporates as they comply with the officer's investigation into a possible crime. For the juvenile, too, while he may claim that he is being treated unfairly, it is clear as he listens to his Miranda Rights that he is in a whole new ball game. For some youths, this may be a kind of initiation into the lifestyle they have anticipated for some time. For others, it is a brutal realization that they have been on the wrong track and that things will have to change.

Studies in several states have shown that of all juveniles referred for the first time to juvenile court, only about two in five return for another referral (Snyder and Sickmund 1995). If we take such arrest or referral to court as a form of treatment, then these data appear to represent a respectable success rate. Many established therapeutic methods have success rates no better than about 60 percent.

Molly and Andrea, both 13, had been sharpening their shoplifting skills for several months, stealing mostly candy and makeup from local drug stores, and their confidence was building. They began to steal larger and more expensive items such as clothing and costume jewelry from the larger department stores. Finally, they were caught on camera taking several shirts. Store security handcuffed the girls and paraded them through the store to the security office. Two police officers arrived and talked sternly about a future behind bars if such behavior were to continue. The girls' parents were not at home, so they were transported to the local police station in the squad car. They were held for several hours and were exposed to intoxicated and intimidating adults who were being held in a nearby jail cell. Both girls cried almost the entire time. When their parents arrived, they swore they would never steal anything again, and by all accounts they never did. They were not prosecuted and did not have to go to court.

Many adults who have been living healthy and productive lives can tell tales of adolescent misadventures that led to arrest. The typical comment is, "I really learned my lesson."

Juvenile Court

Roughly two-thirds of juveniles who are arrested are referred to juvenile court. In many cases, such as the girls described above, the case is handled within the police department and there is no referral to court and no prosecution. There may or may not be any time in detention, depending on the nature of the alleged crime, the youth's history of police contacts, the appearance of remorse, and the family's response.

For the two-thirds of arrested juveniles who are referred to juvenile court, there are several possible routes their cases may take and several choice points along the way: the case may be diverted out of the justice system by law enforcement and/or the prosecutor; it may go through formal court intake procedures (by the probation department and/or the prosecutor); it may be handled informally (e.g., restitution, probation, community service) or dismissed (for lack of evidence); it may be *waived* to adult court;

or it may be processed formally and proceed to prosecution and adjudication.

Diversion

The aim of diversion programs is to target mildly antisocial youths and first-time offenders to prevent the development of more serious and chronic delinquent behavior while avoiding formal processing through the juvenile justice system. A variety of social services are usually available to the youth and his family with the intention of addressing the issues thought to contribute to the youth's antisocial behavior. The most common referral is for individual or family counseling. Unfortunately, many families of antisocial youths do not follow through on treatment referrals or they stop treatment prematurely, resulting in little change in the youths' behavior. Evaluations of diversion programs have not shown this to be an effective treatment strategy. This is likely due to the vague treatment referrals, the lack of monitoring, and early termination.

Restitution

As part of an informal handling of a case or of a diversion agreement, the youth may be required to compensate the victim for losses the youth has caused. This can mean monetary reimbursement or performing some useful service for the victim. Some offenders may be required to perform community service (volunteer work) such as cleanup of roadsides or parks, or tutoring younger children. Restitution has a logical appeal, and judges can be creative in making restitution arrangements. It is unclear just how effective restitution is as a treatment for antisocial behavior because good research data are not available. However, it carries a strong appeal and there surely are cases in which restitution makes good sense, and it probably will continue to serve as one component in efforts to alter antisocial behaviors.

Prosecution

The process of being prosecuted for a crime can extend over many months. It can involve numerous meetings with the lawyer and the parents, hearings in court, and plenty of time to consider possible punishments if found guilty. The youth may be held in detention awaiting trial, or he may be living at home under probation. The court may mandate certain conditions for the youth's remaining out of detention, such as school attendance and curfews. During this long process, there are countless opportunities for the youth and his family to reflect upon the trajectory he has been on—if they are able to do so. In many instances, the focus on the legalities and the lawyers may distract from the more important work of coming to terms with one's attitudes and patterns of behavior. But when arrest and the ominous events involved in prosecution do break through the wall of denial and angry rejection, there can be a grand opportunity for some psychological change. For some youths in this predicament, therefore, a referral to individual and/or family counseling can be most useful.

Because the process of prosecution can vary so dramatically from one case to the next, systematic study of its efficacy as a treatment modality is impossible. There can be little doubt, however, that for some juveniles and their families, prosecution is a powerful corrective experience. As with other data on the trajectories of antisocial behavior, the age of onset and the number of referrals for prosecution strongly predict which youths are likely to benefit from this treatment and which are not. Youths on their fifth prosecution at age 16 are far less likely to benefit than are youths of the same age who are on their first such prosecution. This is not to say that youths who have been prosecuted several times cannot make good use of the experience. There surely are some individuals and families, now facing likely commitment to corrections, who finally do come to terms with how they have lived their lives and who make serious resolves to do things differently. In some cases, prosecution and commitment enable the youth finally to overcome a dependence on drugs and alcohol, then to change course in school and work.

Probation

Young offenders may be placed on community supervision (probation) for a specified period of time. They can reside at their own home and attend their own school, but remain under the supervision of the court. There usually are restrictions placed on their behavior, and violation of those conditions (e.g., school truancy, drug use, rearrest) may lead to more time in juvenile detention. This can be a strong motivating factor to stay clear of illegal behavior, at least for the period of supervision. Most probation officers (sometimes termed probation counselors) carry an unrealistically large caseload. It would be naive to think that a probation officer meeting with a youth once a month or sporadically monitoring a youth's behavior will have a significant effect on an antisocial youth's lifestyle. In fact, some studies have shown that probation is similar to not receiving any treatment at all (Lipsey 1992), because checking in with the probation officer is so infrequent that some youths are willing to take the risk and continue to use drugs and engage in criminal behavior, hoping they will not get caught. It is critical that the youth's family talk with the probation officer and involve themselves with the probation process. Families should assist in monitoring the youth and assist their child in complying with probation requirements if necessary (e.g., drive them to substance abuse treatment, remove alcohol from the house, monitor school attendance).

There are several treatment-oriented interventions that are frequently mandated by the juvenile court, such as referral to mentoring, alternative schooling, wilderness programs, social skills training, and anger management. Each of these treatments can be useful at any level—for juveniles who have never been arrested, for those under the authority of the court, even for those who have been committed to corrections. Because these interventions are commonly mandated by the court, they will be reviewed here.

Referral to a Mentoring Program

Mentors are typically trusted volunteers (adults or college students) from the youth's community who spend time with the youth and offer encouragement and support, while serving as a positive role model. Mentors assist youths in setting and accomplishing goals in education, vocation, and living an alcohol- and drug-free lifestyle. Mentors usually encourage youths by sharing their own personal goals and experiences, and help youths develop realistic beliefs and standards for their behavior. Prosocial adult role models can have a positive influence on a youth's development, especially a youth at high risk for delinquent behavior. Research thus far has been unable to demonstrate the positive effects of mentors on more chronic antisocial youths (Office of Juvenile Justice and Delinquency Prevention 1995). For them, mentoring may be an effective component of a more comprehensive treatment intervention, but not sufficient when provided as the only treatment component.

Referral to Alternative Schooling

Many antisocial youths have had repeated difficulty in public school. Due to repeated incidents of truancy or disruptive behavior, some youths have been suspended or expelled and are not allowed to return to their local school. If truancy is a prominent difficulty, the judge may order the youth to attend a different type of educational program. Home schooling is an option for youths who require the constant supervision of their parent(s). Parents serve as teachers; schooling takes place in the family home, and the youth can receive credits toward graduation. However, the majority of parents of antisocial youths do not have the time or desire to undertake such an arduous task. The parent–child relationship may not be able to withstand the hours and stress related to schooling a child at home. Contract schooling is more common than home schooling for antisocial youths. Contract schooling involves having a certified teacher from the school come to the youth's home for a few hours per week, working with the youth and providing additional assignments to complete individually. The youth may not take classes at the actual school building, but his work is regularly checked and monitored.

Although many youths prefer their education at home (e.g., not having to get up as early, less structure, no interpersonal conflict), this type of schooling can be counterproductive. Antisocial youths typically need a great deal of monitoring and support in order to complete their schoolwork. Without the structure of the school environment they tend to go through their academic assignments quickly and sloppily, resulting in an increase of unstructured free time. Schooling in the home environment also deprives the youths of opportunities to interact with prosocial peers and increase their social skills. Although less stressful for the youths in the short-term, home-based education can reinforce feelings of alienation and of being different from others.

Alternative high school programs are designed for adolescents who have been unsuccessful in the regular public school system. These programs offer a more activities/project-based educational experience than traditional high school programs. There are fewer students per classroom in alternative schools and each student has an individualized education contract that takes into account his particular academic strengths and weaknesses. Students can earn regular school credits and work toward obtaining a high school diploma or take general equivalency diploma (GED) preparatory courses.

Although earning educational credits is one goal of alternative school programs, there is an overarching goal of helping students identify areas of personal interest and use their innate curiosity and creativity to make the learning process more personal. A typical school day would involve individual work on a core curriculum (e.g., English, American history, mathematics), followed by a group format where time is devoted to interactive projects, field trips, goal setting, and guest speakers. Many alternative school programs offer a variety of experiential educational experiences including having the youths participate in a challenge (ropes) course involving physical activity.

A student must earn a minimum number of school credits to be eligible for graduation. Many antisocial youths are lacking credits due to missing classes or dropping out of school for a while. Alternative school programs can help many such students become re-involved with the educational system and work toward graduation. For some, the individualized, hands-on, experiential programming of alternative schools is the hook that keeps them from dropping out of school entirely. Furthermore, some students report that alternative schools provide their only opportunity for emotional and creative expression in a safe and contained environment. Many alternative schools have strict attendance requirements and zero-tolerance policies regarding antisocial behavior on campus. Alternative schools often serve as "last chance" opportunities, and if a student is expelled from an alternative school, she is unlikely to return anytime soon to an academic setting, which raises the odds or drifting deeper into a deviant lifestyle.

Some alternative school programs devote classroom time to issues such as conflict resolution, social and communication skills, and alcohol and drug education, and they often work closely with mental health and chemical dependency treatment facilities. In some cases, psychiatric and substance abuse treatment goals are integrated into the youth's educational program.

Referral to Wilderness Programs

These programs typically remove a youth from his natural environment and place him in a novel and challenging wilderness setting. Personal growth and group bonding can result from an emphasis on achieving individual and group goals in difficult and challenging circumstances. Wilderness programs are typically highly structured two- to four-week programs that focus on helping youths identify personal strengths and goals; they are encouraged to reevaluate personal responsibility to family members and others. There are often group wilderness expeditions, a solo experience, and other outdoor programs. They typically include a great deal of journal writing and group problem-solving activities as well.

Many antisocial youths and their family members report positive changes in the youth's beliefs and behaviors after returning home from a wilderness program. Reported changes include a decline in drug use, fewer absences from school, and less contact with the juvenile justice system (Shannonhouse 1997). Wilderness programs appear to be effective for youths at the mild end of the antisocial continuum, possibly after their initial brush with the law. Adolescents who still have attachments to family members and the school system can utilize this type of program as a productive "time-out" period for reflection and self-appraisal. It may be particularly helpful for the neurotic type of delinquent, whose antisocial behavior is related to feelings of low self-esteem or a lack of social skills. However, these programs seem to have little lasting impact on more seriously antisocial youths (Mulvey et al. 1993). In addition, wilderness programs are more expensive than most families can afford.

Referral to Anger Management

Anger management programs typically run from six to twelve weeks, and they focus on teaching the youths specific and practical skills to use in situations where they are likely to get angry (Goldstein and Glick 1987). The emphasis is on educating the youths about the physiological and psychological factors underlying their anger and helping them to identify internal cues that can alert them to potential trouble. Attitudes about anger and violence are identified and often challenged by the leader and by group members. The youths are taught new ways to cope with difficult situations, including engaging in new self-statements (e.g., "Hitting that kid will only get me in trouble") and adaptive behaviors (e.g., count to ten, walk away, talk calmly and firmly). Some programs include a relaxation component.

Rather than just talking about new skills, the group models appropriate responses, engages in role plays with the youths, and provides feedback. During role plays, students can play themselves and practice anger management skills. In addition, role plays are often used to help youths understand the perspective of others. When a peer plays the role of the antisocial youth, the others experience firsthand how their own behavior may be impacting those around them.

Anger management programs have had mixed results with antisocial youths. They have been helpful for some youths with regard to better anger control and decreased aggressiveness (Feindler et al. 1986); however, many antisocial youths find this type of treatment contrived and unrealistic. This is especially true for the more serious antisocial youths. They complain that the techniques do not take into account the context of their lives. For example, they have difficulty monitoring their physiological cues, and "walking away" is viewed as being weak and unworthy of respect in some subcultures.

Another obstacle is that many antisocial youths are attached to their anger. In a world where they often feel powerless and out of control, anger lends a sense of power and strength. They often feel they would be weak and vulnerable without it. In addition, anger is often a large part of some antisocial youths' self-identity. It also is a coping mechanism that has helped them survive their family and their neighborhood. Motivation in anger management groups is low among this subset of youths.

Research on anger management training has shown positive results during the period of treatment, but long-term benefits are more elusive. Most youths are able to comply with the demands of a group. But it is much more difficult to help these youths take new anger management skills into their communities and actually change the way they interact with their families or peers.

Referral to Social Skills Training

Antisocial youths often lack the social skills necessary for appropriate and positive interactions with peers, teachers, and potential employers. Antisocial youths may never have learned how to achieve their goals in an adaptive and legitimate manner, and instead learn to manipulate or coerce others as a means of getting what they want (Davis and Boster 1992). Social skills training directly teaches youths the interpersonal skills needed for everyday living, including communication skills and social problem-solving skills. Depending on the environment in which the youths were raised, some will experience this as a reeducation process, while others will be learning these skills for the very first time.

Skills addressed by this type of treatment include social participation (e.g., how to join a group, how to initiate conversation), negotiation, conflict management, compromise, social problem solving, self-control, and communication. Students are taught how to read social cues, how to listen to others, and how to communicate in a give-and-take manner (versus monopolizing the conversation). Treatment is delivered in a concrete and practical manner, utilizing a variety of techniques such as modeling, role playing, feedback, and positive reinforcement. Similar to anger management training, the adult leading the group models appropriate social behavior. A group member is encouraged to role-play with the counselor or with peers, who, in turn, give feedback on how the youth was perceived, where she demonstrated appropriate social skills, and which skills still need work. Between training sessions, the youths are encouraged to practice newly learned social skills with their peers. This type of treatment can be provided in an individual or group format, and in community or residential settings.

Social skills training has been shown to be successful among delinquent youths, particularly during the period they are involved in the training. Antisocial youths who receive this type of treatment often increase their prosocial behavior and decrease their delinquent behavior (Bank et al. 1991), and these positive effects have been observed in both community and residential settings. Unfortunately, after leaving the program, many youths return to their old patterns of behavior. It appears especially difficult for some to generalize the skills learned in training to real-life interactions at home and school.

Serious Crimes or Multiple Arrests Are Likely to Lead to Juvenile Detention

When a youth is charged with a serious offense such as assault with a weapon or sexual assault, or when he has multiple recent arrests, the judge is likely to order that he be held in juvenile detention for a specific period of time. Juvenile detention centers are analogous to adult jail: they are highly secure, with double-locked iron doors, electronic surveillance, and a no-nonsense security staff. Detention is designed for short-term stays, from a few days to a month; however, an individual may remain in detention much longer, awaiting trial on serious charges or awaiting hearings on waiver to adult court. Depending on the county, juvenile detention centers house anywhere from a dozen to 250 youths.

Because of the short length of stay and the rapid turnover of new offenders, most detention centers offer little programming. Instead, they provide a high level of structure, and closely scheduled activities, duties, and meal times. There usually is some form of reward-and-punishment system in place. Youths are rewarded for following the rules, and they often exchange earned points for special privileges. Some facilities provide anger management training, substance abuse groups, and Bible study classes. Most detention centers try to incorporate some form of educational component for the residents, in addition to recreational activities and crafts. All these activities notwithstanding, much of the incarcerated youth's time is spent sitting in a jail cell, left alone with her thoughts, her worries, and her emotions.

Spending time in a juvenile detention facility can be an effective intervention for modifying the behavior of some antisocial youths. However, for adolescents who have only experimented with deviant behavior or for those with a psychiatric disorder, detention can be an especially aversive experience, giving rise to depression, anxiety, and remorse. Individuals are often placed in crowded units with many other juvenile offenders, and some of those other offenders are essentially hardened criminals. The youths are housed in very small cells with none of the conveniences of home. All personal belongings are taken away, including personal clothes. For some, this is the first time anyone has told them when to wake up, when and what to eat, where to go, and what to do. Misbehavior is not tolerated, and consequences for transgression are swift and substantial. Communication with friends and family is very difficult and visits are limited and monitored.

For youths who are not deeply involved in antisocial habits and an antisocial lifestyle, detention can serve as a powerful deterrent. The threat of returning to detention can motivate a boy to get to school every day, to avoid a bad crowd, to restrain himself when angry. The threat of detention can motivate good-faith efforts in family counseling or in attending Alcoholics Anonymous (AA) meetings.

Unfortunately, for the more serious and chronic juvenile offender, detention does not serve as punishment or as a real deterrent. Instead, each encounter with the court and detention seems to deepen the alienation and distrust. Ironically, some youthful offenders who have been locked up many times seem to feel quite comfortable there. For many, it is like "coming home" when arriving back in detention—back where staff members are attentive, consistent, and at least mildly supportive. Needless to say, this strict but benevolent setting is an improvement over home for some particularly unfortunate youths.

Conviction for a Serious Crime or Multiple Stays in Detention Will Likely Lead to Commitment to Juvenile Corrections (Prison)

If a youth is found guilty of a serious crime or has a history of multiple stays in juvenile detention, the court may commit him to the juvenile correctional system—a network of facilities designed for long-term, usually secure treatment. A youth's sentence to corrections can range from a few months to a few years. In most states, a youth committed to the juvenile justice system can be held only until he turns 21, at which point he is released to the community or transferred to the adult correctional system.

In contrast to adult corrections, whose focus is security and safety, the juvenile correctional system emphasizes rehabilitation. Besides keeping the community safe, the mission of most juvenile correctional facilities is to help juvenile offenders alter their atti- tudes and behavioral habits and to develop the skills to participate in socially acceptable activities. Some correctional institutions offer many treatment groups, individual counseling, and psychiatric services. Other facilities take a more security-based approach and offer minimal opportunities for treatment.

The juvenile correctional system offers a variety of residential placements that vary according to the level of security. These can range from a work-oriented forestry camp or a group home (low security) to full-scale, high-security prison. Placement depends on the youth's committing offense, age, and history of criminal behavior.

Nonsecure Residential Placements

There is a subset of antisocial youths who require long-term place- ment in a residential program, but whose crimes are not severe enough to warrant a locked, high-security placement. A judge may rule that the youth needed to be removed from the community to ensure safety, but due to the nature of the offense or low escape risk, he does not require a maximum security prison. The juvenile justice system attempts to place youths in the least restrictive place- ment possible, while ensuring community safety. Antisocial youths committed to nonsecure residential placements often are near the beginning of their criminal career and have repeatedly engaged in nonviolent criminal behavior (e.g., property damage). This type of antisocial youth may be sentenced to placement in various resi- dential programs.

Group Homes

Group homes typically house a small number of youths (six to six- teen) and provide a more home-like setting than the larger correc- tional facilities. Although residents are not allowed to live with family during the the their time of correctional commitment, they are able to utilize several services in the community. They are typically able to attend the local school (especially the alternative schools), and to attend vocational programs, drug and alcohol treatment, and mental health counseling in the local community. Group homes typically have strong behavior management programs, and many offer individual and group counseling. The most effective group homes encourage parental involvement in the all aspects of the youth's rehabilitation.

Boot Camps
This type of rehabilitative program follows a military model and is often led by current and former military personnel. The primary focus is on strict discipline, leadership, physical conditioning, and military drill. A primary goal is to replace the negative norms learned on the streets with positive, pro-social attitudes. Some boot camp programs offer individual and group counseling, and most emphasize extensive aftercare services. Although these types of programs are often favored by both the public and politicians, there is little evidence that they are effective in reducing antisocial behavior (Greenwood 1996).

Work Camps
The correctional facilities known as work camps provide a work-oriented experience for juvenile offenders. Residents spend most of their time working at assigned tasks such as landscaping, kitchen duty, forestry, or maintenance. They may also be required to complete educational requirements by participating in academic classes in the evening. There have not been many formal evaluations of these programs, but juvenile offenders who reside at the work camps gain real-world skills to use when they return to the community. Youths from work camps often leave the facility with marketable skills and appear to have less difficulty finding substantive work. Even if the work skills they have learned do not directly transfer to a particular job, their experience in the work camp often leads to gains in self-confidence, development of a work ethic, and feelings of self-worth.

Secure Residential Facilities

Antisocial youths who have been judged to pose a significant threat to society or whose antisocial ways have not responded to lesser sanctions are often placed in a locked, secure facility. Secure correctional facilities for juveniles house 20 to over 300 offenders. Most programs offer a very structured setting with clear, firm limits and rules. The majority of programs utilize some form of contingency management (e.g., point system or token economy), rewarding positive and prosocial behavior, while punishing unwanted and antisocial behavior. Privileges (e.g., wearing their own clothes, having personal items, receiving a later bedtime) are typically earned by active participation in prosocial activities and following institution rules.

Secure correctional facilities are concerned first and foremost with safety and security. The juveniles placed in such facilities are there because of the risk they pose to others. Once incarcerated, there is continued concern regarding the safety of staff and the other residents. Staff monitor almost all activities and there is minimal tolerance for misbehavior. Punishment for negative behavior may include having points deducted off a daily reward sheet, not being allowed to participate in a desired activity, or having to spend time alone in one's room (cell). If youths are assaultive or out of control, they may be housed for a short time in a room located away from the other residents (e.g., quiet room, isolation room). These rooms are barren in order to provide minimal stimulation. The goal is to help the youths regain control over emotions and behavior. Some antisocial youths find these rooms helpful in calming themselves. Others, however, find them intolerable, and they can actually escalate the level of arousal and anger. In addition, most facilities have special rooms for youths who become suicidal or otherwise in danger of harming themselves. These rooms allow staff to closely monitor the youths and their actions.

Most secure correctional facilities offer a variety of educational, vocational, and rehabilitation programming. Residents attend classes taught by certified teachers, including special education teachers. Students can receive class credits to be used when they return to the school in their community. They can earn a high school diploma or GED if they remain in the residential facility long enough. There is often an emphasis on preparing the older youths for employment. Basic workplace and prevocational skills are taught to increase the likelihood of job placement once youths return to their community.

Many institutions offer an array of treatment groups, each targeting a specific set of issues, such as victim awareness, anger management, social skills, grief and loss, and sexual abuse. These groups may be psychoeducational (primarily didactic) or process-oriented, where residents explore their own thoughts and feelings in interaction with other group members. Treatment interventions are carried out within the context of an offense-specific framework—aimed at helping the youths grasp the relationship between their individual treatment issues and the crime that resulted in their incarceration.

Many of the residential facilities offer special programming for juvenile offenders with specific needs. For example, there is often specialized programming for juvenile sex offenders, with a core treatment curriculum focusing on issues specific to this population (e.g., victim empathy, defining and taking responsibility, sex education, relapse prevention). Special programs dealing with drug and alcohol abuse are usually available. Depending on the severity of a youth's substance abuse, outpatient treatment or inpatient treatment may be offered. A substantial proportion of youths incarcerated in correctional facilities are suffering from psychiatric disorders such as major depression, attention deficit/hyperactivity disorder, or posttraumatic stress disorder. Many juvenile correctional facilities offer some type of mental health screening and treatment, and some facilities offer specific units designated for youth with psychiatric problems.

It is difficult to determine the effectiveness of secure correctional facilities for juvenile offenders. Only a few programs have been evaluated systematically and findings vary a great deal. Critics of the large juvenile correctional institutions point to the sometimes

minimal amount of rehabilitative programming, the artificial setting for youths to learn new skills, the ample opportunity for juvenile offenders to associate with strongly antisocial characters, and
the lack of family involvement. Most incarcerated juveniles will
eventually be released from the correctional facility and most of
these will be involved in some ways with their families; hence the
importance of family involvement, whenever possible.

Responding to some of these concerns, some large facilities are
divided into cottages or units of sixteen to twenty inmates each.
Additionally, some of these training schools have developed more
sophisticated rehabilitation programs that emphasize individual and
group counseling, as well as skill-building groups that teach the
practical skills needed to function on return to the community.
Unfortunately, some states are going the wrong direction in this
regard; they are building larger institutions, some of which hold
over 300 juvenile offenders and with minimal programming.

There currently is a move throughout the juvenile justice facilities toward an outcomes-based model of treatment. This model
requires youths to demonstrate in everyday activities the new prosocial thinking and behaviors they have learned. Merely attending
counseling groups is no longer sufficient. Youths must demonstrate
behaviorally that they have acquired the new skills, whether they
be related to problem solving, victim empathy, self-monitoring and
restraint, or anger management. The ultimate test, of course, is
whether these new competencies and skills are maintained after
the youth returns to the community, and this is the focus of outcomes research.

Transition Back to the Community

Regardless how effective treatment appears to be within the correctional facilities, treatment gains usually are short-lived without
good aftercare. Many juvenile corrections programs are able to
positively influence antisocial youths' behavior while they are incarcerated, but the delinquent behaviors often return after release
to the community. Without ensuring that the youth has a stable

place to live, a school willing to accept him, and at least one supportive adult, a return to juvenile justice system is likely. Studies of correctional programs have documented their effectiveness within the institution (Burchard and Tyler 1965, Phillips et al. 1971). However, maintaining long-term behavior change is another matter. Allotting additional time and resources for the transition back into the community can help to maintain gains made while incarcerated.

Most youths committed to a secure correctional facility are placed on *parole* upon release to the community. An assigned parole officer monitors them for a specified period of time. If they engage in any antisocial behavior while on parole (e.g., drug use, truancy, criminal behavior), they usually are returned to the correctional facility.

CLINICAL TREATMENTS FOR ANTISOCIAL BEHAVIOR

Most of the interventions described above involve institutional responses. That is, diversion from prosecution, detention, alternative school placement, and anger management training all are often mandated by the courts or other authorities. Some interventions (e.g., commitment to corrections) are triggered only by a high level of antisocial behavior. Clinical treatments, by contrast, have traditionally involved an alliance between clinician and patient; and they can be useful at any level of antisocial development.

Individual Psychotherapy/Counseling

Individual psychotherapy has been the most prevalent form of psychosocial treatment of mental disorders for the past century. The term *psychotherapy* now encompasses dozens of different theoretical and technical approaches to helping individuals to think, feel, and function better. Traditional psychotherapy derives primarily from *psychoanalysis*, the intensive free-association and interpretation method developed by Sigmund Freud. Traditional, psychodynamic psychotherapy still is widely studied and practiced, and it is effective for many of the difficulties individuals encounter. However, newer methods of cognitive-behavior therapy (CBT) have gained support in clinical and research settings, especially for well-defined sets of problems (e.g., anxiety disorders, depression). In CBT, the individual is taught how to identify and to modify patterns of thinking that keep her stuck in some pathological state. For example, by breaking the cycle of negative attributions about the self and one's life, depression can be relieved.

The key, common ingredient in all effective forms of psychotherapy is the treatment alliance. This is the "contract" (written or otherwise) between the patient and the therapist wherein each commits to working together honestly to resolve or alleviate the patient's difficulties. The patient agrees to make a good-faith effort to cooperate in the endeavor to relieve her suffering. Without a treatment alliance, there is no treatment, and it is right here that the difficulties arise in treating antisocial youths.

The most obvious impediment to individual psychotherapy with antisocial youths is that they typically do not feel afflicted within themselves. Most often, they locate the source of their troubles outside the self, between the self and the others—between self and parents, police, and judges. It is in the nature of antisocial character not to feel that the locus of trouble is within, which runs counter to the basic premise of individual psychotherapy. A treatment alliance to examine and amend individual attitudes and behaviors usually makes little sense to an antisocial juvenile.

It should be no surprise, then, that individual psychotherapy of antisocial behavior has not fared well when examined in controlled studies. Indeed, in the 1960s a series of studies pronounced, essentially, that nothing works with the antisocial character. Subsequent research and study has shown the picture to be more complex. For example, going back to August Aichhorn's 1925 book, *Wayward Youth*, we see the effective treatment of antisocial juveniles, but these boys were largely unhappy and neurotic characters (conflicted within themselves) and not what we would mean today by seriously antisocial. This is an important lesson, as we see today, too, that some antisocial behavior is performed by unhappy, neurotic, or agitated youths. These juveniles can benefit from psychotherapy because they are motivated to change something about themselves—how they feel, how they act, and where they are headed in life.

Psychotherapy can be beneficial for antisocial individuals who have come to a crisis in life, perhaps the first stay in detention or release from a stay in juvenile corrections. Many youths who, at some crisis point, would like to make positive changes still may be stuck in the old habits. Such youths, who may have some genuine motivation to change for the better but who also harbor deep anti-social habits, are most likely to benefit from a focused, cognitive approach to solving real-world problems (e.g., keeping away from drugs, staying in school, avoiding conflict).

Family Therapy

Family therapy represents a great leap forward in the treatment of young people. This is primarily due to the fact that adolescents cannot be counted on to bring into individual sessions the most salient problems. Thanks to denial and other defenses, individual sessions can drag along for weeks without getting to the point. Bring in the parents and siblings, and the picture often changes dramatically. Now there is lots to talk about, and the therapist may learn the most astonishing facts and events.

The aims of family therapy can vary widely depending on the circumstances. In some cases, the goals must be quite modest, for example, to mobilize the family to provide basic support and guidance to a boy who is returning from corrections. At the other extreme, in some cases an adolescent's antisocial acts may be an expression of family conflict and tension. Regular, systematic exploration of individual behavior and family history can, in some instances, relieve an adolescent of some of the pressure to act out. More often, though, the family is considered in family therapy as a potential resource. Blaming the family is not useful, although occasionally a parent needs to acknowledge some of the ways he has let his child down. In any case, it is best to approach the family with the positive expectation that past difficulties can be put aside in order to do the right thing for the child who now is in trouble.

Behavior Management Training (for Parents)

Numerous studies have found strong associations between child maladaptive behaviors, such as aggressiveness, and maladaptive interaction patterns between parents and child (see Chapter 3). Indeed, a whole host of poor parenting practices is associated with deviant child behavior—lax supervision, harsh and inconsistent discipline, and unwitting reinforcement of maladaptive behaviors. Lax supervision, alone, in some studies, is highly predictive of antisocial outcomes.

Behavior management training for parents is aimed at just these kinds of deficiencies in parenting. Training can take place in an individual or a group format, and it is designed to teach specific child-management techniques. Parents usually work with a therapist for eight to fifteen sessions. This is not family therapy, and the youth is not included in the training. Parents are taught the principles of behavior management—reinforcement, time-out from reinforcement, and the place of punishment. They are taught how to recognize the ways in which they may be unwittingly reinforcing unwanted behaviors, and they are taught strategies to avoid struggles and arguments. They are taught how to work collaboratively, for example, how to avoid undermining the parental authority of one another. The parents who benefit from behavior management training are not necessarily incompetent or careless. Many intelligent and well-socialized, middle-class parents also find themselves embroiled in maladaptive cycles with their children, and they can benefit from such training.

Behavior management training for parents has been shown to be effective in reducing maladaptive child behaviors (Kazdin 1994). It has been found to be superior to some other strategies, such as leaderless parent discussion groups and traditional psychotherapy.

Moreover, these positive effects often last for years (Bank et. al. 1991). In some cases, where the child or adolescent is also motivated to make real changes (where a treatment alliance is possible), concurrent individual or family therapy may be helpful in making long-term gains.

Psychiatric Hospitalization

Families, judges, and others sometimes turn to inpatient psychiatric hospitalization as a treatment option for antisocial youths. Inpatient psychiatric hospitals are typically staffed with a variety of mental health professionals, including psychiatrists, psychologists, nurses, and social workers. An antisocial youth may partake of a variety of treatment modalities including psychiatric medication, individual counseling, family counseling, group counseling, occupational therapy, and recreational therapy. If a youth's antisocial behavior stems primarily from an underlying psychiatric disorder, then time in a psychiatric hospital may be useful in order to accomplish a thorough psychiatric/psychological evaluation and possibly a trial of psychiatric medication.

The majority of young people who engage in antisocial acts, however, do not have an underlying psychiatric disorder, and the services provided by psychiatric hospitals have not been shown to be effective in ameliorating delinquent behavior (U.S. Congress 1991). In fact, hospitalization is clearly inappropriate for an antisocial youth who does not show evidence of psychiatric liabilities. Even if psychiatric issues are present, significant behavior change from inpatient hospitalization is rare today, as insurance and managed care severely limit the time a person can remain in inpatient care. Whereas several years ago a person may have been able to reside at a psychiatric hospital for several months, the current average length of stay is only a few days. This is not much time to treat any type of psychiatric disorder, much less to impact problems as complex and multidetermined as antisocial behavior. Studies of hospital treatment of antisocial children are not encouraging. While gains are sometimes made in-hospital, those gains usually are not maintained long after discharge (Kazdin 1989).

Despite the pressures of managed care to keep individuals out of hospitals, there continue to be some misuses of psychiatric hospitalization for antisocial adolescents. Juvenile offenders are sometimes transferred from detention to a psychiatric hospital—a move usually arranged by the family's lawyer and a cooperative doctor. Such moves appear to support claims of psychiatric involvement in alleged crimes, which may turn up in court as a plea of insanity or diminished capacity. Occasionally, if a judge is convinced by a doctor's testimony, he may order the case dismissed or diverted. These are legal maneuvers and should not be confused with legitimate clinical intervention.

Multisystemic Therapy

Throughout the discussion of treatment of antisocial behavior, reference has been made to levels of involvement in antisocial character. Many treatments are useful for children and adolescents who are early in their antisocial careers; some are helpful for juveniles with psychiatric involvement; some are helpful for youths whose families can rally around them, or for those whose commitment to crime is shallow. But what about the more serious and chronic antisocial youth? What about that small proportion of juvenile delinquents who account for the majority of serious and violent crimes? Again and again in discussions of treatment of antisocial behavior, caveats are inserted, to indicate that a given interventions works well "except for the more deeply antisocial youths" or "except for the truly sociopathic." So, a fair question would be whether there are any interventions that work with this group of serious and chronic offenders.

We know that many approaches usually are not effective with the serious offenders—traditional psychotherapy, medications, anger management, arrest, prosecution, and detention. Are we then to write off the tens of thousands of youthful offenders who commit serious and violent crimes or who find themselves committed to correctional institutions? Is this large segment of a generation beyond hope? Should we, as some argue, pour ever more resources into our expanding system of prisons for juveniles and adults? It would simplify matters to conclude that serious and violent young offenders are hopeless and incorrigible.

This reasoning is brought up short with the recognition that the majority of serious and violent young offenders can, in fact, be rehabilitated through newly developed comprehensive, community-based treatment programs. The best known and tested of such programs is termed multisystemic therapy (MST), developed by psychologist Scott Henggeler and his colleagues (Henggeler and Borduin 1990). MST is a comprehensive treatment program that begins with a family preservation approach. It avoids costly out-of-home placement, and it views the young offender as part of a larger system that includes the family, peer group, school, and neighborhood. Because of the complex nature of antisocial behavior, treatment may be directed at any and all of these domains of functioning. Involvement in community-based activities is encouraged. Schoolwork is monitored, in that many antisocial youths are deficient in basic academic skills, and real-world work skills are encouraged through closely monitored work experiences.

The first feature of MST is that treatment is based in the youth's natural environment of home, school, and community. Skills that are learned in MST therefore do not need to be transferred from an institutional or treatment setting to the real world. They are learned in the client's real world. Second, MST works directly with the strengths and weaknesses of the youth and his family, his set of peer relations, his school, and his job. In other words, MST addresses the broad range of skills and processes that are implicated in the development and maintenance of antisocial behavior. There is a particular emphasis on family functioning and the impediments to effective family communication and behavior management. Rather than blame the family for letting the child down in the past, the family is seen as a resource, and efforts are made to support and strengthen parental functioning (e.g., setting reasonable limits and supervision).

The services that make up MST are planned and implemented by a therapist who carries a realistic case load of just four to six families. Therapists are available 24 hours a day, seven days a week. Family counseling may take place in the youth's home, and every effort is made to make participation feasible for the family. In addition, there is a strong monitoring function. The therapist ensures that she is in regular contact with the juvenile's school, his boss at work, his tutor, and his youth group leader.

By the age of 16, Joey had accumulated a record of arrests for shoplifting, selling drugs (two convictions), and at least two assaults. But when he was arrested and charged with systematically stealing cars and selling them to "chop shops," the scenario became more ominous. This time, he was held in detention for several weeks, and he faced the likelihood of long-term commitment to corrections. Despite his history of infractions, Joey had managed to perform adequately in school (i.e., passing grades), and his family remained hopeful that he would pull out of his troubling trajectory.

Both of Joey's parents worked full time. However, his mother watched over Joey's four younger siblings in the evenings while his father situated himself at the local tavern, often until late at night. He had essentially abdicated his role as father for several years, and his wife was depressed, overwhelmed, and worn out by Joey's troubles and her husband's absence. The big break for Joey and his family came when the judge offered the option of participating in MST instead of commitment to corrections.

Because of transportation and child-care limitations, the MST therapist conducted family sessions at Joey's home in the evenings. Joey's father was referred (strongly) to alcohol treatment and AA, and he complied. At the same time, the therapist began training both parents in behavior management techniques, and helped them stop undermining their own authority and one another. They were coached in how to present a united front and how to define and implement consequences for Joey's associating with antisocial peers or other violations. Communication improved among all three, and even the younger siblings were helpful. Joey was assigned to a problem-solving skills group. His schoolwork and attendance were closely monitored, and he was enrolled in a basketball team at the Boys' and Girls' Club. A part-time job filled what free time remained in Joey's week. Close contact was maintained between the therapist and Joey's school, his group leader, his coach, and his boss at work. Any hint of associating with his old antisocial peers triggered immediate sanctions. The threat of return to court served as a constant motivator.

Joey exemplifies the application of MST to young offenders whose antisocial career is well developed. His antisocial attitudes and habits had been developing for several years. When the MST option was presented, Joey's only friends were peers involved in antisocial behaviors of one kind or another. Some had felony convictions and had been committed to corrections. Despite the depth of his antisocial involvement, however, there were substantial resources for MST to mobilize—a family that, while quite dysfunctional, was present and capable of rallying; a school where he was still welcome, with teachers and administrators willing to communicate with the therapist; some extended family willing to assist with transportation; an employer willing to give Joey a chance at learning some work skills; and, perhaps most important, a juvenile court willing to give therapy a chance to make a difference.

Several controlled studies have concluded that MST is effective in substantially reducing criminal activity among serious and even violent juvenile offenders (Guerra et al. 1994). For example, Henggeler and his colleagues (1992) reported that MST, when compared with typical intensive probation services, produced significantly lower recidivism rates. Antisocial youths who received the MST package are described as showing fewer behavior problems and being less aggressive with peers. Four years after treatment, these youths are less likely to have been rearrested, and when they are arrested, it is for less serious offenses. Such positive effects were found for families of antisocial youths regardless of gender, race, social class, and age.

The institutional interventions and the clinical treatments described above are addressed to antisocial behavior and antisocial character in general. The treatment of two subgroups of antisocial youth will now be reviewed—sex offenders and substance abusers.

Treatment of Juvenile Sex Offenders

Both the mental health and juvenile justice systems are coming into contact with an increasing number of juvenile sex offenders. Although there has always been a subset of juveniles engaging in sexually aggressive behavior, society's view toward this behavior has changed. In past years, some sexually offending behavior was seen as innocent experimentation or passed off as "boys will be boys." Some saw the harm in this type of behavior, but viewed sexual offending as part of a larger problem with delinquency and not an issue of its own. Since the 1980s, there has been increased awareness about this population and more treatment programs specifically designed to address and ameliorate this type of behavior.

Recent estimates indicate that adolescent males commit 20 percent of all rapes and between 30 and 50 percent of child molestations (Brown et al. 1984). According to experts on sex offender behavior (Abel et al. 1984), the average juvenile sex offender will commit over 350 sexual offenses throughout his lifetime if he receives no treatment. Because a large proportion of adult sex offenders have engaged in deviant sexual behavior as children or adolescents, it is imperative to begin treating juvenile sex offenders as early as possible.

There is considerable heterogeneity among sex offenders, for example, in the types of offensive sexual behaviors and the long-term trajectory of sexual offending behaviors. Some offenders are physically aggressive and threatening toward victims, while others exploit younger children through nonviolent coercion. A teenage boy may be involved in a public, romantic relationship with a female schoolmate who is younger than himself. Although sexual relations between them may be consensual, they may be illegal according to local laws and he may be arrested and labeled a sex offender. This contrasts with a boy who deliberately seeks out younger, vulnerable boys or girls whom he can coerce into secret sexual behavior with him. He would also be labeled a sex offender. Because many juvenile sex offenders have been sexually and/or physically abused themselves, or may have observed this type of behavior in their family environment, they may be confused about what constitutes appropriate and inappropriate touching of others. A large proportion of juvenile sex offenders lack basic social and communication skills. They often are severely lacking in self-knowledge, and are unable to think realistically about their own future or the needs and emotions of others. Because of the heterogeneity among juvenile sex offenders, it is important to obtain a specialized, comprehensive assessment of the youth's behavior. Assessing the youth's impulse control, social competence, cognitive ability, and family environment is as important as assessing the history of sexually aggressive behavior when designing individualized treatment programs. Continual reassessment throughout treatment will help inform treatment providers about areas that require increased or decreased focus.

Denial and minimization is the norm among the majority of adolescent sex offenders. They may deny they committed the offense at all, deny the offense was sexual in nature, or deny it was an offense because the victim did not resist. Juvenile sex offenders often minimize the harm done to their victim or minimize the extent of their past sex-offending behavior. Because of these defenses, very few youths seek treatment on their own or voluntarily attend treatment programs focused on sex-offending behavior. Court-mandated treatment is often necessary to prompt the youths to attend treatment and to keep them attending once treatment becomes difficult. Some mental health clinics and inpatient hospitals offer sex-offender treatment programs, but without the external motivator of the juvenile justice system attendance and participation are typically inconsistent. Motivation is not a prerequisite for successful treatment (Groth et al. 1981).

Depending on the nature of the crime and previous sex-offending behavior, some youths are offered treatment in place of incarceration. They are monitored by the court, but live at home and attend treatment on an outpatient basis. Other youths are committed to a juvenile correctional facility and receive their sex-offender treatment while incarcerated. Because of the necessity for strong incentives for both youths and their family, it has been suggested that sex-offender treatment is not effective unless it is delivered under the framework of the criminal justice system (Barbaree and Cortoni 1993). Regardless of where treatment is provided, an extensive period of follow-up and monitoring is required upon completion of sex-offender treatment.

Outpatient sex-offender treatment is typically provided by a mental health professional who is certified as a sex-offender specialist. These specialists have received extensive training in the area of sexually aggressive behavior. Treatment may be provided individually or the youth may be required to attend sex-offender treatment groups. Inpatient treatment can occur in a correctional facility or a psychiatric facility and includes both individual treatment and participation in sex-offender treatment groups.

Sex-offender treatment is focused on helping the youths identify and gain control over their sex-offending behavior. There are several steps in successful treatment of youthful sex offenders: (1) helping the youth accept responsibility for his sexually aggressive behavior; (2) identify the nature and history of the youth's unique cycle of aggression; (3) identify the unique, reinforcing characteristics of the youth's pattern of sex-offending behavior; (4) assist the youth in changing the focus of his patterns of sexual arousal; (5) help the youth develop empathy for his victims and for people in general; and (6) work with the individual to develop a lifelong strategy to prevent a return to aggression.

Sex-offender treatment involves several organizing principles:

History: Treatment helps the youth explore and understand how his own experiences (e.g., being a victim of sexual abuse, observing sexual aggression as a child) relate to his own pattern of sexual aggression.

Responsibility: Because of the denial and minimization around sexually aggressive behavior, the youth is strongly encouraged to take responsibility for his sex-offending behavior. It is difficult to change the youth's sexually aggressive behavior until he has acknowledged his offensive behaviors and the effects these behaviors may have on victims.

Cycle of aggression: Sex offenders typically have a clear pattern or cycle of thoughts, fantasies, and behavior leading to sexual aggression. Once a youth and his counselor can identify that cycle, he can begin to learn strategies to interrupt the cycle, as early as possible.

Arousal to sexual aggression: Juvenile sex offenders are usually sexually aroused by aggressive sexual behavior. Efforts are made to reduce arousal to aggressive themes and increase arousal to themes of appropriate and mutual sexual behaviors. Most sex offenders need basic sexual education information, for example, on appropriate sexual relationships.

Nonsexual contributions to offending: There are a variety of nonsexual factors that can raise the risk of sexually aggressive behavior, and these too are targets of treatment. Many youths benefit from social skills training, anger management training, and family therapy. Substance abuse treatment also is often essential.

Relapse prevention: The goal of treatment is to increase internal controls in order to prevent sexually aggressive or exploitative behaviors. But juvenile sex offenders require supervision once treatment has been completed. It is important to structure the youth's environment to reinforce appropriate and newly learned behaviors and provide swift, negative consequences for inappropriate sexual behavior. It is important to identify what situations are high risk for the youth, what coping strategies he can use to minimize the chances of a relapse, and what to do if a relapse should occur.

Sex-offender treatment relies on the youths' possessing a minimum level of intellectual functioning. Most treatment programs require the youths to achieve some insight about their own victimization and to understand how that relates to their own sexual acting out. Developing empathy for others, especially their victims, is also an important goal. These tasks are often difficult for an individual who is cognitively limited (e.g., mentally retarded). Because some youths do not have the intellectual capacity to process the treatment tasks in the manner they are intended, sex-offender treatment and the topics discussed may have the unintended effect of actually arousing the youth sexually—not the intended consequence.

Many youths who complete sex-offender treatment are able to talk realistically about their victimizing behavior and accept responsibility for it, identify their offense cycle and how to interrupt it if they start thinking and behaving in those old ways, and verbalize high-risk situations and how they plan to avoid or cope with them.

There is a dearth of formal evaluations of sex-offender treatment programs, so it is difficult to determine just how effective these programs are. Treatment utilizing the above approaches appears to be very helpful for many juvenile offenders, particularly those who do not have a long history of sexually aggressive behavior. However, for offenders with personal histories of severe sexual victimization or extensive histories of victimizing others, the long-term effectiveness of treatment programs is diminished.

Substance Abuse Treatment for Juvenile Offenders

The majority of antisocial youths are involved in drug and alcohol abuse. Up to 80 percent of youths committed to juvenile correctional institutions are substance abusers or chemically dependent, and many report using drugs just prior to committing the crime for which they were adjudicated. Most antisocial youths use more than one substance and many use drugs and alcohol on a daily basis, or even several times daily. It is not clear if using drugs and alcohol causes crime, or engaging in crime leads to the use of drugs and alcohol. There may be a third, underlying factor causing both. Some suggest that drug use and criminal behavior among adolescents stem from similar factors and are all part of a general deviance syndrome (Elliot et al. 1979). If this is true, then treatment of substance-abusing juvenile offenders should target both problems at the same time. Without this simultaneous focus, long-term behavior change would be more difficult.

Alcohol and drug use can impact a youth's behavior in several ways. First, these substances are disinhibiting, meaning that drugs and alcohol undermine normal restraints and judgment, and readily lead to dangerous behaviors. Thoughts of being arrested and being locked up are far from the youth's conscious mind. Also, drug and alcohol abuse increases the likelihood of spending time with deviant peers. In addition, many crimes committed by youths are directly associated with substance use. A youth may engage in burglary or drug dealing in order to pay for his drug.

For many antisocial youths, drug and alcohol abuse is a long-term preoccupation, often beginning in early adolescence or earlier. Such substance abuse can severely undermine normal developmental processes—exploration and consolidation of identity and development of academic, work, and social skills. Self-knowledge is obliterated by long-term substance abuse, and the capacity for sound judgment can deteriorate.

The majority of drug and alcohol treatment services are delivered to "low-end" juvenile offenders. The youth typically receives an assessment of his alcohol and drug use, and a treatment plan is developed. Offenders may be referred to outpatient treatment while they reside at home, and attend substance abuse counseling once or twice a week. If the youth has a more serious drug or alcohol problem, inpatient treatment may be necessary. These youths live at a residential substance abuse treatment facility (private community facility or group home) for thirty to ninety days, then return to their community, most often to the family home. These programs typically utilize educational instruction related to substance abuse, as well as individual, group, and family therapy. Most youths enrolled in any type of formal substance abuse treatment attend Alcoholics Anonymous (AA) or Narcotics Anonymous (NA). These clients are strongly encouraged to continue attending twelve-step meetings after formal treatment is discontinued in order to maintain treatment gains. These meetings focus on abstinence and helping the youths continue to live a substance-free lifestyle. Many low-end offenders elect to enroll in formal substance abuse treatment (inpatient or outpatient) in lieu of time in detention.

Youths who are committed to juvenile correctional facilities usually have access to drug and alcohol treatment. Within the past ten years, most correctional institutions have developed substance abuse treatment programs for their residents, designed on an inpatient or outpatient model. The majority of facilities do some type of assessment to determine the nature and severity of the drug and alcohol problem. After assessment, a youth should be referred to the appropriate treatment setting, taking into account other factors that may impact treatment (e.g., security risk, length of sentence, and age). Due to the large numbers of youths with substance abuse issues, not all youths eligible for treatment receive it while incarcerated. These youths usually are then referred for substance abuse treatment in the community when they are released, but follow-up and compliance generally are poor.

Many juvenile correctional programs are developing specialized inpatient drug and alcohol treatment programs within the institutions. A specific cottage or unit is designated for substance abuse treatment and youths are placed in that program for thirty to ninety days. After completion of the program, they return to general correctional treatment. These programs typically have staff members who are trained in chemical dependency treatment. The majority of these programs are based on the abstinence model of the twelve-step program of AA, and the youths have the opportunity to attend AA meetings. These programs typically offer individual and group counseling, drug and alcohol education, and personal/social responsibility classes. Some programs offer additional treatment groups, academic instruction, and encouragement of family involvement with the youth's treatment. The goal is for offenders to accept that they do not have control over their use of drugs and alcohols, and that they are unable to manage their lives because of their use of drugs and alcohol. Youths are taught to rely on the support of others to maintain their commitment to sobriety. Most programs utilize group discussions and written assignments to help the youths identify the negative impact of drugs and alcohol on their life, and to specify the goals they want to achieve.

Regardless of the type of substance abuse treatment while in the juvenile justice system, aftercare is critical. Youths must identify and commit to the lifestyle changes they will make to support a life of sobriety. Identifying situations that trigger their substance abuse and helping them develop alternative behaviors and coping strategies in these situations is imperative if they are to remain free of drugs and alcohol. Having some type of juvenile justice supervision (probation/parole) is very helpful, especially when utilizing random drug tests on the youths and attaching negative consequences to the use of substances (e.g., incarceration).

Motivation to change is typically low or nonexistent in this population. While some youthful offenders make substantial changes, the effectiveness of treatment programs is not impressive. Many antisocial youths have been using drugs and alcohol for years. Drugs are an integral part of their life; they do not believe they have a problem, and they are not motivated to give this up. In addition, this is one of the main coping mechanisms for most antisocial youths. When they get sad, they use drugs. When they get scared, they use drugs. When they get angry, they fight or they use drugs. Unless treatment providers help antisocial youths to develop alternative coping mechanisms, the moment the youth is placed in a stressful situation he will return to his old habits.

❖ C H A P T E R   8 ❖

Reading the Barometer

There is not much about the development of antisocial behavior that is altogether mysterious. We can understand many of the psychological building blocks of antisocial character and habits—the roots of despair and resentment and the rejection of positive social values, the defense mechanisms that undercut self-knowledge and personal responsibility, the impoverished ego strengths and rigid coping styles, the coercive interpersonal habits, the identification with deviant peers. We can reliably discriminate among several subtypes of antisocial personality. We can describe the various trajectories that antisocial youths tend to follow, and we can prescribe the modifications in their social milieu that are most likely to help. Moreover, we can successfully treat the majority of even seriously antisocial youths in comprehensive, community-based programs. Only the most extreme juvenile offenders require long-term incarceration.

Despite our capacity to understand and to treat antisocial youths, there is cause for humility. Psychological insights from research and from clinical experience take us only so far in accounting for the explosion of juvenile crime over the past generation. Abusive or neglectful parenting, for example, raises the odds that a child will develop antisocial attitudes and habits, but can this risk factor explain why serious juvenile offenders are three times as prevalent today as they were thirty years ago? An aggressive or difficult temperament raises the odds that the child will display aggressive or antisocial behaviors by latency or adolescence, but can this risk factor account for the modern specter of school-yard shootings, the demand for metal detectors at the entrance to many institutions, and the flight of the privileged behind the walls of gated communities?

THE LIMITS OF PSYCHOLOGICAL INQUIRY

Our theories of antisocial behavior turn upon an understanding of risk factors, those conditions that cause or are closely associated with pathological development. There are two reasons, however, why these psychological risk factors cannot account for the surge in juvenile offenders over the past generation. First, we know that the effects of risk factors—even those with some causal weight—are heavily mediated through a broad constellation of socialization practices. There are no direct, causal connections leading from risk factors or root causes to pathological behaviors. Children who are neglected or abused may become resentful and alienated. But for any given child, the long-term effects of mistreatment depend on a host of other conditions—whether there are other adults in the child's life to bond with and to be guided by, whether the neighborhood is stable and cohesive or suffering social and economic decay, whether the educational system provides opportunity and hope or stress and despair, whether the community tolerates minor crime by youngsters or responds promptly to signs of trouble.

The effects of some risk factors, such as poverty, are even more tenuous. While some research shows that poverty is strongly associated with juvenile crime, by itself poverty surely does not cause crime. Countless poor families have raised perfectly well-socialized citizens; indeed, many cultures that we would count as very poor display strikingly low levels of criminal activity. Poverty is strongly associated with crime, however, in the context of late twentieth-century urban America—that is, in the context of socially and economically decaying neighborhoods (urban and suburban), high rates of single mothers and absent fathers, impoverished schools systems, and a heavy national diet of extreme media violence. Contrary to any notion that our nation's strong economy is benefiting all citizens, the poverty rate for juveniles has increased substantially in recent years. Just between 1976 and 1995, the number of juveniles living in poverty increased by over 42 percent (Snyder and Sickmund 1995).

Many of the conditions through which the effects of risk factors are mediated are not readily accessible to psychological inquiry. They involve social, economic, and political forces. The educational opportunities for disadvantaged youth, for example, can have an enormous impact on psychological development. But the level of financial support enjoyed by school systems varies enormously, and that support, in turn, depends entirely on political and economic factors. Jonathan Kozol's *Savage Inequalities* analyzes the enormous disparities in financial support for schools, and the effects of such disparities. Similarly, the social pathology and crime that pervades many neighborhoods was brought about by economic and political forces operating over a period of years and even decades.

The second reason why psychological risk factors cannot account for the escalation of juvenile crime is that the occurrence of those risk factors themselves stems from forces outside the realm of psychological and psychiatric research. The burgeoning of single-parent households and the prevalence of economically desperate neighborhoods and severely underfunded school systems are beyond the scope of traditional psychological inquiry, and they demand other forms of analysis.

The prevalence of risk factors for pathological development, and the ultimate effects of those risk factors, can be understood only in the context of the processes of socialization. The risk factors that we understand via psychological research are shaped by social-historical forces (e.g., economic, political). Those risk factors, in turn, interact with contemporary social conditions of resilience and support to shape the adolescent's personality. The risk factors for pathological development, and their place in the broader context of socialization, are displayed in Figure 8–1. Socialization, including the role of risk and protective factors, interacts with the child's temperament (over many years) to yield the personality attributes of the adolescent or young adult.

There is one more set of mediators between the adolescent/ young adult and his actual behaviors. Even for an aggressive and impulsive 17-year-old, there is a wide range of behavioral options into which his energies might be channeled. Our aggressive young man is more likely to commit a murder if handguns are easily available. The availability of handguns is primarily responsible for the vastly greater number of murders in the United States as compared to other Western nations. All large rises in murder rates from 1989 to 1993 were due to gun violence (Sickmund et al. 1997, p. 7).

FIGURE 8–1. Socialization, personality, and behavior

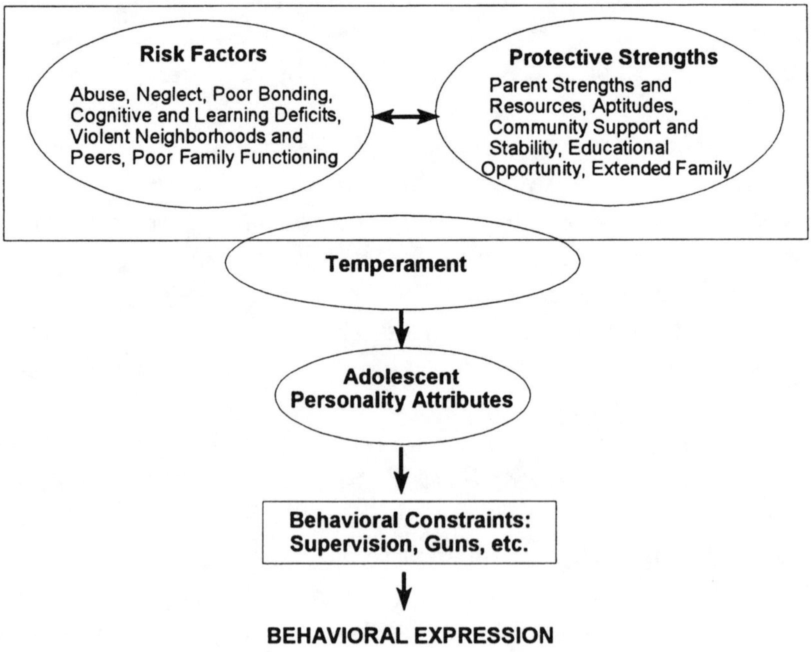

There are no data to support the logical alternative explanation—that there are many times more antisocial individuals in the United States. Parental supervision also plays a crucial role. An adolescent is more likely to get into trouble at night if his parents are not supervising his evening adventures, and if his community tolerates a pattern of low-level transgressions (e.g., loud parties, youth drinking). Moreover, adolescents who may be prone to misadventure are less likely to choose the untoward endeavors if there is something better to do—such as midnight basketball or cultural events or even getting some sleep in preparation for a job early the next morning.

The bright light of psychological research dims considerably when confronted with large-scale societal dynamics. Economic and political forces are largely beyond the realm of psychological inquiry. Does this mean that psychological research cannot help in the endeavor to understand the escalation of juvenile crime? Not at all. It is psychological research that has clarified the role of healthy socialization in protecting against pathological outcome. It is psychological research that has shown how crucial are committed and healthy parents, a stable and supportive community, and a hopeful and promising education. Thus, while psychological research cannot explain societal, economic, and political processes, it decisively indicates the risk factors and protective factors that are directly shaped by those broader social dynamics.

The conditions that promote antisocial development today are the same as the conditions that promoted antisocial development a half century ago, only now we have a deeper understanding of those conditions and how they exert their damaging influences. With understanding comes responsibility. Seeing that many of the conditions that promote antisocial development turn on broad societal factors, we cannot pretend that these are merely technical or clinical matters, the kind best left to the doctors. It was noted in Chapter 7 that an essential ingredient in the treatment of antisocial youth is accountability. But our society, too, must be held accountable for such large historical trends, for the sense that we are all under siege. Pamela Eakes, founder of Mothers Against Violence in America, and her husband, Kenneth Eakes recently wrote, in response to the multiple school murders in Springfield, Oregon, "Long prison sentences and death penalties for children are not solutions, but rather the tragic consequences of our failures" (1998, p. B5). It is not the failure of clinical research and practice that leads to the prevalence of juvenile crime. Clinical research points to the conditions that are responsible, and now there can be no excuse for neglecting such pathogenic conditions.

Adolescents are a good barometer of the health of a society and the effectiveness of child-rearing practices. Psychological deficits that accumulate during the childhood years tend to make themselves felt during adolescence—whether in the form of internalizing disorders such as anxiety and depression or as externalizing problems like aggression and violence. The escalation of juvenile crime in recent decades, and its incursion into virtually every sector of society, expresses a widespread decline in the effectiveness of socialization. The social conditions that would mediate and buffer the effects of risk factors have eroded. There are more children at risk today, and for those who are at risk there are fewer sources of protection and resiliency.

There are many conditions that can reduce the prevalence and expression of the better-understood and more circumscribed psychological risk factors. These are conditions such as family and community cohesiveness, economic viability, family stability (versus mobility and dislocation), neighborhood stability and vitality, exposure to quality media, educational quality and the sense of opportunities, and exposure to cultural and historical institutions. A full review of the conditions affecting socialization is beyond the scope of this chapter. But three social conditions whose effects are clear will be considered: (1) the need for stable, healthy, and committed parents; (2) the need for stable communities that support the development of children and families; and (3) the need for appropriate and prosocial education and entertainment (media).

SINGLE MOTHERS/ABSENT FATHERS

The Office of Juvenile Justice reports a profound social trend in recent decades: from 1960 to 1990, the proportion of births to unmarried women rose from 5 percent to 25 percent. The divorce rate during the same period tripled, and the proportion of children living with a never-married parent jumped from less than 1 percent in 1970 to 8 percent in 1990.

If the foundation stones of personality are laid primarily in the early relationships with loving, protective parents, then the phenomenon of overstressed, unsupported single mothers is a prescription for large numbers of psychologically impaired youngsters—some of whom will find their way into antisocial practices. The fracturing of the traditional two-parent family carries two distinct liabilities from the standpoint of the child's psychological development. First is the phenomenon of young mothers whose children's needs for nurturance, protection, and supervision exceed her capacities as a parent. Overtaxed and unsupported single parents (despite good intentions) are more likely themselves to be depressed and resentful and to lack the personal resources needed to bear the responsibility of parenting. Such young adults are more likely to produce a second or third child—when even a single child was beyond her capabilities. A parent who feels overtaxed and depressed cannot reliably provide the secure bonding along with clear boundaries and limits that children need. Too often, lonely and depressed mothers turn to their children to meet their own emotional needs, and then fail to provide the boundaries and discipline that healthy development requires. Supervision often is lax, and indulgence of misbehavior undermines the child's self-restraint and respect for others. Overtaxed single parents are more likely to resort to harsh punishments, and are more likely to fall into coercive parenting practices that unwittingly encourage aggressive and manipulative habits by the child.

David Lykken (1995) locates the source of the escalation in antisocial development in the breakdown of the two-parent family. "The current trend toward single parent households . . . is beyond doubt the primary source of the concurrent increase in the proportion of sociopaths in our society and in the rates of juvenile crime and violence" (p. 227). While it is hard to argue with Lykken's basic claim, there is more to be said. Many single mothers do manage to raise healthy and well-adjusted children. The effectiveness of child-rearing by single mothers varies a great deal according to the personal resources of the woman and according to the kinds of support she can rely on from others—the child's father, the extended family, friends, and the community. Many a child of single mothers has been rescued from deprivation and even abuse by a grandmother or an aunt or a neighbor. Child-rearing capacity also depends heavily on whether the mother brings her childbearing to a halt. The odds of a single mother providing well for her child diminishes sharply as the number of children rises.

The second major liability for child development in single-parent households is the absence of the father. The father's absence can mean different things. It can mean that the father lives elsewhere yet remains actively involved in the child's life, helping to raise the child, even supporting the mother in practical ways (e.g., financially, helping with transportation). Or, more damaging, it can mean that the father is not regularly involved in the child's life and is not a source of support to the mother. A common tale told by mothers of antisocial adolescents is of fathers who "took off," who never paid child support, whose whereabouts are unknown, and who never made much effort to act like a father. In such instances, not only is the mother left unsupported with this profound responsibility, but, equally damaging, the child has no father to look up to, to be guided and disciplined by, and to identify with. The child is left to his imagination and fears as to why the father would not stay involved. Hypotheses entertained by children in such circumstances include, "Is there something wrong with me that made my dad not want to be my dad?" "Is there something wrong with my dad, and if so does that mean there's something wrong with me?" "Did my mom drive my dad away?" The psychological lesson may be even more disturbing: "Connections to parents just don't mean much."

The toll on children of such deprivation and turmoil is immeasurable. The resentment and hostility that children feel when one parent has abandoned them is often directed against the parent who has remained involved and responsible—while "protecting" the absent parent. The missing parent often is idealized while the functioning parent may be seen as deficient, mean, and unfair.

A full analysis would consider why the single mother/absent father syndrome has become so prevalent in recent decades. There probably are several reasons, including increased social and geographic mobility, the destruction of many city neighborhoods, welfare policies that denied benefits to two-parent households, and societal acceptance of lifestyle differences. Part of the acceptance of such configurations has been the simple failure to appreciate the child's needs and the notion that one could make up for such losses.

The ultimate effect on the child of having a single mother and an absent father depends on the co-occurrence of other social and economic conditions. Obviously, it will be more difficult for a single mother living in poverty than for one with reasonable financial support. Also, if the mother is to be the sole parent, then her health is crucial. Depressed or addicted mothers, for example, are less capable of healthy bonding with their young children and are more likely to use their children to meet their own needs. They are less capable of firm discipline and supervision of older children.

Whether or not the child is raised in a single-parent household, there are several other social and economic factors that can undermine healthy child rearing. Some of these conditions affect children at all levels of socioeconomic status; some strongly affect only more vulnerable segments of the population. When these factors intersect with specific vulnerabilities such as absent fathers or depressed mothers, then the effects are more pronounced.

EROSION OF COMMUNITY

Parent and child do not exist in a vacuum. That crucial bond that forms the foundation stone of personality is embedded in a matrix of relationships and support that make possible the healthy development of the child. Mother can provide the holding environment only if she, too, is supported and held—by the father, by her extended family, and by her community. The child's relationships with the father, with uncles and grandparents, with neighbors, and eventually with teachers enrich the child's psychological strengths.

Reflecting on the period of American history since the end of the Second World War, we bear witness to a terrible irony. It is during this fifty-year period that we have gained a broad scientific appreciation for how the deepest layers of personality and cognitive development emerge from the stable, protective bonds the child enjoys with parents and others. We have learned how the child can be protected even from adverse circumstances by relationships with other adults in the community and at the school. Yet during this same historical period, we have recorded an alarming decline in exactly those social institutions that provide for normal, healthy development. It is no accident of history that the widespread decline of socialization we endure today coincides with the wasting of our most fundamental social institutions—the decline of the two-parent family, the dispersion of the extended family, and the erosion of stable communities that nurture parent and child alike.

The prevalence of inadequate child rearing in recent decades is sometimes attributed to a lapse of values. The single mother and the uninvolved father are said to lack "family values." Faulty attitudes in society are said to accommodate such nontraditional—and often dysfunctional—lifestyles. These assertions about values surely capture part of the truth, specifically, that as a society we have failed to appreciate and to cherish the most fundamental social structures that provide for normal development. And yet all the talk of values does not begin to account for the problem. It does not explain why we have seen such adverse social transformations over a half century, and it does not provide any guidance for what to do about it. Lecturing the single mother about her values will not get us anywhere. Campaigning against the welfare mother will only deepen social divisions while contributing nothing toward a solution.

American society in the past half century has neglected and even destroyed an alarming proportion of the social and economic ground upon which families could flourish. City, and especially inner city, have become synonymous with social decay, poverty, and crime. Many of the older suburbs—those built just a generation ago—follow the same path toward degradation and flight of the middle class. The decay and crime in many suburban areas now rivals that of the inner city. Such pathology—whether in the city or the suburbs—directly undermines the socialization of children and makes more likely an antisocial outcome.

Historically, the decline of cities has accompanied the decline of a nation. In the last half century in the United States, it has been different. "Twentieth-century America has turned its cities inside out, releasing industry, population, and commerce from the core, leaving ruinous environments behind" (Moe and Wilkie 1997). In too many urban neighborhoods today, the only viable businesses are liquor stores and state lottery counters. Architectural historian Vincent Scully (1995) describes the fate of our cities and their inhabitants: "Our cities lie destroyed all around us, and, of course, as the cities were destroyed, the terrible thing in American society and politics is that the communities of the center of the city were destroyed with them" (p. 10).

There is a convenient fiction about the demise of our urban areas that goes something like this: the draining of people and resources from the cities, and the resulting social decay, is a natural result of demographic and economic transformations in modern society, perhaps the result of a collision of market forces and the rise of the middle class. By this reasoning, the ruin of the urban areas and the destruction of urban communities are merely the unfortunate consequences of otherwise benign processes.

There is no set of individuals or organizations that set out intentionally to turn our cities into ruins. Yet beginning in the 1930s there have been numerous programs and projects that systematically destroyed many city neighborhoods and the communities they had sustained for decades or for generations. Since the 1950s, economic policies at the local, state, and federal level have ensured a steady drain of financial and human resources, in short, have ensured the death of city neighborhoods and the incursion of decay and crime. As tax bases have plummeted, education and infrastructure fell into disrepair and neglect. The resulting feeling of underclass entrapment has violently undermined social cohesion and stability at all levels.

Federal Housing Administration (FHA) policies beginning in the 1930s set strict criteria for which urban locations were worthy of mortgage insurance and which were not. They favored new locations over old ones, and they systematically undervalued those qualities of locations most directly related to community health and vitality. Ranked last in the FHA's set of criteria were "adequacy of civic, social and commercial centers"—those very qualities that most directly influence the stability and health of families and children. Most destructive for many urban neighborhoods, FHA policies employed racial criteria. Neighborhoods with African-Americans or other racial minorities often were "redlined"—marked off as financially risky and therefore not suitable for financial backing. FHA-backed subdivisions also employed blatantly racist barriers—"covenants"—to protect the racial purity of the new developments. In the city, Moe and Wilkie (1997) report,

> A single house occupied by a black family in an urban neighborhood, even one tucked away on an inconspicuous side street, was enough for the FHA to label a predominantly white neighborhood as unfit for mortgage insurance. Areas that failed to meet the test were "redlined" on confidential maps shared with bankers [which] doomed many of them to eventual decline. [p. 48]

About these processes, Moe and Wilkie wrote, "federal home mortgage insurance policies helped guarantee the conversion of once sound urban areas to urban slums" (p. 50). Even in neighborhoods with decades of social stability and economic health, such policies ensured a gradual but steady drop in property values and an erosion of tax bases. Residents who wanted to remain in their own neighborhoods, because of ties to extended family and friends or because of their personal history in that locale, found it difficult to do so, as services declined, as schools were underfunded, as signs of social decay spread like a blight.

Should anyone doubt the potency of these mortgage insurance policies and the difficulties securing home loans, he need only consider how many middle-class families today would be able to pay cash up front for their homes or even for major home improvements. The long-term health and stability of virtually all sound neighborhoods depends on the availability of such financial resources.

The most violent paradigm for the destruction of cities and their neighborhoods was provided by Robert Moses, called the most influential road builder in American history. Moses controlled the largest statewide empire of public works projects in America, in New York State. His specialty was expressways, and in his long career, "He tore out the hearts of a score of neighborhoods, communities the size of small cities themselves, communities that had been lively, friendly places to live" (Caro 1974, p. 19). Moses's priority was highways, big highways, expressways—not people, not families, not communities. Unfortunately for American families and children, his model for ramming highway projects through neighborhoods without regard for the affected communities was replicated from New York to Los Angeles to Seattle.

Policymakers might argue that there was no intention to destroy the cities, that FHA policies were meant only to ensure stability in the home loan industry, that the expressways were only intended to provide fast, efficient transportation. The aims of urban renewal, laid out in the Housing Act of 1949, were benign, too—the clearing of slums and replacement with more livable conditions. The destruction of living, breathing communities was unintended. What these various policies make clear, however, is how little regard there has been for the social and economic base on which families and children can thrive. By the time it was widely recognized how much was being lost to these forms of "progress," it was too late to do much about it. So many communities were either carved up by highways or drained of economic vitality that the move was on. As the cities became increasingly troubled and unlivable, the middle class moved out. Those who were left behind struggled to get out, too. Thus was set into motion the momentum of urban sprawl—that formless form of building that sucks the life out of existing cities and towns.

As urban ills accumulated from the 1930s to the 1950s, a great migration was set into motion, a migration from the city to the suburbs, and more recently from the old suburbs to the new ones. Several books have examined the phenomenon of urban sprawl and its physical, economic, and social consequences. Excellent works include Joel Garreau's *Edge City* (1991), Kenneth Jackson's *Crabgrass Frontier* (1985), and Moe and Wilkie's *Changing Places* (1997). One measure of sprawl is just how much land area is occupied by urban and suburban development. For example, between 1970 and 1990 the population of Los Angeles grew by 45 percent, but during that same period the metropolitan land area ballooned by 300 percent! The American Farmland Trust estimates that one million acres of productive farmland are lost each year to sprawl development. Surrounding every city in America, low-density building for new homes, office parks, warehouses, and malls gobbles up the countryside at breathtaking speed. There is little hope that any of these formless places might ever become the locus of a stable, rooted community. Architect Peter Calthorpe (1993) writes, "Americans moved to the suburbs largely for privacy, mobility, security and ownership. Increasingly they now have isolation, congestion, rising crime and overwhelming costs" (p. 18). In short, the suburbs are now suffering the same social pathologies that have afflicted the cities over the past several decades.

The irreversible damage to the countryside resulting from sprawl development is only its most obvious consequence. The loss of valuable farmland and the loss of any sense of place in our neighborhoods constitute oppressive visual and aesthetic damage. What is less obvious are the destructive social consequences of sprawl.

Sprawl development has not advanced on a level economic playing field, and existing cities and towns have paid the price. Beginning with the FHA and the banking industry, financial incentives favored new locations over old. While families in urban environments could not get loans for building or for home improvements, developers out on "edge city" could arrange for easy credit. Sprawl development has been heavily subsidized by public money at every level. Tax dollars that were unavailable for maintaining infrastructure in the cities were readily distributed to build the expensive new highways and water and sewer systems for the new subdivisions. Local subsidies for suburban development and tax benefits for real estate construction have ensured that resources would be directed away from the city, away from existing small and medium-sized towns. Tax dollars funding the interstate highway system helped to promote the illusion of economic advantage for suburban expansion. Such subsidy programs, usually poorly understood by those paying the bills, severely distort the market economics, and "do violence to concepts of taxpayer fairness, and to sound land-use planning" (Moe and Wilkie 1997, p. 257). The economic system has been rigged, in short, in a way that promotes sprawl at the same time that cities are being economically strangled. Citizens everywhere pay for grand new highways to feed new subdivisions and malls that, in turn, drain the economic life out of existing cities and towns.

The second social consequence of sprawl is found within the suburbs themselves. I wrote in 1995 about the human landscape in many western suburban areas: "These suburbs have been built not by design to meet the needs of children and families, but by default—to accommodate the demands of economic growth . . . We have created towns that are old after a single generation" (Young 1995, p. E1). The physical configuration of our suburban towns militates against the evolution of stable and cohesive communities. The formlessness of most suburbs means there can be no center and no coherence. Lewis Mumford observed, "As long as the railroad stops and walking distances controlled suburban growth, the suburbs had some form" (quoted in Jackson 1985, p. 101). Often there is no public open space. What passes for town centers too often is the newest, biggest mall, where the agenda is altogether different from that of a traditional civic gathering place. Moreover, suburban towns are regularly carved up by five-lane highways needed to feed the malls and superstores, and no one can go anywhere without a car. When teenagers claim that they have to have a car to do anything, too often they are right. None of this is an altogether new insight. Sociologist Herbert Gans, who lived in Levittown in the 1950s, reported that the environment isolated Levittown's youths, who then grew restless, alienated, and rebellious.

The majority of suburban areas do not age well. It is ironic that many families have moved out of the city because of the city's reputation for being old and riddled by problems. But many of our suburban towns lose their appeal in a few short years. Within a generation, the malls are run down and seedy, property values decline, and the fortunate move out to even-newer suburbs. Following close on the heels of such economic decline is social decay. Indeed, crime and arrest statistics bear out this end result: rates of serious and violent crime by juveniles has escalated in suburban areas, just as they have in the cities.

In our disposable culture, we have first thrown away much of our city areas and the people who were left behind. Now we are in the process of throwing away our older suburbs—the ones built just thirty to forty years ago. Again, the people who remain tend to be those who cannot get away; so they too are more or less discarded.

It is instructive to observe some of the Eastern suburbs, such as those near Boston and Philadelphia, many of which are four or five generations old yet show none of the physical and social decay of forty-year-old suburbs around Los Angeles, Denver, and Seattle. These Eastern suburbs, like Newton, Massachusetts, and towns on the Mainline outside Philadelphia, were built along the commuter rail lines. As Lewis Mumford observed, they display some physical coherence.

THE MEDIA

The statistics on American TV viewing are familiar: children ages 2 to 11 watch an average of twenty-eight hours of TV each week, and teenagers an average of twenty-three hours per week. TV viewing accounts for more than half of children's leisure time—more than any other activity. Children from low-income families are often the heaviest viewers.

The statistics on TV violence are also familiar: TV violence has remained nearly constant over the past twenty years. By the age of 12, the average child has witnessed 8,000 murders and 100,000 other acts of violence, and these numbers rise with so-called cable premium channels or VCR watching of R-rated films. Popular violent films (e.g., *Die Hard*) display dozens if not hundreds of violent deaths (Donnerstein et al. 1994). Compounding the preoccupation with fictional violence, we now see TV stations aggressively exploiting the most tragic real events for display on the evening news. Even worse, whole programs now are devoted to encouraging the most prurient instincts by displaying actual tragedies captured on film—individuals falling to their death from burning buildings, helicopters crashing and burning their occupants to death, violent police busts.

To listen to debates over the effects of media violence on children's behavior, one might conclude that there is some uncertainty about those effects. There is not. In fact, there has been no real doubt about these effects for more than two decades. Numerous well-designed studies almost universally point to the same conclusion. For example, the American Psychological Association's (1993) summary report, *Violence and Youth*, concluded, "There is absolutely no doubt that higher levels of viewing violence on television are correlated with increased acceptance of aggressive attitudes and increased aggressive behavior" (p. 33). As early as 1972, the U.S. Surgeon General's report, after reviewing existing and commissioned research, concluded that there was "a significant and consistent correlation between television viewing and aggressive behavior" and that "there was a *direct causal link* between exposure to televised violence and subsequent aggressive behavior on the part of the viewer" (Donnerstein et al. 1994, p. 223, emphasis added). Subsequent research has repeatedly confirmed these conclusions. The National Institute of Mental Health, for example, concluded in a 1982 report, "In magnitude, television violence is as strongly correlated with aggressive behavior as any other behavioral variable that has been measured" (p. 6). The glamorization of and the desensitization to violence, the modeling of aggressive strategies for problem solving, and the failure to appreciate the actual consequences of violence—all these carry an unmistakable and potent effect on the attitudes and the behavioral repertoire of children and adolescents.

Besides the unarguably damaging effects of heavy TV viewing on children's attitudes toward violence, there is also a nonspecific effect—the substantial proportion of children's time that is occupied in a passive and unproductive endeavor. Inherent in TV programs and movies is that the viewer need contribute nothing. His reactions may vary somewhat, but he is expected to passively absorb the images, the plots, and the outcomes. Increasingly, with children's television programming, the child is also expected to absorb the wish for certain product lines, easily purchased at the nearest big-box toy store.

Passive absorption of media programming is the antithesis of the natural and healthy leisure-time activity of children—play. Play is not passive. Even the most ordinary play is active and creative, and numerous important skills are being developed. Through play of all kinds the child develops a wide range of cognitive, physical, and interpersonal skills—none of which can happen when the child spends the afternoon in front of the TV. Healthy play can involve elaborate and expensive toys, even high-tech gadgets, but none of that is necessary. In fact, many of the most elaborate and expensive toys that are popular today put the child in an essentially passive role. All of the moves and options are programmed by the toy, and the child is reduced to enacting prescribed actions. Such toys deprive the child of exercising her own inventiveness. It is little wonder that so many of the newest and most expensive toys hold the child's interest only briefly. Children are the original innovators, and they make the most productive and creative play devices even out of simple objects.

Many dedicated individuals have toiled for years to put some limits on the violence on television. However, there are vast amounts of money to be made in violent media programming. Where large quantities of money are at stake, real reform is difficult or impossible. An example of the effects of financial forces on the politics of television violence was provided in the 1972 Surgeon General's report on TV violence. The conclusions of many scientists were strong on the causal relation of viewing TV violence and subsequent aggressive behavior. However, the report's summary was substantially weakened and qualified in order to appease the industry interests (Donnerstein et al. 1974). Tepid agreements reached in 1997 with the industry to put certain constraints on violence during certain hours underscored the difficulty in bringing about real improvement.

There is at least one other way to look at the whole matter of children's exposure to media violence and the surrender to passive attention. If violence on TV is not going to abate (every indication is that it will not), and if children are going to continue to fall into the easy habits of passivity, then the TV can be turned off. There is something disingenuous about parents complaining about all the violence on TV, wondering why the government cannot put some curbs on what comes over the airways. For those same parents could pull the plug on the TV, could keep watch over the videos that come into the house and the movies that come in via the cable. One of the sorriest tales to hear from the families of antisocial adolescents is how the boy has had what amounts to an entertainment center in his bedroom—a TV (usually with cable and often with no supervision), a stereo system, a video game system. Ironically, it often is the families with the least financial resources who ensure that their children's rooms are outfitted with a full range of high-tech entertainment.

In older children and adolescents one of the best predictors of antisocial behavior is lax parental supervision. This parallels the situation regarding TV in the home. If the normal parental functions of supervision and guidance are being fulfilled, then the children will not be watching TV more than a few hours per week—and then it will be educational programs or largely nonviolent entertainment. This is not to say that children must be shielded from any and all violence in movies and TV. Like all profound matters in life, children are curious about violence, just as they are curious about love, birth, death, and the history of the earth. Violent acts sometimes are an integral component in a worthy plot. This is very different from the gratuitous violence that is the norm in much current media. It is not hard to tell the difference.

RESPONSIBILITY

A great deal been learned about antisocial development through psychological and psychiatric investigations, so much, in fact, that we now realize that the problem of antisocial youth cannot be left entirely to clinicians. Antisocial youths cannot be considered just a clinical problem. As citizens, we cannot pretend that the problem is adequately accounted for through studies of psychosocial risk factors, resiliency, and temperament. Antisocial youth is a social problem, with roots in social, economic, and political processes and policies.

Psychological research is doing its job well, by delineating the factors that predispose the child to pathological development, or buffer the child from negative influences or even from innate liabilities. We can rehabilitate the vast majority of antisocial youths. But therapeutic measures are directed at the existing population of troubled kids. This does not take account the kids in the pipeline. In other words, all the clinical expertise in the world will have little or no effect on the production of the next cohort of antisocial youth. The exception is what are called primary prevention programs. Primary prevention, usually designed by clinically trained professionals, aims to prevent the development of psychopathology in vulnerable populations.

There is a responsibility at every level of society to respect and to protect the conditions that encourage healthy child development. The conditions that encourage antisocial development are not a clinical problem—despite the fact that clinical research clarifies the nature and effects of those conditions. If we are responsible as a society, then we will promote policies and projects that support protective conditions—healthy two-parent families, stable communities and livable neighborhoods, adequately supported school systems, and appropriate media entertainment. If we are responsible as a society, then we will work to halt the destructive influences. We will work to ensure that unsupported single mothers and absent fathers are the exception, and that the trend toward increasing numbers of children growing up in such households is reversed.

If we are responsible as a society, we will work to oppose projects and policies that undermine the health and stability of existing communities. Community is a living, breathing system that takes years, even decades to develop. It cannot be replaced. In the modern era, the most pernicious projects are always made to look appealing at first. Local communities, whether in small towns or inner cities, are especially vulnerable to promises of economic growth and more jobs. As one National Public Radio (NPR) commentator put it, "Some small towns feel so thirsty for new tax revenues that they will drink poison." Insensitive location of large highways, suburban tracts, and retail malls can drain the life out of existing commercial centers, slowly strangling the social vitality of communities that had thrived for decades.

If we are responsible as a society, we will work to ensure that all school districts are adequately funded. In an era when many cities can afford to spend a half billion dollars of taxpayer money on sports stadiums, it is scandalous that schools must struggle to provide the most basic educational necessities.

If we are responsible as parents and neighbors and teachers, then we will ensure that TV and video games and other passive preoccupations occupy a small proportion of children's time. They will not grow up watching hours of violent programming each week, and they will have discovered at an early age the richness of books and projects and play that has not been packaged for them. They will enjoy time with their parents, whether in work and chores or in sports and hobbies. Boredom will not trigger a rescue through the purchase of the newest toys, but instead will impel the child and parent to be inventive.

❖ REFERENCES ❖

Abel, G. G., Becker, J. V., Cunningham-Rathner, J., et al. (1984). *Treatment Manual: The Treatment of Child Molesters*. Tuscaloosa, AL: Emory University Clinic, Department of Psychiatry.

Achenbach, T. M., and Edelbrock, C. (1983). *Manual for the Child Behavior Checklist and Revised Child Behavior Profile*. University of Massachusetts.

Aichhorn, A. (1925). *Wayward Youth*. New York: Viking.

Akiskal, H. (1995). Mood disorders: introduction and overview. In *Comprehensive Textbook of Psychiatry*, ed. H. I. Kaplan and B. J. Sadock, pp. 1067–1079. Baltimore: Williams & Wilkins.

Allison, J., Blatt, S., and Zimet, C. (1968). *The Interpretation of Psychological Tests*. New York: Harper & Row.

American Academy of Child and Adolescent Psychiatry (1997). Practice parameters for the assessment and treatment of children, adolescents and adults with attention-deficit/hyperactivity disorder. *Journal of the American Academy of Child and Adolescent Psychiatry* 36:85S–121S.

American Psychiatric Association (1994). *Diagnostic and Statistical Manual of Mental Disorders*, 4th ed. Washington, DC: Author.

American Psychological Association Commission on Violence and Youth (1993). *Violence and Youth: Psychology's Response. Vol. 1: Summary Report of the American Psychological Association Commission of Violence and Youth*. Washington, DC: American Psychological Association.

Armistead, L., Wierson, M., Forehand, R., and Frame, C. (1992). Psychopathology in incarcerated juvenile delinquents: Does it extend beyond externalizing problems? *Adolescence* 27:309–314.

Arnold, L. E., and Jensen, P. S. (1995). Attention deficit disorders. In *Comprehensive Textbook of Psychiatry*, vol. 6, ed. H. I. Kaplan and B. J. Sadock, pp. 2295–2310. Baltimore: Williams & Wilkins.

Ayers, W. (1997). *A Kind and Just Parent: The Children of Juvenile Court*. Boston: Beacon.

Bailey, S. (1996). Adolescents who murder. *Journal of Adolescence* 19:19–39.

Bank, L., Marlowe, J. H., Reid, J. B., et al. (1991). A comparative evaluation of parent-training interventions for families of chronic delinquents. *Journal of Abnormal Child Psychology* 19:15-33.

Barbaree, H. E., and Cortoni, F. A. (1993). Treatment of the juvenile sex offender. In *The Juvenile Sex Offender*, ed. H. E. Barbaree, W. L. Marshall, and S. M. Hudson. New York: Guilford.

Bates, J. E., Bayles, K., Bennett, D. S., et al. (1991). Origins of externalizing behavior problems at eight years of age. In *The Development and Treatment of Childhood Aggression*, ed. D. J. Pepler and K. H. Rubin, pp. 93-120. Hillsdale, NJ: Lawrence Erlbaum.

Bateson, M. C. (1994). *Peripheral Visions: Learning Along the Way*. New York: HarperCollins.

Berkowitz, L. (1994). Guns and youth. In *Reason to Hope: A Psychosocial Perspective on Violence and Youth*, ed. L. D. Eron, J. H. Gentry, and P. Schlegel, pp. 251-279. Washington, DC: American Psychological Association.

Biederman, J., Faraone, S. V., Haatch, M., and Mennin, D. (1997). Conduct disorder with and without mania in a referred sample of ADHD children. *Journal of Affective Disorders* 44:177-188.

Biederman, J., Faraone, S. V., and Mick, E. (1996a). Attention deficit hyperactivity disorder and juvenile mania: an overlooked comorbidity? *Journal of the American Academy of Child and Adolescent Psychiatry* 35:997-1008.

Biederman, J., Faraone, S., Milberger, S., and Jetton, J. (1996b). Is childhood oppositional defiant disorder a precursor to adolescent conduct disorder? Findings from a four-year follow-up study of children with ADHD. *Journal of the American Academy of Child and Adolescent Psychiatry* 35:1193-1204.

Blackburn, R., and Maybury, C. (1985). Identifying the psychopath: the relation of Cleckley's criteria to the interpersonal domain. *Personality and Individual Differences* 6:375-386.

Blanck, G., and Blanck, R. (1979). *Ego Psychology*, vol. 2. New York: Columbia University Press.

Bleiberg, E. (1994). Borderline disorders in children and adolescents: the concept, the diagnosis, and the controversies. *Bulletin of the Menninger Clinic* 58:169-196.

Block, J. H., and Block, J. (1980). The role of ego control and ego resiliency in the origins of behavior. In *Development of Cognition/Minnesota Symposia on Child Psychology*, ed. W. A. Collins, vol. 13, pp. 99-128. Hillsdale, NJ: Lawrence Erlbaum.

Block, N. (1995). How heritability misleads about race. *Cognition* 56:99–128.

Blomhoff, S., Seim, S., and Friis, S. (1990). Can prediction of violence among psychiatric patients be improved? *Hospital and Community Psychiatry* 41:771–775.

Blumstein, A. (1995). Youth violence. *Journal of Criminal Law and Criminology* 86:10.

Bowlby, J. (1940). The influence of early environment in the development of neurosis and neurotic character. *International Journal of Psycho-Analysis* 21:154–178.

―――― (1944). Forty-four juvenile thieves: their character and home life. *International Journal of Psycho-Analysis* 25:10–52

―――― (1958). The nature of the child's tie to his mother. *International Journal of Psycho-Analysis* 39:350–373.

Breuer, J., and Freud, S. (1895). Studies on hysteria. *Standard Edition* 2:1–305.

Bronfenbrenner, U. (1977). Toward an experimental ecology of human development. *American Psychologist* 32:513–531.

Brooks, R. (1991). *The Self-Esteem Teacher*. Circle Pines, MN: American Guidance Services.

Brown, E. J., Flanagan, T. J., and McLeod, M. (1984). *Sourcebook of Criminal Justice Statistics—1983*. Washington, DC: Bureau of Statistics.

Burchard, J. D., and Tyler, V., Jr. (1965). The modification of delinquent behavior through operant conditioning. *Behavior Research and Therapy* 2:245–250.

Butts, J., Snyder, H., Finnegan, T., et al. (1993). *Juvenile Court Statistics 1993*. Washington, DC: Office of Juvenile Justice and Delinquency Prevention.

Cadoret, R. J. (1978). Psychopathology in adopted away offspring of biologic parents with antisocial behavior. *Archives of General Psychiatry* 35:176–184.

Cadoret, R. J., Cain, C., and Crowe, R. R. (1983). Evidence for a gene-environment interaction in the development of adolescent antisocial behavior. *Behavior Genetics* 13:301–310.

Cadoret, R. J., Yates, W. R., Troughton, E., et al. (1995). Genetic-environmental interaction in the genesis of aggressivity and conduct disorders. *Archives of General Psychiatry* 52:916–924.

Calthorpe, P. (1993). *The Next American Metropolis: Ecology, Community and the American Dream*. New York: Princeton Architectural Press.

Cantwell, D. P. (1996). Attention deficit disorder: a review of the past 10 years. *Journal of the American Academy of Child and Adolescent Psychiatry* 35:978–987.

Carey, G. (1992). Twin imitation for antisocial behavior: implications for genetic and family environment research. *Journal of Abnormal Psychology* 101:18–25.

Caro, R. (1974). *The Power Broker: Robert Moses and the Fall of New York*. New York: Knopf.

Caspi, A., Henry, B., McGee, R., et al. (1995). Temperamental origins of child and adolescent behavior problems: from age 3 to 15. *Child Development* 66:55–68.

Cicchetti, D. (1996). Integrating developmental risk factors: perspectives from developmental psychopathology. In *Threats to Optimum Development: Biological, Psychological and Social Risk Factors*, ed. C. Nelson, pp. 285–325. Hillsdale, NJ: Erlbaum.

Cleckley, H. (1941). *The Mask of Sanity*. St. Louis: C. V. Mosby.

——— (1982). *The Mask of Sanity*, rev. ed. St. Louis: C. V. Mosby.

Cloninger, C. R., and Gottesman, I. I. (1987). Genetic and environmental factors in antisocial behavior. In *The Causes of Crime: New Biological Approaches*, ed. S. A. Mednick, T. E. Moffit, and S. A. Stack, pp. 92–109. Cambridge, England: Cambridge University Press.

Cobb, J. A. (1972). The relationship of discrete classroom behavior to fourth grade academic achievement. *Journal of Educational Psychology* 63:74–80.

Compas, B. E., Hinden, B. R., and Gerhardt, C. A. (1995). Adolescent development: pathways and processes of risk and resilience. *Annual Review of Psychology* 46:265–293.

Crowe, R. R. (1974). An adoption study of antisocial personality. *Archives of General Psychiatry* 31:785–791.

Davidson, J. R. (1995). Posttraumatic stress disorder and acute stress disorder. In *Comprehensive Textbook of Psychiatry*, ed. H. I. Kaplan and B. J. Sadock, vol. 6, pp. 1227–1236. Baltimore: Williams & Wilkins.

Davis, D. L., and Boster, L. H. (1992). Cognitive-behavioral-expressive interventions with aggressive and resistant youths. *Child Welfare* 71:557–573.

Dawes, M. (1979). The robust beauty of improper linear models in decision making. *American Psychologist* 34:571–582.

DiLalla, L. F., and Gottesman, I. I. (1989). Heterogeneity of causes for delinquency and criminality: Lifespan perspectives. *Development and Psychopathology* 1:339–349.

Dishion, T. J., Loeber, R., Stouthamer-Loeber, M., and Patterson, G. R. (1983). Social skills deficits and male adolescent delinquency. *Journal of Abnormal Child Psychology* 12:37–54.

Dodge, K. A., Bates, J. E., and Pettit, G. S. (1991). Mechanism in the cycle of violence. *Science* 250:1678–1683.

Donnerstein, E., Slaby, R. G., and Eron, L. D. (1994). The mass media and youth aggression. In *Reason to Hope: A Psychosocial Perspective on Violence and Youth*, ed. L. D. Eron, J. H. Gentry, and P. Schlegel, pp. 219–250. Washington, DC: American Psychological Association.

Drope v. Missouri (1975). 420 U.S. 162.

Dugan, T. F., and Coles, R. (1989). *The Child in Our Times: Studies in the Development of Resiliency*. New York: Brunner/Mazel.

Dusky v. United States (1960). 362 U.S. 402.

Eakes, P., and Eakes, K. (1998). We are responsible for their behavior. *The Seattle Times*, June 4, p. B5.

Earls, F. (1989). Epidemiological strategies in child mental health. In *Children's Mental Health Policy: Building a Research Base. Proceedings from the Second Annual Conference*, ed. P. Greenbaum, R. Friedman, A. Duchnowski, et al. Tampa: Florida Mental Health Institute, University of South Florida.

Ellason, J. W., Ross, C. A., Sainton, K., and Mayran, L. W. (1996). Axis I and II comorbidity and childhood trauma history in chemical dependency. *Bulletin of the Menninger Clinic* 60:39–51.

Elliott, D. S., Ageton, S. S., and Canter, R. J. (1979). An integrated theoretical perspective on delinquent behavior. *Journal of Research in Crime and Delinquency* 16:3–27.

Elliott, D. S., Huizinga, D., and Ageton, S. S. (1985). *Explaining Delinquency and Drug Use*. Beverly Hills, CA: Sage.

Elliott, D. S., Huizinga, D., and Morse, B. (1986). Self-reported violent offending: a descriptive analysis of juvenile violent offenders and their offending careers. *Journal of Interpersonal Violence* 1:472–514.

Erikson, E. (1968). *Identity: Youth and Crisis*. New York: Norton.

Eron, L. D., and Huesmann, L. R. (1984). The relation of prosocial behavior to the development of aggression and psychopathology. *Aggressive Behavior* 10:201–211.

——— (1990). The stability of aggressive behavior—even unto the third generation. In *Handbook of Developmental Psychopathology*, ed. M. Lewis and S. M. Miller, pp. 147–156. New York: Plenum.

Exner, J. (1986). *The Rorschach: A Comprehensive System, vol. 1. Basic Foundations*. New York: Wiley.

———— (1991). *The Rorschach: A Comprehensive System, vol. 2. Interpretations.* New York: Wiley.

Exner, J., and Weiner, I. (1982). *The Rorschach: A Comprehensive System, vol. 3. Assessment of Children and Adolescents.* New York: Wiley.

Eysenck, H. J., and Eysenck, S. B. (1978). Psychopathy, personality and genetics. In *Psychopathic Behavior: Approaches to Research,* ed. R. D. Hare and D. Schalling, pp. 197–224. London: Wiley.

Fairbairn, W. R. (1952). *An Object Relations Theory of the Personality.* New York: Basic Books.

Farrington, D. P. (1986). Stepping stones to adult criminal careers. In *Development of Antisocial and Prosocial Behavior: Research, Theories and Issues,* ed. D. Olweus, J. Block, and M. Radke-Yarrow. New York: Academic Press.

———— (1991). Childhood aggression and adult violence: early precursors and later-life outcomes. In *The Development and Treatment of Childhood Aggression,* ed. D. J. Pepler and F. H. Rubin, pp. 5–29. Hillsdale, NJ: Lawrence Erlbaum.

Farrington, D. P., Gallagher, B., Morley, L., et al. (1986). *Cambridge study in delinquent development: long term follow-up.* Unpublished annual report, Cambridge University Institute of Criminology, Cambridge, England.

Farrington, D., Loeber, R.,and Van Kammen, W. (1990). Long-term criminal outcomes of hyperactivity-impulsivity-attention deficit and conduct problems in childhood. In *Straight and Devious Pathways from Childhood to Adulthood,* ed. L. N. Robins and M. Rutter, pp. 62–81. New York: Cambridge University Press.

Federal Bureau of Investigation (1992). *Crime in the United States 1991.* Washington, DC: U.S. Department of Justice.

———— (1996). *Uniform Crime Reports for the United States, 1995.* Washington, DC: U.S. Department of Justice.

Feindler, E. L., Ecton, R. B., Kingsley, D., and Dubey, D. R.(1986). Group anger-control training for institutionalized psychiatric male adolescents. *Behavior Therapy* 17:109–123.

Florsheim, P., Tolan, P., and Gorman-Smith, D. (1996). Family processes and risk for externalizing behavior problems among African-American and Hispanic boys. *Journal of Consulting and Clinical Psychology* 64:1222–1230.

Forth, A., Hart, S., and Hare, R. (1990). Assessment of psychopathy in male young offenders. *Psychological Assessment: A Journal of Consulting and Clinical Psychology* 2(3):342–344.

Frazier, C. (1997). *Cold Mountain*. New York: Atlantic Monthly.

Freud, A. (1936). *The Ego and the Mechanisms of Defense*. New York: International Universities Press, 1966.

Gacono, C. B., and Meloy, J. R. (1994). *The Rorschach Assessment of Aggressive and Psychopathic Personalities*. Hillsdale, NJ: Lawrence Erlbaum.

Gardner, H. (1983). *Frames of Mind: The Theory of Multiple Intelligences*. New York: Basic Books.

Garmezy, N. (1981). Children under stress: perspectives on antecedents and correlates of vulnerability and resistance to psychopathology. In *Further Explorations in Personality*, ed. A. I. Rabin, J. Arnoff, A. M. Barclay, and R. A. Zucker, pp. 196–270. New York: Wiley.

Garmezy, N., Masters, A., and Tellegen, A. (1984). The study of stress and competence in children: a building block for developmental psychopathology. *Child Development* 55:97–111.

Garreau, J. (1991). *Edge City: Life on the New Frontier*. New York: Doubleday.

Geller, B., and Luby, J. (1997). Child and adolescent bipolar disorder: a review of the past 10 years. *Journal of the American Academy of Child and Adolescent Psychiatry* 36:1168–1176.

Gladwell, M. (1996). The tipping point. *The New Yorker*, June 3, pp. 32–38.

Goldstein, A. P., and Glick, B. (1987). *Aggression Replacement Training: A Comprehensive Intervention for Aggressive Youth*. Champaign, IL: Research Press.

Goodman, R., and Stevenson, J. (1989a). A twin study of hyperactivity: I. An examination of hyperactivity scores and categories derived from Rutter teacher and parent questionnaires. *Journal of Child Psychology and Psychiatry and Allied Disciplines* 30:671–689.

——— (1989b). A twin study of hyperactivity: II. The aetiologic role of genes, family relationships and perinatal adversity. *Journal of Child Psychology and Psychiatry and Allied Disciplines* 30:691–709.

Gottesman, I. I., and Goldsmith, H. H. (1994). Developmental psychopathology of antisocial behavior: Inserting genes into its ontogenesis and epigenesis. In *Threats to Optimum Development: Biological, Psychological and Social Risk Factors*, ed. C. Nelson, pp. 69–104. Hillsdale, NJ: Erlbaum.

Gottfredson, S. D., and Gottfredson, D. M. (1988). Violence prediction methods: statistical and clinical strategies. *Violence and Victims* 3:303–324.

Greenspan, S. I. (1997). *The Growth of the Mind and the Endangered Origins of Intelligence*. New York: Addison-Wesley.

Greenwood, P. W. (1996). Responding to juvenile crime: lessons learned. *The Future of Children* 6:75–85.

Grisso, T. (1986). *Evaluating Competencies: Forensic Assessments and Instruments*. New York: Plenum.

—— (1998). *Forensic Evaluation of Juveniles*. Sarasota, FL: Professional Resource Press.

Grisso, T., and Appelbaum, P. S. (1992). Is it unethical to offer predictions of future violence? *Law and Human Behavior* 16:621–633.

Groth, A. N., Hobson, W. F., Lucey, K.P., and St. Pierre, J. (1981). Juvenile sexual offenders: guidelines for treatment. *International Journal of Offender Therapy and Comparative Criminology* 25:265–275.

Guerra, N. G., Tolan, P. H., and Hammond, W. R. (1994). Prevention and treatment of adolescent violence. In *Reason to Hope: A Psychosocial Perspective on Violence and Youth*, ed. L. D. Eron, J. H. Gentry, and P. Schlegel, pp. 383–403. Washington, DC: American Psychological Association.

Gunderson, J. G., and Phillips, K. (1995). Personality disorders. In *Comprehensive Textbook of Psychiatry*, ed. H. I. Kaplan and B. J. Sadock, pp. 1425–1461. Baltimore: Williams & Wilkins.

Gunderson, J. G., and Sabo, A. N. (1993). The phenomenological and conceptual interface between borderline personality disorder and PTSD. *American Journal of Psychiatry* 150:19–27.

Gutheil, T. (1995). Legal issues in psychiatry. In *Comprehensive Textbook of Psychiatry*, ed. H. I. Kaplan and B. J. Sadock, pp. 2247–2767. Baltimore: Williams & Wilkins.

Haapasalo, J., and Hamalainen, T. (1996). Childhood family problems and current psychiatric problems among young violent and property offenders. *Journal of the American Academy of Child and Adolescent Psychiatry* 35:1394–1401.

Hare, R. D. (1991). *The Hare Psychopathy Checklist–Revised*. Toronto: Multi-Health Systems.

—— (1993). *Without Conscience: The Disturbing World of the Psychopaths among Us*. New York: Pocket Books.

Harris, G. T., Rice, M. E., and Quinsey, V. L. (1993). Violent recidivism of mentally disordered offenders: the development of a statistical prediction instrument. *Criminal Justice and Behavior* 20:315–335.

Harter, S. (1990). Self and identity development. In *At the Threshold: The*

Developing Adolescent, ed. S. S. Feldman and G. D. Elliott, pp. 352–387. Cambridge, MA: Harvard University Press.

Hartmann, H. (1958). *Ego Psychology and the Problem of Adaptation*. New York: International Universities Press.

Hauser, S. T., Vieyra, M. A. B., Jacobson, A. M., and Wertlieb, D. (1989). Family aspects of vulnerability and resilience in adolescence: a theoretical perspective. In *The Child in Our Times: Studies in the Development of Resiliency*, ed. T. F. Dugan and R. Coles, pp. 109–133. New York: Brunner/Mazel.

Hawkins, J. D., and Lishner, D. M. (1987). Schooling and delinquency. In *Handbook on Crime and Delinquency Prevention*, ed. E. H. Johnson, pp. 179–221. New York: Greenwood.

Hawkins, J. D., Von Cleve, E., and Catalano, R. F. (1991). Reducing early childhood aggression: results of a primary prevention program. *Journal of the American Academy of Child and Adolescent Psychiatry* 30: 208–217.

Heilbrun, K., Hawk, G., and Tate, D. C. (1996). Juvenile competence to stand trial: research issues in practice. *Law and Human Behavior* 20:573–578.

Henggeler, S. W., and Borduin, C. M. (1990). *Family Therapy and Beyond: A Multisystemic Approach to Treating the Behavior Problems of Children and Adolescents*. Pacific Grove, CA: Brooks/Cole.

Henggeler, S. W., Melton, G. B., and Smith, L. A. (1992). Family preservation using multisystemic therapy—a effective alternative to incarcerating serious juvenile offenders. *Journal of Consulting and Clinical Psychology* 60:953–961.

Henry, B., Caspi, A., Moffitt, T., and Silva, P. (1996). Temperamental and familial predictors of violent and non-violent criminal convictions: age 3 to 18. *Developmental Psychology* 32:614–623.

Herman, J. L. (1981). *Father-Daughter Incest*. Cambridge, MA: Harvard University Press.

——— (1992). *Trauma and Recovery*. New York: Basic Books.

Hernstein, R., and Murray, C. (1994). *The Bell Curve: Intelligence and Class Structure in American Life*. New York: Free Press.

Huesmann, L. R., Eron, L. D., Lefkowitz, M. M., and Walder, L. O. (1984). Stability of aggression over time and generations. *Developmental Psychology* 20:1120–1134.

Hutchings, B., and Mednick, S. A. (1977). Criminality in adoptees and their adoptive and biological parents: a polot study. In *Biosocial Bases of Criminal Behavior*, ed. S. A. Mednick and K. O. Christiansen, pp. 127–141. New York: Gardner.

Jackson, K. T. (1985). *Crabgrass Frontier: The Suburbanization of the United States*. New York: Oxford University Press.

Janet, P. (1919). *Psychological Healing*, trans. C. Paul and E. Paul. New York: Macmillan, 1925.

Kagan, J. (1996). Temperament. In *Handbook of Child and Adolescent Psychiatry*, ed. J. D. Noshpitz, pp. 268–275. New York: Wiley.

Kaplan, H. I., Freedman, A. M., and Sadock, B. J., eds. (1980). *Comprehensive Textbook of Psychiatry*, 2 vols. Baltimore: Williams & Wilkins.

Kardiner, A. (1941). *The Traumatic Neuroses of War*. New York: Hoeber.

Kaufman, J., and Zigler, E. (1987). Do abused children become abusive parents? *American Journal of Orthopsychiatry* 57:186–192.

Kazdin, A. E. (1987). Treatment of antisocial behavior in children: current status and future directions. *Psychological Bulletin* 102:187–203.

—— (1989). Hospitalization of antisocial children: clinical course, follow-up status, and predictors of outcome. *Advances in Behavior Research and Therapy* 11:1–67.

—— (1994). Interventions for aggressive and antisocial children. In *Reason to Hope: A Psychosocial Perspective on Violence and Youth*, ed. L. D. Eron, J. H. Gentry, and P. Schlegel, pp. 341–382. Washington, DC: American Psychological Association.

Kent v. United States (1966). 383 U.S. 541, 86 S.Ct. 1045.

Kernberg, O. F. (1975). *Borderline Conditions and Pathological Narcissism*. New York: Jason Aronson.

Klein, M. (1934). A contribution to the pathogenesis of manic depressive states. In *Contributions to Psychoanalysis 1921–1945*. London: Hogarth, 1948.

Kobak, R. R., and Sceery, A. (1988). Attachment in late adolescence: working models, affect regulation, and representations of self and others. *Child Development* 59:135–146.

Kochanska, G. (1993). Toward a synthesis of parental socialization and child temperament in early development of conscience. *Child Development* 64:325–347.

Kohlberg, L. (1964). Development of moral character and moral ideology. *Review of Child Development Research* 1:383–433.

Kolvin, I., Miller, F. J. W., Fletting, M., and Kolvin, P. A. (1988). Social and parenting factors affecting criminal-offense fates: findings from the Newcastle Thousand Family Study. *British Journal of Psychiatry* 152:80–90.

Kovacs, M., and Pollock, M. (1995). Bipolar disorder and comorbid conduct disorder in childhood and adolescence. *Journal of the American Academy of Child and Adolescent Psychiatry* 34:715–723.

Kozol, J. (1991). *Savage Inequalities: Children in America's Schools.* New York: Harperperennial Library.

Krisberg, B. (1992). *Juvenile Justice: Improving the Quality of Care.* San Francisco, CA: National Council on Crime and Delinquency.

Kurcinka, M. S. (1991). *Raising Your Spirited Child.* New York: Harper-Collins.

LaBruzza, A. L., and Mendez-Villarrubia, J. M. (1994). *Using DSM-IV: A Clinician's Guide to Psychiatric Diagnosis.* Northvale, NJ: Jason Aronson.

Lally, R., Mangione, P. L., and Honig, A. S. (1988). The Syracuse University Family Development Research Program: long-range impact of early intervention with low-income children and their families. In *Parent Education as Early Childhood Intervention: Emerging Directions in Theory, Research, and Practice,* ed. D. Powell, pp. 79–104. Norwood, NJ: Ablex.

Levy, F., Hay, D. A., McStephen, M., and Wood, C., et al. (1997). Attention deficit hyperactivity disorder: a category or continuum? Genetic analysis of a large-scale twin study. *Journal of the American Academy of Child and Adolescent Psychiatry* 36:737–744.

Lewis, D. O. (1996). Diagnostic evaluation of the child with dissociative identity disorder/multiple personality disorder. *Child and Adolescent Clinics of North America* 5:303–331.

Lipsey, M. W. (1992). Juvenile delinquency treatment: a meta-analytic inquiry into the variability of effects. In *Meta-analysis for Explanation,* ed. T. Cook, H. Cooper, D. S. Cordray, et al., pp. 83–126. New York: Russell Sage Foundation.

Lipsitt, P., Lelos, D., and McGarry, A. l. (1971). Competency for trial: a screening instrument. *American Journal of Psychiatry* 128:105–109.

Litwack, T. R. (1985). The prediction of violence. *Clinical Psychologist* 38:87–91.

Litwack, T. R., Kirschner, S. M., and Wack, R. C. (1993). The assessment of dangerousness and predictions of violence: recent research and future prospects. *Psychiatric Quarterly* 64:245–273.

Loeber, R. (1982). The stability of antisocial and delinquent child behavior: a review. *Child Development* 53:1431–1446.

———— (1990). Development and risk factors of juvenile antisocial behavior and delinquency. *Clinical Psychology Review* 10:1–41.

———— (1991). Antisocial behavior: More enduring than changeable? *Journal of the American Academy of Child and Adolescent Psychiatry* 30:393–397.

Loeber, R., and Dishion, T. J. (1983). Early predictors of male delinquency: a review. *Psychological Bulletin* 94:68–99.

Loeber, R., Green, S., Keenan, K., and Lahey, B. (1995). Which boys will fare worse? Early predictors of the onset of conduct disorder in a six-year longitudinal study. *Journal of the American Academy of Child and Adolescent Psychiatry* 34:499–509.

Loevinger, J. (1969). Theories of ego development. In *Clinical-Cognitive Psychology: Models and Integrations*, ed. L. Breger. Englewood Cliffs, NJ: Prentice-Hall.

Loevinger, J., and Wessler, R. (1970). *Measuring Ego Development*, vol. 1. San Francisco: Jossey-Bass.

Loevinger, J., Wessler, R., and Redmore, C. (1970). *Measuring Ego Development*, vol. 2. San Francisco: Jossey-Bass.

Lonie, I. (1993). Borderline disorder and post-traumatic stress disorder: an equivalence? *Australian and New Zealand Journal of Psychiatry* 27:233–245.

Lykken, D. T. (1957). A study of anxiety in the sociopathic personality. *Journal of Abnormal and Social Psychology* 55:6–10.

———— (1995). *The Antisocial Personalities*. Hillside, NJ: Lawrence Erlbaum.

Matsakis, A. (1994). *Post-Traumatic Stress Disorder*. Oakland, CA: New Harbinger.

McGue, M. (1994). Why developmental psychology should find room for behavioral genetics. In *Threats to Optimum Development: Biological, Psychological and Social Risk Factors*, ed. C. Nelson, pp. 105–119. Hillsdale, NJ: Lawrence Erlbaum.

McGue, M., Bacon, S., and Lykken, D. T. (1992). Personality stability and change in early adulthood: a behavioral genetic analysis. *Developmental Psychology* 29:96–109.

Melton, G. (1994). Expert opinions: not for cosmic understanding. In *Psychology in Litigation and Legislation*, ed. B. D. Sales and G. R.

VanderBos, pp 59–99. Washington, DC: American Psychological Association.

Menninger, K. (1963). *Man Against Himself.* New York: Harcourt-Brace.

Menzies, R. J., Jackson, M. A., and Glasberg, R. E. (1982). The nature and consequences of forensic psychiatric decision-making. *Canadian Journal of Psychiatry* 27:463–472.

Merikangas, K. R., and Kupfer, D. J. (1995). Mood disorders: genetic aspects. In *Comprehensive Textbook of Psychiatry*, ed. H. I. Kaplan and B. J. Sadock, vol. 6, pp. 1102–1116. Baltimore: Williams & Wilkins.

Merleau-Ponty, M. M. (1962). *Phenomenology of Perception.* London: Routledge & Kegan Paul.

Merriam-Webster's Collegiate Dictionary, Tenth Ed. (1993). Springfield, MA: Merriam-Webster.

Miller, M., and Morris, N. (1988). Predictions of dangerousness: an argument for limited use. *Violence and Victims* 3:262–283.

Moe, R., and Wilkie, C. (1997). *Changing Places: Rebuilding Community in the Age of Sprawl.* New York: Henry Holt.

Moffitt, T. E. (1993). Adolescent-limited and life-course persistent antisocial behavior: a developmental taxonomy. *Psychological Review* 100:674–701.

Moffitt, T. E., Caspi, A., Diskson, N., and Silva, P. (1996). Childhood onset versus adolescent-onset antisocial conduct problems in males: natural history from ages 3 to 18 years. *Development and Psychopathology* 8:399–424.

Moffitt, T. E., and Silva, P. A. (1988). Self-reported delinquency, neuropsychological deficit, and history of attention deficit disorder. *Journal of Abnormal Psychology* 16:553–569.

Monahan, J. (1981). *The Clinical Prediction of Violent Behavior.* Rockville, MD: U.S. Department of Health and Human Services.

———— (1984). The prediction of violent behavior: toward a second generation of theory and policy. *American Journal of Psychiatry* 141:10–15.

Mossman, D. (1994). Assessing predictions of violence: being accurate about accuracy. *Journal of Consulting and Clinical Psychology* 62:783–792.

Mulvey, E. P., Arthur, M. W., and Repucci, N. D. (1993). The prevention and treatment of juvenile delinquency: a review of the research. *Clinical Psychology Review* 13:133–167.

Nanson, J. L., and Hiscock, M. (1990). Attention deficits in children exposed to alcohol prenatally. *Alcoholism: Clinical and Experimental Research* 14:656–661.

National Center for Educational Statistics (1995). Student victimization at school. *Statistics in Brief*. Washington, DC: U.S. Department of Education.

National Institute of Mental Health (1982). *Television and Behavior: Ten Years of Scientific Progress and Implications for the Eighties, Summary Report*, vol. 1. Washington, DC: U.S. Government Printing Office.

Office of Juvenile Justice and Delinquency Prevention (1993). *Comprehensive Strategy for Serious, Violent, and Chronic Juvenile Offenders*. Washington, DC: Author.

——— (1995). *Guide for Implementing the Comprehensive Strategy for Serious, Violent, and Chronic Juvenile Offenders*. Washington, DC: U.S. Department of Justice.

Ogloff, J. R., and Wong, S. (1990). Electrodermal and cardiovascular evidence of a coping response in psychopaths. *Criminal Justice and Behavior* 17:231–245.

Olweus, D. (1979). Stability of aggressive reaction patterns in males: a review. *Psychological Bulletin* 86:852–875.

——— (1980). Familial and temperamental determinants of aggressive behavior in adolescent boys: a causal analysis. *Developmental Psychology* 16:644–660.

O'Malley, K. D. (1994). Fetal alcohol effect and ADHD. *Journal of the American Academy of Child and Adolescent Psychiatry* 33:1059–1060.

Patrick, C. (1994). Emotion and psychopathy: startling new insights. *Psychophysiology* 31:319–330.

Patterson, G. R. (1982). *Coercive Family Processes*. Eugene, OR: Castalia.

——— (1992). Coercion and the early age of onset for arrest. In *Coercion and Punishment in Long-Term Perspective*, ed. J. McCord and R. E. Tremblay, pp. 81–105. Cambridge, England: Cambridge University Press.

Patterson, G. R., and Capaldi, D. M. (1991). Antisocial parents: Unskilled and vulnerable. In *Family Transitions*, ed. P. A. Cowan and M. Hetherington, pp. 195–217. Hillsdale, NJ: Lawrence Erlbaum.

Patterson, G. R., DeBaryshe, B., and Ramsey, E. (1989). A developmental perspective on antisocial behavior. *American Psychologist* 44:329–335.

Patterson, G., Reid, J. B., and Dishion, T. J. (1992). *A Social Learning Approach. Vol. 4: Antisocial Boys*. Eugene, OR: Castalia.

Pepler, D. J., and Rubin, K. H., eds. (1991). *The Development and Treatment of Childhood Aggression*. Hillsdale, NJ: Lawrence Erlbaum.

Pfefferbaum, B. (1997). Posttraumatic stress disorder in children: a review of the past 10 years. *Journal of the American Academy of Child and Adolescent Psychiatry* 36:1503–1511.

Phillips, E. L., Phillips, E. A., Fixsen, D. L., and Wolf, M. M. (1971). Achievement place: modification of the behaviors of pre-delinquent boys within a token economy. *Journal of Applied Behavior Analysis* 4:45–59.

Piaget, J. (1952). *The Origins of Intelligence in Children*, trans. M. Cook. New York: Norton.

Postman, N. (1995). *The End of Education: Redefining the Value of School*. New York: Vintage.

Pritchard, J. (1835). *A treatise on insanity*. London: Sherwood, Gilbert & Piper.

Putnam, F. W. (1989). Diagnosis and treatment of multiple personality disorder. New York: Guilford Press.

Quinsey, V. L., and Maguire, A. (1979). Variables affecting psychiatrists' and teachers' assessments of the dangerousness of mentally ill offenders. *Journal of Consulting and Clinical Psychology* 47:353–363.

Rabinivitch, R. D. (1950). Psychogenetic factors. Round table: The psychopathic delinquent child. *American Journal of Orthopsychiatry* 20:223–265.

Raine, A., and Duncan, J. (1990). The genetic and psychophysiological basis of antisocial behavior: implications for counseling and therapy. *Journal of Counseling and Development* 68:637–644.

Raine, A., and Jones, F. (1987). Attention, autonomic arousal and personality in behaviorally disordered children. *Journal of Abnormal Psychology* 15:583–599.

Reid, J. B., and Patterson, G. R. (1989). The development of antisocial behaviour patterns in childhood and adolescence. *European Journal of Personality* 3:107–119.

Reid, W. H. (1978). Genetic correlates of antisocial syndromes. In *The Psychopath: A Comprehensive Study of Antisocial Disorders and Behaviors*, pp. 244–257. New York: Brunner/Mazel.

Reiss, A. J., Jr., and Roth, J. A., eds. (1993). *Understanding and Preventing Violence*. Washington, DC: National Academy Press.

Reiss, D. (1981). *The Family's Construction of Reality*. Cambridge: Harvard University Press.

Rice, M. E., and Harris, G. T. (1995). Violent recidivism: assessing predictive validity. *Journal of Consulting and Clinical Psychology* 63:737–748.

Richters, J., and Martinez, P. (1993). Community violence, family choices, and children's chances: an algorithm for improving the odds. *Development and Psychopathology* 5:609–627.

Rivera, B., and Widom, C. S. (1990). Childhood victimization and violent offending. *Violence and Victims* 5:19–35.

Robins, L. N. (1966). *Deviant Children Grown Up: A Sociological and Psychiatric Study of Sociopathic Personality*. Baltimore: Williams & Wilkins.

——— (1978a). Etiological implications in childhood histories relating to antisocial personality. In *Psychopathic Behavior: Approaches to Research*, ed. R. D. Hare and D. Schalling, pp. 255–272. Chichester, UK: Wiley.

——— (1978b). Sturdy childhood predictors of adult antisocial behavior: replications from longitudinal studies. *Psychological Medicine* 8:611–622.

——— (1985). The epidemiology of antisocial personality. In *Psychiatry*, ed. J. O. Cavenar, vol. 3, pp. 1–14. Philadelphia: Lippincott.

——— (1988). Changes in conduct disorder over time. In *Risk in Intellectual and Psychosocial Psychiatry*, ed. D. C. Farran and G. Curtiss. Orlando, FL: Academic Press.

Robins, L. N., and Regier, D. A. (1991). *Psychiatric Disorders in America*. New York: Free Press.

Rush, B. (1812). *Medical Inquiries and Observations Upon Diseases of the Mind*. Philadelphia: Kimber and Richardson.

Rushton, J. P. (1996). Self-report delinquency and violence in adult twins. *Psychiatric Genetics* 6:87–89.

Rutter, M. (1979). Protective factors in children's responses to stress and disadvantage. In *Primary Prevention of Psychopathology, vol. 3, Social Competence in Children*, ed. M. W. Kent and J. E. Rolf, pp. 49–74. Hanover, MA: University Press of New England.

——— (1997). Nature-nurture integration: the example of antisocial behavior. *American Psychologist* 52:390–398.

Sabo, A. N. (1997). Etiological significance of associations between childhood trauma and borderline personality disorder: conceptual and clinical implications. *Journal of Personality Disorders* 11:50–70.

Schneider, S. M., Atkinson, D. R., and El-Mallakh, R. S. (1996). CD and

ADHD in bipolar disorder. *Journal of the American Academy of Child and Adolescent Psychiatry* 35:1422–1423.

Scully, V. (1995). The civilizing force of architecture. *Humanities* 16(3): 10.

Shannonhouse, K. (1997, Fall). Why three weeks? *SUWS News*, vol. 1(2). Shoshone, ID: Z Publishing.

Sherman, D. K., McGue, M. K., and Iacono, G. (1997). Twin concordance for attention deficit hyperactivity disorder: a comparison of teachers' and mothers' reports. *American Journal of Psychiatry* 154: 532–535.

Sickmund, M., Snyder, H. N., and Poe-Yamagata, E. (1997). *Juvenile Offenders and Victims: 1997 Update on Violence*. Washington, DC: Office of Juvenile Justice and Delinquency Prevention.

Slipp, S. (1988). *The Technique and Practice of Object Relations Family Therapy*. Northvale, NJ: Jason Aronson.

Sloan, J. H., Kellermann, A. L., Reay, D. T., et al. (1988). Handgun regulations, crime, assaults and homicide: a tale of two cities. *New England Journal of Medicine* 319:1256–1262.

Snyder, H. N., and Sickmund, M. (1995). *Juvenile Offenders and Victims: A National Report*. Washington, DC: Office of Juvenile Justice and Delinquency Prevention.

Snyder, H. N., Sickmund, M., and Poe-Yamagata, E. (1996). *Juvenile Offenders and Victims: 1996 Update on Violence*. Washington, DC: Office of Juvenile Justice and Delinquency Prevention.

Spaccarelli, S., Coatsworth, J. D., and Bowden, B. S. (1995). Exposure to serious family violence among incarcerated boys: its association with violent offending and potential mediating variables. *Violence and Victims* 10:163–182.

Spitz, R. A. (1945). Hospitalism: an inquiry into the genesis of psychiatric conditions in early childhood. *Psychoanalytic Study of the Child* 1:53–74. New York: International Universities Press.

——— (1949). The psychopathic delinquent child, chair B. Karpman. *American Journal of Orthopsychiatry* 20:240–248.

——— (1950). Possible infantile precursors of psychopathy. Round table: the psychopathic delinquent child. *American Journal of Orthopsychiatry* 20:223–265.

——— (1965). *The First Year of Life*. New York: International Universities Press.

Steiner, H., Garcia, I., and Matthews, Z. (1997). Post-traumatic stress disorder in incarcerated juvenile delinquents. *Journal of the American Academy of Child and Adolescent Psychiatry* 36:357–365.

Steiner, H., and Huckaby, W. (1989). Adaptation in incarcerated juvenile offenders. In *Scientific Proceedings, Annual Meeting of the American Psychatric Association*, p.110. Washington, DC: American Psychiatric Association.

Surgeon General's Scientific Advisory Committee on Television and Social Behavior (1972). *Television and Growing Up: The Impact of Televised Violence.* Washington, DC: U.S. Government Printing Office.

Swets, J. A. (1988). Measuring the accuracy of diagnostic systems. *Science* 240:1285–1293.

Tarasoff v. Regents of the University of California (1976). 131 Cal.Rptr. 14,551 P.2d 334.

Thomas, A., and Chess, S. (1989). Temperament and its functional significance. In *The Course of Life, 2nd Edition. Vol. 2: Early Childhood,* ed. S. I. Greenspan and G. H. Pollock, pp. 163–227. Madison CT: International Universities Press.

Thompson, L. L., Riggs, P. D., Mikulich, S. K., and Crowley, T. J. (1996). Contribution of ADHD symptoms to substance abuse problems and delinquency in conduct-disordered adolescents. *Journal of Abnormal Child Psychology* 24:325–347.

Tinklenberg, J., Steiner, H., and Huckaby, W. (1996). Criminal recidivism predicted from narratives of violent juvenile delinquents. *Child Psychiatry and Human Development* 27:69–79.

Turecki, S. (1985). *The Difficult Child.* New York: Bantam.

U.S. Congress, Office of Technology Assessment (1991). *Adolescent Health, vol. 2, Background and the Effectiveness of Selected Prevention and Treatment Services.* Publication number OTA-H-466. Washington, DC: U.S. Goverment Printing Office.

Vaillant, G. (1993). *The Wisdom of the Ego.* Cambridge, MA: Harvard University Press.

van der Kolk, B. (1996). The body keeps the score: approaches to the psychobiology of posttraumatic stress disorder. In *Traumatic Stress: The Effects of Overwhelming Experience on Mind, Body and Society,* ed. B. van der Kolk, A. McFarlane, and L. Weisaeth, pp. 214–241. New York: Guilford.

van der Kolk, B., and McFarlane, A. (1996). The black hole of trauma. In *Traumatic Stress: The Effects of Overwhelming Experience on Mind, Body and Society*, ed. B. van der Kolk, A. McFarlane, and L. Weisaeth, pp. 3–23. New York: Guilford.

van der Kolk, B., van der Hart, O., and Marmar, C. R. (1996a). Dissociation and information processing in posttraumatic stress disorder. In *Traumatic Stress: The Effects of Overwhelming Experience on Mind, Body and Society*, ed. B. van der Kolk, A. McFarlane, and L. Weisaeth, pp. 303–327. New York: Guilford.

van der Kolk, B., Weisaeth, L., and van der Hart, O. (1996b). History of trauma in psychiatry. In *Traumatic Stress: The Effects of Overwhelming Experience on Mind, Body and Society*, ed. B. van der Kolk, A. McFarlane, and L. Weisaeth, pp. 47–74. New York: Guilford.

Vitiello, B., and Jensen, P. (1995). Disruptive behavior disorders. In *Comprehensive Textbook of Psychiatry*, ed. H. I. Kaplan and B. J. Sadock, pp. 2311–2318. Baltimore: Williams & Wilkins.

Wechsler, D. (1991). *Wechsler Intelligence Scale for Children–3rd Edition*. New York: The Psychological Corporation, Harcourt Brace Jovanovich.

Werner, E. E., and Smith, R. S. (1982). *Vulnerable but Invincible: A Study of Resilient Children*. New York: McGraw-Hill.

——— (1992). *Overcoming the Odds: High Risk Children from Birth to Adulthood*. New York: Cornell University Press.

Widom, C. S. (1989a). The cycle of violence. *Science* 244:160–166.

——— (1989b). Does violence beget violence? A critical examination of the literature. *Psychological Bulletin* 106:3–28.

Wilson, H. (1974). Parenting in poverty. *British Journal of Social Work* 4:241–254.

Winnicott, D. W. (1958). *Through Pediatrics to Psycho-Analysis*. New York: Basic Books, 1975.

Wolfgang, M., Figlio., R. M., and Sellin, T. (1972). *Delinquency in a Birth Cohort*. Chicago: University of Chicago Press.

Wooden, W. (1995). *Renegade Kids, Suburban Outlaws: From Youth Culture to Delinquency*. Belmont, CA: Wadsworth.

Young, D. (1994). Behaviors and attributions: family views of adolescent psychopathology. *Journal of Adolescent Research* 9:427–441.

——— (1995). Suburban disconnect. *Seattle Post-Intelligencer*, November 12, pp. E1–2.

Young, D., and Larue, C. (1998). *Aggression in a middle class high school: prevalence, effects and protective factors.* Unpublished research report.

Zimring, F. (1995). Reflections on firearms and the criminal law. *Journal of Criminal Law and Criminology* 86:1–9.

Zuckerman, M. (1990). Some dubious premises in research and theory on racial differences: Scientific, social and ethical issues. *American Psychologist* 45:1297–1303.

Zweig, M. H., and Campbell, G. (1993). Receiver-operating characteristic (ROC) plots: a fundamental evaluation tool in clinical medicine. *Clinical Chemistry* 39:561–577.

❖ INDEX ❖